Aboriginal Australia

An Introductory Reader in Aboriginal Studies

Edited by Colin Bourke,
Eleanor Bourke and Bill Edwards

University of Queensland Press

First published 1994 by University of Queensland Press
Box 42, St Lucia, Queensland 4067 Australia

© University of South Australia 1994
The copyright in readings remains with the individual contributors

Typeset by University of Queensland Press
Printed in Australia by McPherson's Printing Group, Victoria

Distributed in the USA and Canada by
International Specialized Book Services, Inc.,
5804 N.E. Hassalo Street, Portland, Oregon 97213-3640

Cataloguing in Publication Data
National Library of Australia

Aboriginal Australia: An introductory reader in Aboriginal studies.

[1.] Aborigines, Australian. [2.] Aborigines, Australian —
Ethnic identity. [3.] Aborigines, Australian — Cultural
assimilation. [4.] Aborigines, Australian — Social life and
customs. [5.] Aborigines, Australian — Social conditions.
6. Australia — Race relations — History. I. Bourke, Colin.
II. Bourke, Eleanor. III. Edwards, W.H. (William Howell).

305.89915

ISBN 0 7022 2684 X

Contents

About the Editors

Colin Bourke is Professor and Dean of the Faculty of Aboriginal and Islander Studies, University of South Australia. A former primary school principal, he has a Master of Education degree from Canberra and has undergraduate qualifications in commerce and education from the University of Melbourne. He is currently undertaking an LLB at the University of Adelaide. He has written numerous published and unpublished papers on Aboriginal issues and was co-author of *Before the Invasion!*

Eleanor Bourke has a Master of Educational Studies from the University of Adelaide, where she is a PhD candidate. She is Director of the Aboriginal Research Institute (ARI) in the FAIS, University of South Australia where she oversees a publications program which has recently produced:

- Tertiary Education in Australia: How well is it serving the needs of Aborigines? (Dr Mary Ann Bin-Sallik)
- Accessing the Dreaming (Dr Olga Gostin)
- The *Kaurna Higher Education Journal.*

Bill Edwards is a graduate of the University of Melbourne. From 1958 to 1972 he was Superintendent of Ernabella Mission in the north-west of South Australia and remained in the area as Minister of the Pitjantjatjara Parish of the Uniting Church until 1980. He is a Senior Lecturer in Aboriginal Studies at the University of South Australia. He is the author of *An Introduction to Aboriginal Societies* (Social Science Press, 1988) and edited *Traditional Aboriginal Society: A Reader* (Macmillan, 1987).

The other contributors include:
- Franchesca Alberts, Curator of Anthropology, South Australian Museum;
- Rob Amery, Senior Secondary Assessment Board South Australia and Project Officer for the Australian Indigenous Languages Framework;
- Christopher Anderson, Director, South Australian Museum;
- Jenny Burden, Lecturer, School of Aboriginal and Islander Administration, University of South Australia;
- Alwin Chong, Lecturer, University of South Australia;
- Helen Cox, Lawyer, Norwood Community Legal Service;
- Olga Gostin, Lecturer, University of South Australia;
- Howard Groome, Lecturer, University of South Australia;
- Steve Hemming, South Australian Museum; and
- David Roberts, Lecturer, University of South Australia.

Editors' Note

Throughout this book, some Aboriginal words are spelt in more than one way, reflecting the alternative spellings often employed by linguists and others.

Introduction

Rarely in Australia's history of contact between indigenous Australians and their non-Aboriginal counterparts has there been a favourable representation of Aboriginal and Torres Strait Islander culture and lifestyle. This book presents some positive perspectives of indigenous people on a range of issues which affect their everyday lives.

The central aim of the book is to present a realistic view of Aboriginal and Torres Strait Islander people. However, the chapters offer more than this. Their purpose is also to encourage readers to examine their own knowledge and ideas about Australia's indigenous people and to provoke critical thinking.

These two objectives depend on a third objective, which is to reveal the cultural and linguistic diversity of indigenous Australians and to demonstrate to other Australians their great versatility, resilience and adaptability. This book should assist the Australian community to access the wealth of Aboriginal and Islander experience and to gain a greater appreciation of the contribution that indigenous people have made, and are making, in so many areas of Australian life.

Each chapter concentrates on a particular facet of the lives of indigenous Australians. It examines their struggle to maintain a strong identity and heritage while actively participating in Australian society. Reflected throughout the book are the ways in which indigenous Australians enrich Australian culture as a whole.

Chapter 1, "Images and Realities", takes up the issue of who defines and speaks for Aboriginal and Torres Strait Islander people. Most Australians have stereotypical images of Aboriginal people which are the result of non-Aboriginal concepts built on views of European superiority. Chapter 2, "Changing History: New Images of Aboriginal History" outlines the challenges of Aboriginal people to the history of European and Aboriginal relations since 1788 as written by the "victors". It traces the determination of Aboriginal people to be heard and to present their own versions of what has happened in the past 200 years.

Chapter 3, "Australia's First Peoples: Identity and Population", examines how, from the beginning of British settlement, the cultures and identity of Aboriginal people have been under enormous pressure from non-Aboriginal actions which have fragmented and undermined that culture. Today Aboriginal people are still fighting to retain their identity as the original Australians. This identity is intimately bound to the land, as examined in Chapter 4, "Two Laws: One Land". The land issue highlights the clash between two incompatible systems of law. Aboriginal law is derived from the land and encompasses all aspects of spiritual, social and economic life. On the other hand, Australian law is based on the ideologies associated with capitalism. Indigenous Australians have been disadvantaged before Australian law, but the Mabo case may herald a new phase in the Aboriginal struggle for land rights and social justice for some indigenous people.

The land and the people are bound together by traditional Aboriginal concepts of spirituality which Europeans might classify as religion. Chapter 5, "Living the Dreaming", introduces these concepts and explores the roots of contemporary Aboriginal religious experience. The impact of Christian missionary activities is outlined with a focus on Aboriginal Christianity and some other movements which have developed in response to these influences.

The Aboriginal extended kinship system and family ties have survived, albeit in many cases in a modified form, through two centuries of dispossession, discrimination, urbanisation and traumatisation due to children being removed from their families. Aboriginal concepts of kinship, community and family and the ways in which they differ from non-Aboriginal people's concepts, particularly as they relate to co-operation, sharing and responsibility, are the subjects of Chapter 6, "Family and Kin".

Chapter 7, "Australian Languages: Our Heritage", emphasises the rich linguistic heritage of indigenous Australians, which is now in danger of being lost. These languages, with their rich complexities and subtleties, have been either denigrated or ignored. Efforts are being made by Aboriginal people and linguists to redress this by implementing language programs through communities and education systems.

Chapter 8, "Living Wisdom: Aborigines and the Environment", explores indigenous Australian systems of knowledge and their wide range of application. It is a story of adaptation, change and development demonstrating the effectiveness of a lifestyle in which Aboriginal and Torres Strait Islander people lived in harmony with their environment.

Aboriginal people, no less than non-Aboriginal Australians, appreciate the importance of education in maintaining and passing on culture and in helping to adapt to the demands of modern life. Chapter 9, "Education: The Search for Relevance", traces the history of the Aboriginal struggle to make schools and education systems meet Aboriginal needs.

Major issues for Aboriginal people are health and the delivery of health services. Chapter 10, "Health: A Holistic Approach", looks at the major factors that have contributed to the poor health status of Aboriginal people following their enforced lifestyle changes since European occupation.

Chapter 11, "Economics: Independence or Welfare", presents an outline of Aboriginal economic life in pre-contact times and the effects of colonisation and government policies. It also considers the efforts of Aboriginal people to break a cycle of economic dependency and the contributions they have made and are making to the overall Australian economy.

Traditionally, art has been integral to all facets of Aboriginal life. Chapter 12, "Art: Interpreting Reality", reveals the rich diversity of Aboriginal art forms and styles from pre-colonial times to the present. It considers the success of Aboriginal art on a world scale and shows how it has changed in the last 100 years, reflecting the political and economic realities of the day.

Chapter 13, "Self-determination and the Struggle for Aboriginal Equality", explores aspects of the contemporary struggle of Aboriginal and Torres Strait Islander peoples for control over their affairs. It also highlights the different ways in which Aboriginal people seek to achieve self-determination.

As a collection, these chapters are intended to introduce facets of indigenous Australia to a wide readership. For many, it will be their first experience of the "other" Australia. The book is not definitive; it aims to encourage readers to explore further and discover the rich heritage that exists almost undetected in contemporary Australian life.

The editors wish to thank the authors for their dedication to the cause of presenting, as authentically as possible, these perspectives of indigenous Australia.

Chapter 1

Images and Realities

Eleanor Bourke

Introduction

In Australia today, Aboriginal people are still held hostage, in the main, to images created by non-Aboriginal Australians. The power of a people to say who they are, to define their own identity and to relate their own history is fundamental to their existence and the perpetuation of their cultures. To deny a people their law, languages and the use of their land is a denial of basic human rights. These fundamentals and other trappings of civilisation were systematically stripped away from most of the indigenous people of Australia.

This chapter looks at the historical and contemporary Aboriginal images and issues from Aboriginal and non-Aboriginal perspectives.

Some material in this series may serve to illustrate the "nothing has changed" attitude of non-Aboriginal people to Aborigines. For example, it is well documented that Captain Cook wrote that Joseph Banks saw "naked, treacherous Aborigines armed with lances, but extremely cowardly Aborigines who consistently retired from our people when they made the least appearance of resistance".

From 1788, which Aboriginal people call the invasion and non-Aboriginal people call British settlement, most representation of Aboriginal people has been produced and controlled by non-Aboriginal people. This representation has been biased and culturally prescriptive. It is biased because those newly arrived to this continent did not see any positive attributes among the Aboriginal people and believed in their own superiority. There was little, if any, communication between these two sides about culture, language and beliefs. The land was declared *terra nullius* (uninhabited) and the various Aboriginal nations declared uncivilised.

Creating the images

Source materials which illustrate the European beliefs prevailing in 1770 reveal the "imperial/colonial" attitude to indigenous people. Such sources include :

- the writings of early arrivals;
- diaries;
- official documents;
- education and school textbooks ; and
- paintings.

Museums now house various artefacts which support the early representations of the "noble savage" image which was used to represent "Australianness" to the rest of the world.

There were alternative positive perceptions, such as Edward Eyre's comment in 1845:

> Australia is so vast, and the customs of its inhabitants so varied in detail, though similar in outline, that it will require the lapse of many years, and the labours of many individuals, to detect the links connecting the habits and history of tribes so remotely separated.

and

> Despite the brutality they suffered at the hands of Europeans, Aborigines usually cared for the white people lost, or distressed, in the bush ... Sometimes white men — and white women — lived with an Aboriginal tribe for many years.

But some of these more positive perceptions have been ignored and forgotten. It is the negative attitudes and stereotypes that have persisted and become incorporated into popular culture — or, in many cases, Aboriginal people have been left out of Australian culture altogether.

It is interesting to note, however, that the first Australian cricket team to tour England was "Eleven Aboriginal Black Australians", as reported by *The Times* on 26 May 1868. The members of the team were reported as representing various states and having "beards and hair long and wiry" (Ward and Robertson, 1980: 190).

Issues surrounding ownership of the land are illustrations of how Aboriginal people have been misrepresented in Australian history. Land and labour exploitation were used to advance British colonisation and became the rationale for European land ownership. This led to misrepresentations of Aboriginal people in their relationship with the land. As the flora and fauna were systematically classified, so was the natural environment tamed. The Aborigines had become less troubling and were cast in a role as primitive human beings. The study of anthropology in the second half of the nineteenth century placed Australia in the vanguard of study of a fossilised society.

When European missionaries from Christian denominations started to arrive in the 1820s, they targeted various Aboriginal groups for converts. They must have been viewed with some perplexity by the Aborigines, because they were different from the other white settlers. They didn't seek to control the land and they didn't show the same interest in obtaining Aboriginal women.

They were a paradox in that, while they expressed goodwill and concern for Aboriginal people, they were more intrusive and disruptive than other Europeans because they endeavoured to break down belief systems, destroy ceremonies and wreck the very fabric of Aboriginal society. They represented Aborigines as heathen children who needed to be saved.

In 1901 the Australian Constitution's only reference to Aboriginal people was one of exclusion. Aboriginal people were referred to in a number of state acts and the commonwealth's exclusion from any responsibility towards Aboriginal people only served to confuse the status of Aboriginal people and alienate them from aspects of Australian life. Aboriginal people had no citizenship under British law and were thought to be doomed (McIntyre, 1986: 79).

The 1901 *Constitution Act* resulted in Aboriginal people being excluded from some Commonwealth services and programs until the 1970s. This had the effect of making Aboriginal people invisible within society for most Australians. However, selective representations were projected to the Australian public, such as a "corroboree — for the amusement of American tourists" in Darwin in 1936 and the re-enactment of the landing of the British Fleet in 1938 by a group of Aborigines kept in Sydney Gaol.

Even though the Constitution excluded Aborigines from being counted as citizens in their own land, some Aboriginal men were soldiers in World War I. Upon returning to Australia, they were not prepared to accept being treated as being less than human and started to discuss the possibility of becoming organised and asserting their citizenship rights and entitlement to land.

Most Australians have had only limited personal exposure to Aboriginal people or to studies and media which show Aborigines in a favourable light. Consequently, most Australians have attitudes towards Aborigines which are based on very little knowledge or which are only partially accurate because of over-generalisation. The Australian education system's past attitude toward Aborigines and Torres Strait Islanders is reflected in the textbooks that have been used in schools, such as the Victorian Education Department's series of readers developed from 1927 and in use until the 1960s.

Many Australian textbooks did not include Aborigines at all. A book on Australian history may refer to Aborigines only in passing or briefly in the first chapter. In 1977, Professor Noel Loos wrote that the history of frontier contact between white settlers and Aborigines in Australia had been glossed over (Loos, 1977: 508). He noted the tendency to treat Aboriginal Australia as an episode in early Australian history. Aboriginal oral history draws attention to a universal awareness of illegal dispossession.

Loos also noted that:

> the few ethnohistorians who have researched in the area have understandably concentrated on the destruction of the pre-existing or traditional Aboriginal society. The "doomed race" theory has thus had its effect on historians, who marched the survivors from the battlefields and the disease ridden "blacks' camps" to the concentration camps of the reserves, out of Australian society and its history. [Loos 1977: 510]

Professor Colin Bourke (1979) categorises the representation of Aborigines in early texts on Australian history as:

- **the colonial presumption**
  where Aboriginal people are represented as being appropriate subjects for colonisation and civilisation.
- **inadequate treatment**
  a failure to take account of Aboriginal peoples' presence in Australian history and to mention Aboriginal dimensions only in passing.
- **stereotypes and derogatory concepts**
  notions of superiority expressed in stereotypes such as childlike, simple, savage and primitive.
- **the exotic stress**
  draws attention to superficial differences but infers groups inferiority through words such as corroboree, cannibal, polygamy and bone pointing.
- **objects for study and discussion**
  references such as they, them, these people aligned with physical

descriptions emphasizing stereotypes such as medium stature, wiry hair, thick lips, prominent lower jaw and broad nose.

- **distortion and euphemism**
  where Australian history begins in 1788, Cook discovered Australia, first settled, the Aboriginal problem, and pioneers.

The European belief that a society continues to develop towards an ideal civilisation failed to distinguish between biological evolution and cultural development. The Social Darwinist theory invariably puts forward the view that those who are less fit fail to survive. Indigenous Australian people were regarded as quite appropriate subjects for colonisation and civilising. Possessive terms such as "our Aborigines" are often used. Cannibalism, savages and tribal fighting are abhorred. Indeed, such images of the original Australians supported the argument that the new settlers were members of a superior culture and the rationalisation that their acquisition of the land would lead to the creation of a superior nation. This argument was further supported by stereotyping Aboriginals as "simple, primitive, dirty and ugly".

Books containing such misinformation affect the attitudes of teachers and students. Despite increased Aboriginal involvement in education systems, school texts written by non-Aboriginal people remain an influential educational tool. Early texts making any reference to Aboriginal people focused on the appearance of Aboriginal people and their eating habits.

- They eat animals, grubs, fruit, fish anything.
- These dark skinned people need our help and care. When they smile at us, showing their lovely white teeth, they want to be friendly, and
- we must always try to make them happy in this land which once belonged to them.
  [Bundy, 1961: 8–10]

Such statements can be linked to racism and the function of racism in the broader society. They are reflected in more contemporary media — for example, cartoons (there may be some difficulty in interpretation because of licence allowed to political cartoonists), journalism, narrative films and documentaries.

Prejudice and bias in relation to Aboriginal perspectives of history have been taught in Australian schools and supported by the media. Studies of race relations by Lorna Lippman, while at Monash University, and other researchers, have found that Australians hold negative attitudes toward Aborigines. To overcome prejudice, Aboriginal Studies programs have been developed since 1968. Such programs have spread slowly from the then Teachers' Colleges into schools and universities. The emphasis has moved from traditional life and culture to contemporary situations.

In Thomas Keneally's *The Chant of Jimmie Blacksmith* (1973) there appears to be a rationalisation of white superiority and Aboriginal dispossession. Michael Cotter (1977) wrote that Jimmie Blacksmith is represented as being disenchanted with Aboriginal society as he knows it. The destruction of his people is evident to his sensibilities and he inherits a share in white contempt for Aboriginal culture [Cotter, 1977: 583]. In the novel, Jimmie is shown to aspire to equality on white terms. These are, of course, based on the institutions of Western society — for example, owning his own property and marrying a white woman.

More recently, there have emerged many Aboriginal writers telling their stories and, therefore, trying to balance the scales of history.

Similarly, there has been a bias in the representation of Aboriginal people in film. Early ethnographic films depicted aspects of Aboriginal life of those groups who were thought to be disappearing. Early feature films did not include Aboriginal people at all, except occasionally as primitives. After World War II there were a few films featuring Aboriginal characters, usually made by visiting British or American directors. *Jedda* was made in 1955, starring Rosalie Kunoth Monks and Robert Tudawali, who was not required to speak any lines.

Dealing with realities

Aboriginal Studies has been strongly supported by Aboriginal educators. In 1975, the Aboriginal Consultative Group to the Schools Commission called for all teacher trainees in Australia to study courses relating to Aboriginal social organisation, traditional and contemporary culture. This was seen as a strategy to gain an appreciation of Aboriginal and Islander culture within Australian society.

In recent years there has been a distinction drawn between the needs of Aborigines for cultural education and the need for Aboriginal Studies for non-Aborigines. The basis for this is that Aboriginal people see Australia as comprising two distinct groups of people:

- Aboriginal and Torres Strait Islanders and their descendants, who are the indigenous people of Australia, and

- People of a number of other races, predominantly European, who have chosen to make their home in Australia.

Aboriginal Studies programs generally aim to increase understanding of traditional Aboriginal life, activities, social organisation, beliefs and values. They provide an opportunity to counteract stereotypes of Aborigines which contribute to racist attitudes and negative behaviour. Intrinsic to such studies is the attempt to present a less ethnocentric view of Australian history and endeavour to create a culturally plural Australia through better understanding of contemporary Aboriginal situations.

"Who should teach Aboriginal Studies?" is a question often raised at conferences of Aboriginal education. The National Aboriginal Education Committee asked for Aboriginal involvement in the planning and teaching of Aboriginal Studies in 1977.

David Hollinsworth (1992) said:

> As a non-Aboriginal person who has taught Aboriginal Studies to both Aboriginal and non-Aboriginal tertiary students for over a decade, these arguments are of intense significance, professionally, personally and politically. Arguments about the nature of Aboriginality and the means of claiming, contesting and authenticating Aboriginal identity are central to both the future of Aboriginal Studies as an academic area of study and to political and ideological struggles over Australian nationalism and the position of indigenous peoples within it. [Hollinsworth, 1992: 137]

Andrew Lattas, commenting on Hollinsworth in the same journal, said that paternal supervision of Aboriginal identity was current. He added that:

> The academic desire to demystify people, to teach them that they are socially and culturally produced, strips from people the myths of their own autonomous being; it disempowers people. [Lattas, 1992: 160]

For this reason, it would appear that Professor Colin Tatz, of Macquarie University, believes Aboriginal aspects should permeate all subjects of the curriculum and that this is a better approach than having explicit Aboriginal Studies programs. However, regardless of how Aboriginal Studies is dealt with in schools or universities, the teaching of it provides another avenue for others to represent Aboriginal views and values. Mudrooroo Nyoongah (1992) noted that "those writing about Aboriginal identity often employ ideology to push their case on us". He warned of engaging in discourses of:

> Aborigines and Aboriginal identity without placing the importance on Aboriginal theories of identity. I believe that such a search and any conclusions reached must come from us, ourselves. We must determine our own identity in parameters established by us. [Nyoongah, 1992: 156]

While words such as *assimilation* and *self-determination* may be mere concepts in some minds, they have been used to describe policies relating to Aboriginal people.

In academic discussions, culture, oppression and racism are simply concepts; in the context of Aboriginal Studies, they are issues at the heart of relationships between Aboriginal Australians and other Australians since European settlement. Many of the misconceptions of the past are still with us today. Not much has changed, and in some ways attitudes are even more entrenched.

Aboriginal people want to retain their languages, culture, social organisation and the management of their lands and their lives. They struggle to retain their identity, values and beliefs. They require that their representation shows them as they see themselves.

Aboriginal people such as Jack Davis, Mudrooroo, Ruby Langton, Sally Morgan and Eva Johnson are writing books, poems, short stories and plays. They are redefining their role in Australia. They see cultural pluralism in their own way, which ignores the mere acceptance of migrants. They are developing their potential to influence all facets of the fabric of Australian society and develop a truly Australian approach in representing themselves and other Australians.

However, the mass media is still controlled by non-Aboriginal people and their organisations. Aboriginal people are moving into radio, television and print. CAAMA radio in Alice Springs and Imparja television have become well known. Radio is widely used among Aboriginal groups to maintain social and cultural links. At Ernabella and Yuendumu, Aboriginal people are developing new uses for communications in support of social and cultural links, service and delivery and commercial activities. Video conferencing, computer links, telephone, radio, facsimile, local video production and broadcasting are being controlled by local groups.

These initiatives appear to be on the margins and not yet able to influence the attitudes of other Australians. For example, the Tanami network covers the Walbiri lands and can be used for family and ceremonial contacts, representations of community viewpoints and community networking. Government agencies are involved in providing health services and education via video links. These kinds of representations are rarely offered to the rest of the Australian community, and therefore remain on the margins and in isolation.

Nevertheless, the extent to which Aboriginal people may develop their own representations is very much controlled by governments. This occurs through various policies such as the reconciliation process or may be derived from occurrences such as the Mabo High Court decision. The reconciliation process has derived from a clear desire to do something, but it is also drawn from a view of Aboriginal peoples' disadvantage. Ron Brunton (1993) has critically analysed the way in which Aboriginal disadvantage has been used to influence the commonwealth government's Aboriginal Affairs policy.

Brunton was concerned with the way in which Aboriginal issues are being dealt with at the taxpayers' expense from a perspective of disadvantage[1] rather than from a more positive position. His observations take account of the following:

- racism and disadvantage;
- protectionism and disadvantage;
- assimilation and disadvantage;
- Aboriginal cultures and disadvantage.

Brunton (1993) criticises the Royal Commission into Aboriginal Deaths in Custody report for its omissions on the impact of Christianity on Aboriginal life. He believes that there is a great silence on the way in which Christianity has been blended into some Aboriginal communities and in some instances has helped place Aboriginal people in control over the direction of their own lives (Brunton, 1993: 51). He is critical of the report for not pursuing the way in which individual self-esteem may be strengthened and communities revitalised by Christianity.

In response to the criticisms directed at popular misconceptions about government policy in relation to Aboriginal affairs, the commonwealth has produced a publication called *Rebutting the Myths*. It deals with the popular issues that form the basis of stereotypes and misinformation relating to Aboriginal Australians — such issues as:

- Aboriginal people and alcohol;
- whether Aboriginal people are really lazy;
- the availability of funds in Aboriginal affairs;
- the "special treatment" of and "special privileges" for Aboriginal people;
- sacred sites, land rights and development; and
- the "free car".

The booklet is produced by the Office of the Minister for Aboriginal and Torres Strait Islander Affairs to banish some of the shocking and absurd prejudices which exist about Aboriginal and Torres Strait Islander people.

The decision to take such a step on behalf of the commonwealth government through the Minister's office raises the question of public opinion about Aboriginal issues generally and about attitudinal shift. Mary Edmunds (1987) refers to the 1967 Referendum, where an impressive 90.77 per cent of electors voted to change the Constitution. She has suggested that this result has been interpreted by some commentators as support for Aboriginal people and recognition that there needed to be a change in the status of Aboriginal people's quality of life.

Ms Edmunds' work was a study of public opinion, the media and attitudes towards Aboriginal people. In a seminar paper given at the Australian Institute of Aboriginal and Torres Strait Islander Studies, Ms Edmunds referred to a study conducted by Malcolm Calley in 1957 on the north coast of New South Wales. This study identified that the attitude of most whites to Aborigines was ambivalent, but identified a list of principal stereotypes which seemed to be used to justify community practices excluding Aborigines. The list was reproduced by Ms Edmunds because the same attitudes kept coming up in other studies. It included:

- Aborigines are dirty and foul smelling, possessing no conception of personal hygiene.
- Aborigines are diseased.
- Mixed-bloods are promiscuous and venereal disease is more common among Aborigines than in white society.
- Aborigines drink more and are unable to hold their alcohol.
- They are lazy, unpunctual and thriftless: that is, also unreliable.

- They are addicted to gambling.
- They are inferior in mental capacity to whites.

In 1988 the Mackay Report was about *Being Australian*. It included a chapter called "The Aborigines: a dimension to the Australian identity". This study found that 1988 had heightened the discussions about Aboriginal people and Aboriginal issues. There was an almost universal awareness that Aboriginal people believe that they are a dispossessed people and that some reparation should be made on their behalf.

The study found that Australians had become more comfortable about discussing the role, plight and future of Aboriginal Australians than a few years ago. However, there was some belief that, having stimulated a free and open discussion about Aboriginal issues, there is no need to do anything more.

> We all seem to be much more prepared to discuss it these days — I suppose that that's a good thing.
>
> There's so much in the media about Aborigines. They have really used the Bicentenary to push their cause. At least we have listened to them ... We are all much more aware than we used to be.
>
> I really wonder about the future for Australia, because I am convinced we haven't come to grips with the past. I don't think we can go on in the right way until we accept what our history really is and not glamorise it.

This study indicated that Australians seemed to regard Aboriginal people as a curious subspecies of Australians; better educated respondents who knew Aboriginal people tended to defend the Aboriginal cause; less educated people pointed out the obvious differences with a mixture of distaste and animosity.

The 1988 Mackay Report indicated that there was an acceptance that Aboriginal people have the right to complain about their historical treatment and about their status in Australian society. There was no knowledge about how Aboriginal people might change the situation themselves, and it was generally accepted that Aboriginal people would not be easily assimilated into urban Australian life.

Respondents to the study made a distinction between "good" and "bad" Aboriginal people. "Good" ones integrated totally into European culture or disappeared to take up a primitive way of life. "Bad" Aborigines were seen to be those who made a "nuisance of themselves" by wanting special rights while claiming all the privileges assumed to go with white civilisation.

A distinction was made by respondents between "full-bloods" and "half-castes". "Full-bloods" were assumed to be much more reliable, responsible and clearer in their goals and it was assumed that they resisted assimilation into white society. "Half-castes", however, were thought to be the "real trouble-makers" because they were presumed to suffer an identity crisis (Mackay Report, 1988: 45).

> Your half-caste doesn't know where he fits in. [Mackay Report, 1988: 46]

Though the respondents acknowledged the legitimacy in many Aboriginal issues, they believed that the Aboriginal way of life had nothing to offer in the way of enrichment or interest. The report concluded that, in spite of a heightened awareness of Aboriginals and Aboriginal issues, Australians generally feel superior to Aboriginal people whom they want to regard as true Australians. It was generally accepted that Aboriginal influences would be negative, that Aborigines tended to drag down the standard of living of those with whom they interacted and that Aboriginal people were committed to "taking from the system" rather than contributing to it.

The studies and attitudes referred to in this chapter have been used to draw attention to the fact that representations help form opinions. The seemingly funny, simple Pelaco shirt advertisement with an Aboriginal man from Casterton saying "Mine tink it fit fine" fulfilled and justified a stereotype. Comic strip characters, such as those of Joliffe and the Aboriginal characters in Mary Grant Bruce's Billabong series, help develop white myths and perpetuate misrepresentation of Aboriginal life.

Aboriginal society and cultures have been given a limited role in influential forms such as Australian history books, Australian movies or popular images. There seems to be some difficulty in accepting the multidimensional nature of Aboriginal life. Aboriginal lifestyles range across a spectrum. Many Aboriginal and Torres Strait Islander people today live in cities and participate in a range of cultural, political and religious activities across Australia. Diversity existed before the Europeans came. It continues today. Diversity does not mean that one Aboriginal group's lifestyle is more or less valid than any other.

Notes

1. Brunton has picked up on the "catalogue of disadvantage", another way in which Aboriginal people have been represented recently. "Disadvantage" could, in fact, be said to be the platform of the reconciliation process.

References

Aboriginal Consultative Group (1975). *Education for Aborigines*. Report to the Commonwealth Schools Commission.

Bourke, C.J. (1979). Prejudice in School Texts: An Aboriginal Viewpoint. Unpublished paper.

Bourke, E.A. (1988). *Whitefulla Ceremonies*. Paper delivered at the ACT Chapter of the Australian College of Education AGM — 1988.

Brunton, R. (1993). *Black Suffering, White Guilt*. IPA: Melbourne.

Bundy, (1961). *My Land*. Adelaide: Rigby.

Cotter, Michael (1977). "The image of the Aboriginal in three modern Australian novels". *Meanjin*, vol. 4, Aboriginal issue.

Edmunds, M. (1987). *Opinion, Ideology and Practice or Do Public Attitudes Exist Rebutting the Myths?* Canberra: AGPS.

Eyre, E. (1845). *Journals of Expeditions of Discovery*. London. 2 vols.

Hollinsworth, D. (1992). "Discourses on Aboriginality and the politics of Aboriginal identity in urban Australia". *Oceania*, vol. 62.

Keneally, Thomas (1973). *The Chant of Jimmie Blacksmith*. Ringwood: Penguin.

Lattas, A. (1992). "Wiping the blood off Aboriginality: the politics of Aboriginal embodiment in contemporary intellectual debate". *Oceania*, vol. 62.

Loos, Noel (1977). "The frontier revisited". *Meanjin*, vol. 4, Aboriginal issue.

MacIntyre, S. (1986). *The Oxford History of Australia*, vol. 4.

Mackay, H. (1988). *Being Australian. The Mackay Report*. Sydney: Mackay Research.

Mudrooroo, Nyoongah (1992). "Self-determining our Aboriginality: a response to Hollinsworth". *Oceania*, vol. 62.

Ward, R. and Robertson, J. (1969). "Such was life". In *Select Documents in Australian Social History, vol. 2, 1831–1913*. Sydney: Ure Smith.

Chapter 2

Changing History: New Images of Aboriginal History

Steve Hemming

Teichelmann (Lutheran Missionary, Adelaide 1842) told the story of how he cornered two recently initiated men and told them that they should fear Jehovah and not the "red kangaroo" (the red kangaroo being the principal Dreaming of the region). One of the Aboriginal men became very angry and replied:

> Why do you charge us with a lie, that is, reject our opinion, we do not charge you with lies; what you believe and speak of Jehovah is good, and what we believe is good.
>
> We replied that only on one side the truth would be, and that side was ours.
>
> Very well, he answered, then I am a liar, and you speak the truth; I shall not speak another word, you may now speak. [Teichelmann, quoted in Foster, 1990:19]

Introduction

In 1988 some Australians celebrated two hundred years of Australian history — "a celebration of a nation". But what of Australia's history before 1788 and what about the last two hundred years as seen through Aboriginal eyes? For Aboriginal people, Australia's Bicentenary was a time of mourning — perhaps a celebration of the survival of Aboriginal people, but not "a celebration of a nation". The year 1788 marked the beginning of great suffering and loss for Aboriginal people: the invasion of their land. In 1939, the year after Australia celebrated its sesqui-centenary, the Aboriginal political activist William Cooper, the Honorary Secretary of the Australian Aborigines League, wrote the following words:

> How much compensation have we had? How much of our land has been paid for? Not one iota! Again we state that we are the original owners of the country. In spite of force, prestige, or anything else you like, morally the land is ours. We have been ejected and despoiled of our God-given right and our inheritance has been forcibly taken from us. [Cooper 1939, quoted in Markus 1988:14]

In 1988 other Aboriginal people repeated Cooper's demands for justice. More recently, the results of the landmark Mabo case have prompted strong statements from contemporary Aboriginal people, echoing Aboriginal pleas for justice made since the first days of European invasion.

The images that Europeans have constructed of Australia's indigenous inhabitants have both shaped the nature of Aboriginal and non-Aboriginal relations and provided the framework within which Aboriginal history has been and is still being written. Western constructs of "race", Christian ideology and the development of Social Darwinism, with its "child" anthropology, have all been critical in the construction of images of Aboriginal people. When reading histories of Australia dealing with Aboriginal people, it is important to recognise these influences and to understand the ways in which the past is constructed by historians and others.

The well-known saying "history is written by the victor" should be kept in mind when understanding the representations of Aboriginal people in Australia's history. A recent and important collection of writings by Australian academics uses the theoretical framework developed by the French historian Michel Foucault to investigate the relationship between power and knowledge in the constructions of images of Aborigines (Attwood and Arnold, 1992). In the introduction to this collection Bain Attwood writes:

> Thus, in Foucault's terms, knowledge or "truth" is not "outside of power" but closely affiliated with it. Indeed, any "truth" depends upon power to make it true. [Attwood 1992: ii]

This understanding of the relationship between knowledge and power is clearly illustrated at the beginning of this chapter in the 1842 interchange in between the missionary Teichelmann and an angry Aboriginal man. To introduce new "truths" into Australia's history, Aboriginal and non-Aboriginal commentators and academics are in the process of challenging contemporary Australian power relations.

In recent years the boundaries between academic disciplines in the humanities have become blurred and this process can clearly be witnessed in the writing of historical works about Aboriginal people. Anthropologists, historians, sociologists and other academics are all involved in the production of what is most often termed Aboriginal history (Cowlishaw, 1992: 20). However, it is perhaps the comparatively recent emergence of a large body of Aboriginal literature that has most directly challenged the old versions of Australian history and, as part of this process, non-Aboriginal constructions of Aboriginality (Narogin, 1990; Davis et al., 1990).

Aboriginal people have started an invasion of their own over the last few decades — challenging the dominant "white" view of Australia's past. They have begun presenting their own versions of what has happened in Australia in the last two hundred years and introduced a new perspective, based on The Dreaming, of Australia's much longer history. Over the last few decades, the increased access that Aboriginal people have had to the sources of power in Australian society has been a critical factor providing support and impetus to the rewriting of Australian history from an Aboriginal perspective.

Challenging "the great Australian silence"

In 1968 the anthropologist W.E.H. Stanner delivered his landmark lecture, "The great Australian silence", as part of the ABC Boyer lecture series (Stanner, 1972). He highlighted Australia's longstanding habit of forgetting Aboriginal people and their views, and he argued that this habit had developed into a cult of forgetfulness practised on a national scale (Stanner, 1972: 25). That twenty years later Stanner's "great Australian silence" made such a dramatic appearance at Australia's Bicentenary is a matter of shame for non-Aboriginal Australians. In 1988 the Australian authorities recreated the past to fit the positive image of Australia that they wanted to project to the world. This image did not include Aboriginal versions of Australia's history.

In his 1968 lecture, Stanner considered the work of Australian historians from the 1930s to the 1960s and commented on the absence of Aboriginal people from the mainstream Australian histories. What these historians did was to locate Aboriginal people in what they saw as a static, primitive and "traditional" past and in so doing excluded them from the changing story of Australian history. Only so-called "full-blood" people were considered to be "real" Aborigines and they were considered to be part of a dying race, being swept aside by the march of civilisation. The majority of Aboriginal people living on reserves, on missions and in fringe-camps did not qualify, for the purposes of these histories, as "real". It was expected that they would eventually merge into the rest of the population (Langton, 1981). They were on the fringes of white Australian society, the fringe dwellers of Australian historiography, and were not considered important in Australia's past (Reynolds, 1972: ix).

The impact of genocide, invasion, institutionalisation and forced assimilation only began to be widely recognised in non-Aboriginal spheres in the 1960s.

In 1988, Aboriginal people and their supporters publicly challenged the "official" version of Australia's past and brought into focus the ways that particular constructions of the past continue the oppression of Aboriginal people in Australia. The celebration of two hundred years of "Australian" history was in direct contrast to the Aboriginal messages of mourning being presented during 1988.

Excerpts from the speeches given at the protest rally were reproduced in *Paperbark: A Collection of Black Australian Writings* (Davis et al., 1990). Aboriginal speakers questioned some of the principal non-Aboriginal concepts at the centre of the Bicentenary and presented opposing Aboriginal perspectives in their place. The following "oppositional pairs" can be identified in the speeches and used as focal points when critiquing conventional Australian history:

- history/dreaming
- settlement/invasion and dispossession
- pioneers/invaders
- progress/subjugation
- civilisation/genocide.

In his opening prayer to the crowd, the Reverend Charles Harris summed up the mood of the gathering:

> God of the Dreamtime, you who are with us for these 40,000 years or more before 1788, you who gave us our ceremonies, and the law, and our stories, and our sacred sites, you who gave us our Dreaming, you who gave us this land; you were with us then; you are with us now. You march with us today as we march through the streets of Sydney in the march for freedom, justice and hope.
>
> You were with us through the last 200 years of onslaught, of terrorism, and of apartheid that has been administered to our people in this land. And you have helped us and enabled us to survive through the odds that were against us.
>
> We pray that you will avenge your people, the Aboriginal and Islander people. Show to the world, today, the evil deeds of those who came and

robbed us, raped our land and our people, murdered and lied to our people. Expose them to the world.

Look and see the chains of oppression that keep your people, the Aboriginal and Islander people, in bondage. Hear the cry, and the call, and the plea for justice to be done in this land. Show the people that you are the God of justice and, Lord be praised, the God of the Dreamtime.

Bring freedom, bring justice, and bring hope. [Davis et al., 1990: 332]

Harris's prayer clearly and forcefully presents an Aboriginal perspective of the meaning of the Bicentenary. His ability to incorporate Christian imagery into an Aboriginal frame, without seriously challenging the concepts associated with The Dreaming, provides a vivid example of Aboriginal resistance to domination by the ideologies brought by the European invaders. Christianity has been an important "site of resistance" and an analysis of its relationship with Aboriginal people provides examples of cultural change and adaptation that are critical to a new understanding of Aboriginal history and Aboriginality (Swain and Rose, 1988: 5).

With the Aboriginal political struggle for power, and the successes that this struggle has achieved, has come the possibility for Aboriginal people to challenge the established versions of Australian history. Aboriginal perspectives have been increasingly published and have started to have an impact on the way that Australians see themselves and Australian history. Film, as a medium, has had a major role in providing a widely accessible forum for new perspectives. Good examples include the documentary *Lousy Little Sixpence*, the television series *Women of the Sun*, the film *Babakuieria* and the work of Aboriginal film-maker, Tracy Moffatt (e.g. *Nice Coloured Girls and Night Cries*). In the film *Babakuieria* the Bicentennial view of Australian history is turned on its head: by placing non-Aboriginal people in the same powerless position that Aboriginal people continually have experienced, the audience is forced to question the "official" version of Australian history.

Charles Perkins has been a prominent participant in the Aboriginal "struggle" and a vocal advocate of Aboriginal political activism, with its principal concern for changing the social, political and economic position of Aboriginal people. During the 1960s, Perkins was a central figure in activities that challenged the policies of the Australian government, such as the Freedom Rides (Perkins, 1975). On these "rides", young Aboriginal activists organised trips into rural New South Wales to gain support from Aboriginal and non-Aboriginal people and to expose "racist" practices. As well as stressing the centrality of the role of Aboriginal activism in forcing positive change, Perkins acknowledges the valuable role that politicians such as Gough Whitlam and Don Dunstan played in bringing about political and social change.

In response to political activism and the publication of Aboriginal viewpoints, academics in the 1960s and 1970s began taking a different approach to writing Aboriginal history and defining Aboriginal people (see Beckett, 1958; Reay, 1964; Lippmann, 1970; Rowley, 1970 and 1971; Barwick, 1972; Reynolds, 1972). Cowlishaw writes about the interest that young anthropology students of the early 1970s took in the Aboriginal political struggle. At the University of Sydney they organised a "Free University" at which there were courses and discussion groups concerning contemporary Aborigines (Cowlishaw, 1992: 22). It was University of Sydney students who, in the 1960s, joined the Freedom Riders on their trips to the New South Wales country towns (Gilbert, 1973: 31–32).

The advent of the contemporary campaign for "land rights" eventually brought anthropologists and other academics into the frontline of the struggle for Aboriginal rights. This was particularly so after the passing of the *Aboriginal Land Rights Act* (NT) in 1976. This inevitably led to a rethinking of many key concepts in the anthropological literature dealing with Aboriginal people and culture (Berndt, 1982; Langton and Peterson, 1983). New understandings of the changing nature of Aboriginal "cultures" emerged from the Aboriginal struggle for land rights. However, although anthropologists began to recognise the realities of Aboriginal Australia since 1788, the legal system, as witnessed by the 1976 Act, did not:

> In particular, there remains an immense reluctance to acknowledge the impact of colonisation and to give recognition to the creative adaptations of the pre-contact land-tenure system by which many Aborigines have ensured the continuity of relationships to the country. The failure of the Northern Territory legislation to recognise these adaptations, forced upon the people by invasion and the consequent disruptions, is its weakest point. [Langton and Peterson 1983: 3]

During the 1970s and 1980s, anthropology in other parts of the world was taking an interest in cultural change and adaptation and moving away from focusing on "traditional" bounded societies

(Ortner, 1984). New approaches in sociology provided a serious critique of Western knowledge systems and approaches to academic work (Foucault, 1974; Lyotard, 1984; Seidman and Wagner, 1992). The development of what has been described as postmodernist thinking, emanating to a large extent from sociology, has revolutionised the approach that anthropology has taken to studying "other" peoples and developing authoritative accounts of their culture. The power relationship between the researcher and their object of study has been questioned by academics such as Edward Said (1978). His analysis of what he terms "Orientalism" has been applied by a number of contemporary Australian academics to the ways that Aboriginal people have been studied, constructed and disempowered in the process (Attwood and Arnold, 1992; Cowlishaw, 1992).

Before the 1960s: The early struggle

Aboriginal political activism has certainly not been restricted to the period from the 1960s. It is also clear that Aboriginal men and women have played significant roles in the political movement. As the historians Jackie Huggins and Heather Goodall point out in a recent paper:

> Aboriginal women have been involved with men in movements to regain land from the earliest struggles. For example, in NSW, a sequence can be found in the records from 1872, at Braidwood, when Kitty, Ellen and their husband, Alick, spoke for their community in demanding land: "We want to get some land which we can call our own in reality ... We think the Blacks are entitled to live in their own country". [Brennan, 1907: 213, cited in Huggins and Goodall, 1992: 403]

Aboriginal people attained some successes at a local level in the earlier periods of political struggle. In the 1920s the Australian Aboriginal Progressive Association was active on the south coast of New South Wales in the defence of Aboriginal land against local farmers (Huggins and Goodall, 1992: 403). However, as Andrew Markus has documented in his history of William Cooper's political life and the Australian Aborigines' League, it was more difficult for Aboriginal people to challenge the government on wider issues involving the oppression of Aboriginal people (Markus, 1988). Such movements were relatively powerless due to the position of Aboriginal people in Australian society and the racist and ignorant views held by the majority of Australians at that time.

Similar earlier moves for political change have been documented in South Australia (Jenkin, 1976; Mattingley and Hampton, 1988). From the late 1800s, Aboriginal people such as Matthew Kropinyeri were directly confronting the government on issues relating to policies and legislation affecting Aborigines (Jenkin, 1979: 174). However, their pleas often fell on deaf ears, as those in authority largely believed that Aboriginal people were a primitive race and destined to die out in the face of the superior Europeans. As Markus points out in his discussion of William Cooper's role in the Australian Aborigines League (AAL):

> There was no tradition of according serious consideration to Aboriginal viewpoints and the dominant assumptions of his [Cooper's] day meant that Aborigines were dismissed as an irrelevancy, an inferior "race" destined for extinction. [Markus 1988: 20]

When Europeans first came to Australia, they held views about Aboriginal people largely informed by developing forms of what has been described as "scientific racism" (McConnochie, Hollinsworth and Pettman, 1988). Captain Cook brought with him images of "native" peoples as "noble savages", largely the antithesis of Europeans. Cook was influenced by the writings of Rousseau, whose followers saw "native" peoples as uncontaminated by the evils of civilisation, closer to nature and therefore God. These idealistic views were modified after 1788 and the nature of contact between invaders and Aborigines led to descriptions of Aboriginal people as "ignoble" savages and barbarous heathens (Mulvaney, 1990: 10). As Social Darwinism became influential, later in the nineteenth century, the status of Aboriginal people was reduced to the level of sub-humans. It was in this intellectual climate that people such as Matthew Kropinyeri struggled for equal rights.

By the turn of the century, a new Australian national identity was developing and Aboriginal people, in the literature of the time, were often depicted as the villains in the story of Australia's pioneer settlers taming a savage and unused land (Newland, 1893; Healy, 1989: 55). In this growing Australian "folklore", Aboriginal people were characterised as primitive, dangerous savages leading an aimless nomadic life. Aboriginal connections with the land did not fit the European model of land ownership. In 1770 Australia had been claimed by Cook and later declared *terra nullius* — a concept only recently overturned by the High Court in the Mabo case (Frost, 1990; Watson, 1992).

Once Aboriginal people came into contact with what was considered the superior European race, it was seen as inevitable that they become extinct. Genocide was largely justified by the application of the concept of the "survival of the fittest" to humans. The Social Darwinists of the late nineteenth and twentieth centuries developed a rigid, racist view of Aboriginal people (McConnochie, Hollinsworth and Pettman, 1988). Those Aboriginal people not living in an "untouched" state were regarded as remnants of a disintegrating culture living on the fringes of white society (Cowlishaw, 1992: 23–24). By the mid-twentieth century an "assimilationist" perspective dominated government policies and legislation (Broome, 1982: 171). It was expected that Aboriginal people would gradually assimilate into the wider society, becoming lighter skinned as they intermarried with Europeans and adopted the "modern", dominant culture.

New approaches to Aboriginal "culture" and history

By the early 1970s, historians had started to change their approach to the writing of Aboriginal history (Rowley, 1972; Reynolds, 1972). The first focus of these new histories was an attempt to provide a new perspective of the events of early contact history. The violence of relations between Aboriginal and non-Aboriginal people became a characteristic feature in what Attwood has called this "revisionist" history (Attwood, 1989: 135). With the publication of Reynolds' *Other Side of the Frontier* in 1981 came an attempt to discover the Aboriginal view of early contact. As Attwood writes:

> Reynolds established a model of dispossession and resistance which became the paradigm in which most scholars explored Aboriginal responses, although he also pointed to patterns of contact other than conflict. [Attwood, 1989: 137]

Historians became interested in Aboriginal responses to invasion, but mainly the violent ones, and usually discussed them in terms of armed resistance and massacres (Robinson and York, 1977; Loos, 1982; Elder, 1988). The dynamics of cultural change and adaptation were not investigated by these historians and a preoccupation with the breakdown of so-called "traditional" culture left contemporary Aboriginal people in the dubious position of being labelled as having "lost" their culture.

The complexities of the interaction between Aboriginal and non-Aboriginal people have often been treated with more insight by anthropologists, who have applied a more sophisticated understanding of the cultures of the peoples that they study. A good example is Chris Anderson's study of Aborigines and the tin mining industry in Northern Queensland (Anderson, 1983). Anderson is critical of the history that was being written by historians such as Reynolds and Loos and has the following to say about this "new history":

> Much of the "new history" of Aboriginal contact with Europeans in Australia lacks an adequate socio-cultural understanding of Aboriginal society and its diversity. Attempts to produce overall models of contact have obscured, too, the diversity of European activity and its impact. The outcome has been too hollow and passive a view of Aboriginal responses to Australian colonial situations. [Anderson, 1983: 473]

Anderson particularly stresses the Aboriginal "agency" in determining the outcome of interaction with non-Aboriginal people. His study is an example of "historical" anthropology, illustrating the continuing blurring of the boundaries between the disciplines involved in the study of Aboriginal history.

In his book, *The Making of the Aborigines*, Attwood (1989) provides an historical background to the "making" of indigenous Australians into "Aborigines" — an identity he argues has largely been constructed by the actions and interests of Europeans. Attwood places less emphasis than Anderson on the "agency" of Aboriginal people in the contact process.

In an earlier paper, the Aboriginal anthropologist Marcia Langton stressed the importance of recognising Aboriginal adaptations to European invasion and a commonality of "culture" among Aboriginal people across Australia in a variety of situations (Langton, 1981).

More recently, other anthropologists have been producing historical accounts of Aboriginal relations with non-Aboriginal people, in particular emphasising the role of the Australian state (Cowlishaw, 1988; Morris, 1989; Trigger, 1992). Cowlishaw sees Morris's account as critical in the more recent attempts to "deconstruct the construction of Aboriginality":

> Perhaps the most important breakthrough, however, is that which insists that the study of "Us" is part of the study of "Them". Morris has achieved this in his work on the Dhan-gadi Aborigines and the state, perhaps the first

detailed analysis of colonialism in Australia. He views colonialism as "the implementation of a distinctive cultural system", and reveals the Dhangadi's cultural responses as creative and complex. [Cowlishaw, 1992: 29]

Mudrooroo Nyoongah (formerly Mudrooroo Narogin and Colin Johnson), Aboriginal author and chairperson of Murdoch University's Aboriginal and Islander program, stresses the importance of Aboriginal "voices" in changing the picture of Aboriginal history (Narogin, 1990). He has recently established a new Aboriginal and Islander degree program where the emphasis is on Aboriginal people presenting Aboriginal perspectives. He sees the role of Aboriginal writers since the 1960s as being critical in challenging the "official" histories and presenting a new version of Aboriginality (see Walker, 1966; Gilbert, 1973; Narogin, 1983).

In the last few decades there have emerged an increasing number of published accounts of the lives of Aboriginal people who have grown up in the rural or urban areas of Australia. Through their very telling, the images of Aboriginal identity are being extended and changed from the static, "traditional" images presented by earlier, conventional anthropology, to the diverse and dynamic images of contemporary Aboriginality (see Walker, 1964; Gilbert, 1973; Davis and Hodge, 1985; Miller, 1985; Narogin, 1983; Morgan, 1987; Langford, 1988). These Aboriginal authors describe the horrors of Australian history, but also call into question the recent past and the present. They make white Australia aware that, for Aboriginal people, the invasion of their country and the violence of the early contact period have continued to the present day.

Nyoongah also attacks the treatment that the Aboriginal oral history tradition has received at the hands of non-Aboriginal historians and anthropologists (Shaw, 1983; Muecke, 1983). He sees oral histories which have been transcribed to the published page as "captured", "calcified" and transformed from living, dynamic tradition to nothing more than "artefacts". He writes:

Increasingly, traditional discourse is becoming fossilised, and the young people are turning away from the remains. The languages of their communities are becoming objects of shame, ridiculous moments of stone-age culture. This is only too evident in a work such as *My Country of the Pelican Dreaming*. If an Aborigine needs help it is to them he applies, and if he does something wrong it is by them that he is punished — and if his story is to be written, it is to be written by the coloniser and in the coloniser's own discourse. [Johnson, 1987: 28]

However, in the collection of Black Australian writings, *Paperbark* (Davis et al., 1990), Muecke's technique for transcribing and present-ing oral texts is used. The value of this approach is recognised, along with a warning that it still contains some restrictions:

> this can only be a partial representation of the complex gestures, inscrip-tions, melodies and intonations which characterise Aboriginal storytelling and singing. [Davis et al., 1990: 1]

New images of Australia's history

New images of Australia's history are emerging and a growing under-standing of the history of Aboriginal people and their relationship to the Australian state is being developed. This process is occurring both through the efforts of Aboriginal people and through contributions by non-Aboriginal people. A different interpretation of Australia's history, from Aboriginal perspectives, is becoming available due to the grow-ing body of Aboriginal literature. The following images of Australia's history graphically depict why Aboriginal people saw 1988 as both a year of mourning and as an opportunity to say that, as a people, "we have survived".

Aboriginal people believe that they have always lived in Australia, since the beginning — The Dreaming. Archaeologists have a different view of history and through excavation they have pushed the dates for the Aboriginal occupation of Australia back past 40,000 years (Flood, 1983). The Western "scientific" approach to constructing the past has caused considerable conflict between archaeologists and Aboriginal people — the case of the reburial of the Lake Mungo human remains is a recent example (Pardoe, 1992: 138). However, it appears that on both sides of this debate accommodations are being made and archae-ologists who recognise Aboriginal ownership of the pre-European, Australian past are finding support for their research from Aboriginal communities. Many Aboriginal people see value in archaeological research and they don't believe that it necessarily challenges their world view (Pardoe, 1992: 139). Western constructs of time, adapted to fit with Aboriginal concepts, can be clearly seen in the prayer of the Reverend Harris quoted at an earlier point in this paper. The popularity of Aboriginal art, in particular the dot paintings of the Western Desert, has led to the widespread exposure of concepts such as The Dreaming (Sutton et al., 1989). New images of Australia as an "ancient land", created in The Dreaming, are competing with scientific images of Australia's past. This has, however, led to problems for Aboriginal people, with the reinforcement of "traditional" stereotypes of Aboriginal culture often the result.

The violence of early contact between Aboriginal people and Europeans has been a major focus for new interpretations of Australian histories, produced by both Aboriginal and non-Aboriginal people. A recognition that the Europeans were invaders and that they forcibly stole Aboriginal lands has emerged from this literature. Many writers have sought to show that Aboriginal people violently resisted this invasion and that a state of warfare existed in many areas. This didn't all occur 200 years ago. In the Western Desert, first contact is still taking place and there is comparatively recent evidence of massacres of Aboriginal people in Central Australia — for example, the Coniston massacre in 1928 (Elder, 1988: 141–53). A focus in many recent studies has been the continued, violent repression of Aboriginal people by the Australian state through institutionalisation, policing and oppressive policies. Many Aboriginal authors have argued that their resistance to invasion has not ended, and that sovereignty was never ceded.

Along with the violence of the frontier came another invasion — the introduction of Christianity through missionaries. This was both a physical invasion and an "invasion of the mind" (Attwood, 1989: 1). Reynolds has this to say about the arrival of the missionaries:

> Religion moved from the background to the foreground in Aboriginal experience of European culture with the arrival of missionaries in the 1820s when the tribes targeted for conversion were directly challenged by the doctrines and practices of the newcomers. Of all Europeans the missionaries must have seemed the most enigmatic. They didn't seek land; they were often, though not always, disinterested in black women. They were so unlike the majority of frontier settlers; and, while they expressed goodwill and concern for the Aborigines, they were far more intrusive and interfering than other Europeans, often seeking to disrupt ceremonies and beliefs that were at the heart of Aboriginal society. [Reynolds, 1989: 155]

For many Aboriginal people, life on a mission was the only alternative as their lands were taken over by the Europeans. Many Aboriginal people were forcibly moved on to missions. However, the reactions of

Aboriginal people to Christianity and to the establishment of missions have been diverse. There are examples of Aboriginal people rejecting Christianity (Tonkinson, 1974), examples of the destructiveness of missionaries (Attwood, 1989) and numerous examples of Aboriginal people adapting Christianity to fit their particular situations (Calley, 1964; Bos, 1988).

Until recently, the significant role that Aboriginal people have played in the Australian economy has been largely ignored. However, in many situations, such as on missions, their labour was often forcibly obtained and wages were very low or non-existent. Through studies by anthropologists, historians and the reminiscences of Aboriginal people, the story has emerged of how Aboriginal people became essential to the survival of one of the most important non-Aboriginal "industries" — pastoralism (Berndt and Berndt, 1987; McGrath, 1987). However, Aboriginal people have not benefited financially from their involvement with industries such as pastoralism, as can be seen from Sally Morgan's family history in her novel *My Place* (Morgan, 1987).

In 1788 the Australian state began its control of Aboriginal people's lives. The police and the prison system have always been instrumental in this control. The recent Royal Commission into Aboriginal Deaths in Custody has clearly mapped out the role of non-Aboriginal institutions in the oppression of Aboriginal people. Policies of protection, segregation and assimilation have been applied to Aboriginal people by Australian governments and resulted in inhuman practices such as the removal of children from parents (Barker, 1977; Howard, 1982; Read, 1984; Mattingley and Hampton, 1988; Edwards and Read, 1989).

It was not until the 1960s that Aboriginal people began to gain some access to "power" in Australian society. Only in 1967, through an Australia-wide referendum, were Aboriginal people recognised as citizens and included in the census. In 1972, a symbolically significant event for the Aboriginal cause took place with the setting up of a Tent Embassy on the lawns of Parliament House in Canberra. This embassy was set up in protest over statements made by the McMahon government over land rights. The earlier "walk off" by the Gurindji people at Wattie Creek, over wages decisions by the Arbitration Commission, was also crucial in the struggle for land rights (Broome, 1982).

Since 1988 there has been ample opportunity for more reflection by non-Aboriginal Australians on Australian history from an Aboriginal perspective. In these few years, Australians have witnessed the Royal Commission into Aboriginal Deaths in Custody, the establishment of the government's new attempt to provide Aboriginal people with more control over their lives — the Aboriginal and Torres Strait Islander Commission — the introduction of the concept of "reconciliation" rather than the immediate development of a "treaty", as proposed in 1988, the establishment of the "Provisional Government" and the landmark case concerning Aboriginal land rights, the Mabo case (Rowse, 1992; Watson, 1993). Out of the Royal Commission into Aboriginal Deaths in Custody and the High Court decision on native title has come a serious questioning of the past images of Australian history. What Australia has to do to develop as a nation, and as a new republic, is to move towards a shared understanding of Australian history. Aboriginal perspectives have to be respected and recognised for their value in developing a mature nation, willing to face its past.

References

Anderson, C. (1983). "Aborigines and tin mining in north Queensland: a case study in the anthropology of contact history". *Mankind*, vol. 13, no. 6, April, pp. 473-98.

Attwood, B (1989). *The Making of the Aborigines*. Sydney: Allen & Unwin.

_____ (1992). "Introduction". In *Power, Knowledge and Aborigines*, edited by B. Attwood and J. Arnold [a special edition of the *Journal of Australian Studies*). Bundoora: La Trobe University Press in association with the National Centre for Australian Studies, Monash University, pp. i-xvi.

_____ & Arnold, J. (eds) (1992). *Power, Knowledge and Aborigines* (a special edition of the *Journal of Australian Studies*). Bundoora: La Trobe University Press in association with the National Centre for Australian Studies, Monash University.

Australian Academy of Humanities Annual Symposium, *Who Owns the Past?* Edited by I. McBryde (1985). Melbourne: Oxford University Press.

Barwick, D. (1972). "Coranderrek and Cumeroogunga: pioneers and policy". In *Opportunity and Responses: Case Studies in Economic Development*, edited by T. Epstein and D. Penny. London: [publisher unknown].

Beckett, J. (1958). "Marginal men: a study of two half-caste Aborigines". *Oceania*, vol. 29, pp. 91-108.

Benterrak, K., Muecke, S. & Roe, P. (1984). *Reading the Country: An Introduction to Nomadology.* Fremantle: Fremantle Arts Centre Press.

Berndt, R.M. (ed.) (1982). *Aboriginal Sites, Rights and Resource Development.* Nedlands: University of WA Press.

_____ & Berndt, C. (1987). *End of an Era: Aboriginal Labour in the Northern Territory.* Canberra: Australian Institute of Aboriginal Studies.

Bos, R. (1988). "The Dreaming and social change in Arnhem Land". In *Aboriginal Australians and Christian Missions,* edited by T. Swain and D. Rose. Adelaide: Australian Association for Religious Studies.

Broome, R. (1982). *Aboriginal Australians: Black Response to White Dominance, 1788–1980.* Sydney: Allen & Unwin.

Calley, R. (1964). "Pentecostalism among the Bandjalang". In *Aborigines Now: New Perspectives in the Study of Aboriginal Communities,* edited by M. Reay. Sydney: Angus & Robertson.

Cowlishaw, G. (1988). *Black, White or Brindle: Race in Rural Australia.* Melbourne: Cambridge University Press.

_____ (1992). "Studying Aborigines: changing canons in anthropology and history". In *Power, Knowledge and Aborigines*, edited by B. Attwood and J. Arnold (a special edition of the *Journal of Australasian Studies*). Bundoora: La Trobe University Press in association with the National Centre for Australian Studies, Monash University, pp. 20-31.

Davis, J., Muecke, S., Narogin, M. & Shoemaker, A. (1990). *Paperbark: A Collection of Black Australian Writings.* St Lucia: University of Queensland Press.

Davis, J. and Hodge, R. (1985). *Aboriginal Writing Today: Papers from the 1st National Conference of Aboriginal Writers — Perth, WA.* Canberra: Australian Institute of Aboriginal Studies.

Elder, J. (1988). *Blood on the Wattle: Massacres and Maltreatment of Australian Aborigines since 1788.* Frenchs Forest: Child & Associates.

Flood, J. (1983). *Archaeology of the Dreamtime: The Story of Prehistoric Australia and its People.* Sydney: Collins.

Foley, G. (1990). "The year of mourning". In *Paperbark: A Collection of Black Australian Writing,* edited by Davis et al. St Lucia: University of Queensland Press, pp. 330-32.

Foster, R. (1990). "The Aborigines' location in Adelaide: South Australia's first 'mission' to the Aborigines". *Journal of the Anthropological Society of South Australia,* vol. 28, no. 1, pp. 38-63.

Foucault, M. (1974). *The Order of Things: An Archaeology of the Human Sciences.* London: Tavistock.

Frost, A. (1990). "New South Wales as terra nullius". In *Through White Eyes,* edited by S. Janson and S. MacIntyre. Sydney: Allen & Unwin.

Gilbert, K. (1973). *Because a White Man'll Never Do It.* Sydney: Angus & Robertson.

Huggins, J. and Goodall, H. (1992). "Aboriginal women are everywhere. Contemporary struggles". In *Gender Relations in Australia: Domination and Negotiation,* edited by K. Saunders and R. Evans. Sydney: Harcourt, Brace, Jovanovich, pp. 398-424.

Mattingley, C. and Hampton, K. (eds) (1988). *Survival in Our Own Land.* Adelaide: Wakefield Press.

Healey, J.J. (1989). *Literature and the Aborigine.* St Lucia: University of Queensland Press.

McConnochie, K., Hollinsworth, D. and Pettman, J. (1989). *Race and Racism in Australia.* Wentworth Falls: Social Science Press.

Howard, M. (1982). "Australian Aboriginal politics and perpetuation of inequality". In *Oceania*, vol. 53, no. 1, pp. 82-101.

Jenkin, G. (1979). *Conquest of the Ngarrindjeri.* Adelaide: Rigby.

Johnson, C. (1987). "Captured discourse, captured lives". In *Aboriginal History*, vol. 11, nos 1-2, pp. 27-32. (Journal of the Anthropological Society of SA).

Langford, R. (1983). "Our heritage, your playground". *Australian Archaeology*, vol. 16, pp. 2-6.

Langton, M. (1981). "Urbanising Aborigines, the social scientists' great deception". *Social Alternatives*, vol. 2, no. 2, pp. 16-22.

____ & Peterson, N. (eds) (1983). *Aborigines, Land and Land Rights.* Canberra: Australian Institute of Aboriginal Studies.

Lippmann, L. (1970). *To Achieve Our Country. Australia and the Aborigines.* Melbourne: Cheshire.

Loos, N. (1982). *Invasion and Resistance.* Canberra: Australian National University Press.

Lyotard, J. (1984). *The Postmodern Condition: A Report on Knowledge.* Manchester: Manchester University Press.

McGrath, A. (1987). *Born in the Cattle: Aborigines in Cattle Country.* Sydney: Allen & Unwin.

Markus, A. (1988). *Blood from a Stone: William Cooper and the Australian Aborigines' League.* Sydney: Allen & Unwin.

Matthews, J. (1977). *The Two Worlds of Jimmie Barker.* Canberra: Australian Institute of Aboriginal Affairs.

Miller, J. (1985). *Koori — A Will to Win: The Heroic Resistance, Survival and Triumph of Black Australia.* London: Angus & Robertson.

Morgan, S. (1987). *My Place.* Fremantle: Fremantle Arts Centre Press.

Morris, B. (1989). *Domesticating Resistance: The Dhan-Gadi Aborigines and the Australian State.* Oxford: Berg.

Mulvaney, D.J. (1990). "The Australian Aborigines 1606–1929: opinion and fieldwork". In *Through White Eyes*, edited by S. Janson and S. MacIntyre. Sydney: Allen & Unwin.

Narogin, M. (1983). *Doctor Wooreddy's Prescription for Enduring the End of the World.* Melbourne: Hyland House.

____ (1990). *Writing from the Fringe: A Study of Modern Aboriginal Literature.* Melbourne: Hyland House.

Newland, S. (1893). *Paving the Way. A Romance of the Australian Bush.* London: Gay & Bird.

Ortner, S. (1984). "Theory and anthropology since the sixties". In *Comparative Studies in Society and History,* vol. 26, no. 1, pp. 126-166.

Pardoe, C. (1992). "Arches of radii, corridors of power: reflections on current archaeological practice". In *Power, Knowledge and Aborigines*, edited by

B. Attwood and J. Arnold (a special edition of the *Journal of Australasian Studies*). Bundoora: La Trobe University Press in association with the National Centre for Australian Studies, Monash University, pp. 132–41.

Perkins, C. (1975). *A Bastard Like Me*. Sydney: Ure Smith.

Read, P. (ed.) (1984). *Down There with Me on the Cowra Mission: An Oral History of Erambie Aboriginal Reserve, Cowra, New South Wales*. Sydney: Pergamon Press.

Read, R. and Edwards, C. (1989). *The Lost Children*. Sydney: Doubleday.

Reay, M. (ed.) (1964). *Aborigines Now: New Perspectives in the Study of Aboriginal Communities*. Sydney: Angus & Robertson.

Reynolds, H. (1972). *Aborigines and Settlers: The Australian Experience 1788–1939*. Melbourne: Cassell Australia.

_____ (1981). *The Other Side of the Frontier: Aboriginal Resistance to the European Invasion of Australia*. Ringwood: Penguin.

_____ (1989). *Dispossession: Black Australians and White Invaders*. Sydney: Allen & Unwin.

Robinson, F. and York, B. (1977). *The Black Resistance*. Camberwell: Widescope International.

Rowley, C. (1970). *The Destruction of Aboriginal Society*. Canberra: Australian Institute of Aboriginal Studies.

_____ (1971). *Outcasts in White Australia*. Canberra: ANU Press.

_____ (1972). *The Destruction of Aboriginal Society*. Harmondsworth: Penguin.

Rowse, T. (1992). *Remote Possibilities: The Aboriginal Domain and the Administrative Imagination*. Darwin: Northern Australian Research Unit.

Said, E. (1978). *Orientalism*. London: Routledge, Kegan Paul.

Seidman, S. and Waggner, D.G. (1992). *Postmodernism and Social Theory: The Debate Over General Theory*. Cambridge: Blackwell.

Shaw, B. (1983). *Banggaiyerri: The Story of Jack Sullivan*. Canberra: Australian Institute of Aboriginal Studies.

Stanner, W.E.H. (1972). *After The Dreaming*. The Boyer Lecture, Sydney: ABC.

Sutton, P. (ed.) (1989). *Dreamings: The Art of Aboriginal Australia*. New York: Viking.

Swain, T. and Rose, D.B. (eds) (1988). *Aboriginal Australians and Christian Missions*. Adelaide: Australian Association for Religious Studies.

Tonkinson, R. (1974). *The Jigalong Mob: Aboriginal Victors of a Desert Crusade*. California: Cummins.

Trigger, D. (1992). *Whitefella Comin': Aboriginal Responses to Colonialism in Northern Australia*. Cambridge: Cambridge University Press.

Walker, K. (1964). *We are Going*. Brisbane: Jacaranda Press.

_____ (1966). *The Dawn is at Hand*. Brisbane: Jacaranda Press.

Watson, I. (1993). "Has Mabo turned the tide for justice?" *Social Alternatives*, vol. 12, no. 1, pp. 5-9.

Chapter 3

Australia's First Peoples: Identity and Population

Eleanor Bourke

Introduction

There continues to be speculation about the actual numbers of Aboriginal people in Australia at the time of European settlement in 1788 — who they were, whether they originated in this continent, how long they had been here and the numbers of languages spoken. Despite this, Aboriginal people believe that they have always been here, that they developed in Australia and did not come from elsewhere. Estimates of the number of Aboriginal people inhabiting the continent when the British arrived vary from around 300,000 to over a million. Radcliffe-Brown developed the lower estimation in 1928, while in 1983 Professor Noel Butlin, geographer and demographer, estimated the population at about a million. In addition, it has been estimated that from 250 languages with up to 600 dialect groups were viable when the British arrived.

These original inhabitants identified themselves to the Europeans in a way that made it possible to discern associations with specific places by name, such as the Tiwi, Walpiri, Gamilaroi and the Wamba Wamba. Many other names, though changed, have become Australian place names: Yarra Yarra, Wagga Wagga, Jung and Mooroopna. Throughout the continent there were territories clearly defined by language, geography, beliefs and descent which divided the land into some hundreds of identifiable nations.

History demonstrates that various civilisations have developed their culture and identity over long periods of time, with writing being a recent development. Up to 1788, Aboriginal people had been developing their culture for millennia in comparative isolation. Notwithstanding the absence of written language, Aboriginal societies were intricately organised, with culture and knowledge being passed on through a system of education which had a strong spiritual base.

Through ancient oral tradition, the intricacies of social organisation and elaboration of stories and rituals which expressed understandings about the origin and purpose of existence were maintained. Aboriginal people ensured the maintenance of social structures and the passing on of the values through each generation. This was accomplished through a deep spiritual relationship with the environment which included a wide range of rights and obligations to guide their daily interaction. Edward John Eyre wrote in 1845 that:

> The Continent of Australia is so vast and the dialects, customs, and ceremonies of its inhabitants so varied in detail, though so similar in general outline and character, that it will require the lapse of years, and the labours of many individuals, to detect and exhibit the links which form the chain of connection in the habits and history of tribes so remotely separated; and it will be long before anyone can attempt to give to the world a complete and well-drawn outline of the whole. [Eyre, 1845: 152]

Throughout the continent there was a characteristically Aboriginal way of life influenced by geography and the climate. Within a common framework there was much cultural diversity. People of one country or region generally stayed in their own area, but they met with other groups on ceremonial occasions or for trading purposes.

As the groups moved over the land they visited significant sites to carry out ceremonies. These were performed because it was believed that such rituals were necessary to sustain the fertility of the species on which Aborigines depended. Such ceremonies were also cultural activities which were important to the maintenance of the identity of groups. Aboriginal peoples' culture and heritage was transmitted through social interaction and was learned by each generation.

Aboriginal people regard land as a spiritual phenomenon. They believe that the earth is formed by the world's creative powers which appear in the form of ancestral beings who mysteriously move over the surface and shape the landscape. This concept, which has come to be known as The Dreaming, is the basis of Aboriginal relationships with the land.

The association of Aboriginal people with the land was disrupted as the white invasion took effect. Aboriginal groups had to struggle to adapt to new situations under extremely adverse circumstances. For example, traditional hunting grounds and sacred sites were selected for sheep and cattle grazing and waterholes were contaminated. This alienation of Aboriginal people from the land disrupted ceremonial life and eroded Aboriginal identity.

The records of the first settlement show that it was the intention of the British government to deal fairly with the original Australians. However, what followed decimated the population, fragmented Aboriginal people and their culture and challenged their identity and survival. Despite this, Aboriginal people adapted and made the changes necessary to survive as a people. This is highlighted by an extract from the Select Committee on Aborigines (British Settlements) from the House of Commons on 26 June 1837 in London:

> These people, unoffending as they were towards us, have, as might have been expected, suffered in an aggravated degree from the planting among them of our penal settlements. In the formation of these settlements it does not appear that the territorial rights of the natives were considered, and very little care has since been taken to protect them from the violence or the contamination of the dregs of our countrymen.
>
> The consequences have been dreadful beyond example, both in the diminution of their numbers and in their demoralization.
>
> Many deeds of murder and violence have undoubtedly been committed by the stockkeepers (convicts in the employ of farmers in the outskirts of the colony), by the cedar cutters, and by the remote free settlers, and many natives have perished by the various military parties sent against them ...
> [Historical records of Victoria 2A: 62]

The impact of protection on Aboriginal identity

The first *Aborigines Protection Act* was legislated in 1869 in Victoria. This Act and subsequent protection acts were based on the racial superiority of the British and the belief that Aboriginal people were uncivilised. The acts were designed to exclude designated or prescribed Aboriginal people from all aspects of modern Australian life as it was evolving. Specific acts deemed that Aboriginal people were not able to be employees, work with food or carry the mail.

The impact of these acts has been far reaching for Aboriginal people. The acts have underpinned official attitudes and legitimated policies which have discriminated against Aboriginal people. They have been used to validate the idea of "real" Aboriginal people meaning "full-bloods", thereby challenging the identity of Aboriginal people in the more densely European occupied parts of Australia.

In Victoria, the *Aborigines Protection Act* 1886 changed the earlier (1869) definition of "Aborigine" to:

full-bloods, half-castes over 34, female half-castes married to Aborigines, the infants of Aborigines and half-castes who were licensed by the Board of Protection for Aborigines to reside on a station.

The *Protection Acts* were used to sanction divisions between Aboriginal people and to legitimate the idea that some Aboriginal people were more Aboriginal than others. They justified discrimination against Aborigines and division among them. John Murray, in the Victorian Parliamentary Debates in 1911, summed up an attitude to the "half-caste" early this century:

A good many people make a mistake about the character of the half-caste. He is really more of a blackfellow than the full blooded Aboriginals. The infusion of blood does not make him more capable than the full blooded Aboriginal to compete with the white man in the battle of life.

The *South Australian Aborigines Act* 1911 emphasised control and expanded segregation. The *South Australian Aborigines Amendment Act* 1939 changed the definition of "Aboriginal" to include all people of Aboriginal descent. However, it introduced the "dog tag" or the exemption certificate which was described in the amending legislation as making possible

the exemption from the provisions of the Act, Aborigines, who, by reason of their character, standard of intelligence, and development are considered to be capable of living in the general community without supervision.

Exemption was also used as punishment to expel Aboriginal people from institutions and reserves in South Australia.

Many Aboriginal people deeply resented having to carry the exemption paper which declared them to be "honorary whites". Exemption classified some Aboriginal people as white people and this caused divisions in many families, with lasting effects. Val Power, a Ngarrindjeri of Rauukan in South Australia, whose mother was exempted, said:

My mother was fair-skinned with blue eyes. A lot of people with fair skins hid their Aboriginality. But my mother didn't want to do that. She didn't want to lose her identity as an Aboriginal person. It was no use saying she was a Maori or something because she still had brothers at Point McLeay who had dark skins. [Mattingley and Hampton, 1988: 50]

The *Queensland Aboriginals Protection and Restriction of the Sale of Opium Act* 1897 had the following notation to the clause defining half-castes:

Note: Offspring of a white woman and Aboriginal father not half-caste.

The subsequent 1939 Queensland Act included in its definition:

a child on a reserve with a mother who is an Aboriginal.

Some commentators have suggested that the purpose of the *Protection Acts* was to facilitate the takeover of land which European settlers saw as being unused. Protection meant that many Aboriginal people were sent to designated areas away from their own country and away from their families.

The "White Australia" policy, which was designed to control the movement and employment of "coloured" aliens, presented another complication for Aboriginal people, jeopardising their place and identity in Australian society. As non-whites who were indigenous to Australia, they, too, were excluded from employment on the basis of race under acts intended to control the employment of aliens. William Cooper argued for Aborigines to be treated fairly:

the full-bloods are the descendants of the original owners of Australia. They are the lineal descendants of their fathers. The change in ownership by conquest should not invalidate their title to reasonable part of those lands and these rights should be admitted without cavil ...

The half-caste is the descendant of the Aboriginal and therefore joint heirs with the full blood. They are also descendants of the white man and thus heirs with the white race for all rights of British nationhood ... [Cooper in Markus, 1988: 48]

In a document called "Aborigines Demand Citizenship Rights" (1938), also known as the Aboriginal Manifesto, the Aborigines Progressive Association wrote about the feelings of Aboriginal Australians:

You are the New Australians, but we are the Old Australians. We have in our arteries the blood of the Original Australians, who have lived in this land for many thousands of years.

The first Aboriginal organisations: Symbols of Aboriginal people's identity and culture

William Cooper, as Honorary Secretary of the Australian Aborigines' League, wrote at least seventy-seven letters to various politicians from 1933 to 1940, promoting the Aboriginal cause. William Cooper tried to form the first national Aboriginal movement and to petition King George V about the plight of Aboriginal Australians. In hindsight, it is obvious that William Cooper and his peers (in New South Wales the Aborigines Progressive Association was active leading up to the ses-quicentenary) had a great impact on the Aboriginal consciousness and identity.

Cooper won endorsement from the National Missionary Council for the first National Aboriginal Day celebrated in 1940. It was to be celebrated annually on the Sunday preceding the Australia Day week-end. It became known as Aboriginal Sunday in the eastern states. National celebrations now occur in the second week of July each year and are regarded by many Aboriginal people as a national celebration of their existence and survival in Australian society. These celebrations strengthen Aboriginal identity by focusing on Aboriginal people, their culture and their contribution to society. Today the word NAIDOC (National Aboriginal and Islander Observance Day Committee) is synonymous with National Aboriginal Week celebrations.

The postwar drift to urban centres found Aboriginal people seeking each other out. Some often went with the name of an Aboriginal contact in the city. Urban Aboriginal identity, apart from skin colour, meant belonging to an Aboriginal community, identifying as Aboriginal and seeking out new values to blend with a common heritage and a proud tradition. This meant acknowledging loss but celebrating survival as well. Some fair-skinned Aboriginal people faced a dilemma. They could deny their identity, compete for jobs and escape racism, or they could identify as Aborigines and be excluded like their darker brothers and sisters.

Colin Bourke of the Gamilaroi wrote in 1978 about the yearning of Aboriginal people in their desire for a place in modern Australian life:

Few Aborigines are completely comfortable with their Aboriginality. There is a large vacuum of unfulfilled Aboriginal needs. It is these unsatisfied desires — to be able to see oneself as a person of value, to be proud to be an Aborigine, to be able to work at one's own identity and heritage in a positive light which negate all the programs derived for Aboriginal advancement. [Bourke, 1978: 3].

Such a feeling of uncertainty came from the exclusion of Aboriginal people from many normal aspects of Australian society. The *Commonwealth Constitution Act* of 1901 specifically excluded Aborigines as citizens and from some entitlements. As a result, they were not eligible for Commonwealth social services like the age pension and unemployment benefits. Until 1966, Aboriginal people who lived away from towns were not counted in the census. However, estimates were made by the various government agencies responsible for Aboriginal welfare after federation. These estimates were included in every national census.

The repeal in 1967 of section 127 of the *Commonwealth Constitution Act* enabled Aboriginal population figures to be included officially from 1971. Since then, census procedures have been improved to try to ensure that Aboriginal people are counted accurately. At the 1986 census, 198 years after the arrival of the British, approximately 230,000 people identified themselves as Aboriginal or Torres Strait Islander. Over half of the Aboriginal population were under twenty years of age in 1986. While Aboriginal people lived in all census regions, the largest populations were in New South Wales and Queensland. Aboriginal population densities were greatest in the northern part of Australia — north-western Australia, the Northern Territory and northern Queensland.

Has the way Aboriginal people identify themselves changed?

Aboriginal organisations, in addition to being formed in response to government policies, are expressions of Aboriginal identity. While they have been established with a view to meeting Aboriginal needs, they also serve to bring to the fore a distinctive Aboriginal cultural heritage and an Aboriginal presence. In this way, Aboriginal cultural heritage has been modified and changed in response to new experiences and knowledge.

Garnet Wilson, Chairman of the South Australian Aboriginal Lands Trust, speaking at a United Nations International Day for the Elimination of Racial Discrimination in 1983, said:

> If you are an Aboriginal Australian — an *Aboriginal* Australian — *you are robbed of your identity and heritage!* Instead of being a proud guardian of a spiritually and physically beautiful country you are captured in poverty and hopelessness! [Mattingley & Hampton, 1988: 265]

Aboriginal people — Kooris, Murris, Nungas, Nyungars, Yappa, Yolgnu, Anangu — all share common backgrounds in storytelling, while Western music is widely popular. Kinship systems provide child minding and support for the elders. There is a widespread and unique tradition of ironic humour about the situations in which they often have found themselves. Various Aboriginal groups have, of course, always identified as specific groups within their own countries. Ronald and Catherine Berndt (1988) affirm that there is:

> A wave of feeling, of Aboriginal identity, pointing toward pan-Aboriginality, [which] seeks to establish a common socio-cultural heritage.

They add that:

> the significance of Aboriginal identity is of considerable importance, because it defines persons of Aboriginal descent in contrast to non-Aborigines ... [Berndt and Berndt, 1978: 528]

There have been some recent challenges to Aboriginal expressions of identity developed by Aboriginal people using their own experiences. The Aboriginal novelist, Mudrooroo Nyoongah has said of this discourse on the topic:

> I believe that such a search for Aboriginal identity and any conclusions reached must come from us, ourselves ... We must determine our own identity within the parameters established by us. [Nyoongah, 1992: 156]

There has developed also a World Indigenous Movement with good networking through indigenous pathways around the world. Dr Thom Alcoze, of Northern Arizona University, has written:

> There is a rebirth experienced by Native Americans today. Expressions of historic understandings and identity as nations, cultures, and societies of great value and sophistication have emerged. [Alcoze, 1992: 75]

Ms Doreen Eatts made the following statement on behalf of the National Committee to Defend Black Rights (NCDBR) to the UN Working Group on Indigenous Population 10th Session, July 1992, Geneva:

> The Declaration must consistently refer to indigenous peoples and nations. It is not for governments to determine who constitutes a nation or a people. It is for the people to decide for themselves.

Lois O'Donoghue, CBE, AM (Chair, ATSIC) said in presenting the Barunga statement to the United Nations Working Group on Indigenous People:

> Australia is a big country. We come from the north, south, east and west of Australia, the Torres Straits and Tasmania ... Point 6 from the Barunga statement seeks respect for and promotion of our Aboriginal (indigenous) identity, including the cultural, linguistic, religious and historical aspects, including the right to educate in our own languages and in our own culture and history.

Who constructs identity?

If identity is a cultural construction, who makes the construction?

The National Report of the Royal Commission for Aboriginal Deaths in Custody reported that Aboriginal people resent non-Aboriginal attempts to define and categorise them.

Brunton (1993) discussed the tensions between public constructions of Aboriginality. He located this discussion within the Aboriginal movement, based on the understandings and experiences of individual Aboriginal people. He identified the following issues which appear as contradictions in discussions about Aboriginality:

- possible pressure to conform to certain ideas of Aboriginality, and
- conflict between local regionalised identity as against a concept of pan-Aboriginality based on a common cultural framework. [Brunton, 1993: 9–17]

Brunton raises these points in a discussion about the consequences of Aboriginality and the idea that Aboriginal identity attracts preferential treatment and benefits. He repeats Dierdre Jordan's observation that:

> It is a commentary on the perceptions of white society that contemporary theorists, even the most enlightened, assume that Aborigines of mixed ancestry should identify with the race of their black parent, rather than their white parent, and that the identity offered by mainstream society is one of exclusion from claims to European ancestry. [Jordan, 1993: 15]

The "new" Aborigines, to use the Berndts' term, are all those who are of Aboriginal descent or who identify themselves as Aboriginal people and who have carved out for themselves a particular niche in Australian society. The Berndts (1988: 526) write of Aborigines being rediscovered by other Australians and that a romantic image of traditional Aboriginal life was portrayed by novelists, poets, artists, musicians and dancers in the 1970s.

This image includes the emergence of national and state spokespersons; it includes a range of opinions designated as "moderate" to "extremist" in political terms. This has been expressed in the espousing of a distinctive Aboriginal contribution to Australian society and Aboriginal ways of doing things.

Aboriginal people do feel compelled to gain the acknowledgment of their prior ownership, their sovereignty and the recognition of a continuous adapting Aboriginal identity. David Suzuki, writing generally about indigenous nations, said:

> Indigenous people are the descendants of a given geographic territory that may have been taken over militarily, politically or by settlement of outsiders ... as historically, politically, and culturally dominated — though not conquered — world wide they know who they are. The sense of self-identification is the single most crucial element of any working definition of indigenous Aboriginal or first peoples. [UN Working Group, 1992: 7]

Schwab commented on the nature of Aboriginal identity in Adelaide:

> Identity among most Aborigines in Adelaide is clear and explicit because it is based in large part, as it was in the past, on a local ground of kinship, sense of self, as well as relation to and identification with other Aborigines in Adelaide ... [Keen, 1988: 79]

Unlike non-Aboriginal constructions of Aboriginality, Aboriginal people believe that their identity is based on their own cultural heritage and is not merely a reaction to non-Aborigines. While it cannot be denied that the policies in relation to Aboriginal people in the main are articulated by non-Aborigines, there must be acknowledgment of many traditional Aboriginal values, as well as an ancient heritage of adaptation and change. Those who say that Aboriginality is new or that "part-Aborigines" have not had enough time to develop a sense of identity or continuity do not really know Australian history, or they choose to misinterpret it.

Europeans have based Aboriginal identity mainly on race, whereas Aboriginal people speak of "my people", representing the notion of peoplehood. This is derived from knowledge of genealogies, and belonging to specific extended family groups. Aboriginal identity and culture is based on a distinctive cultural heritage which incorporates special meanings given to the land and people and is centred on core values. This heritage has modified and adapted to respond to new knowledge and experiences brought in by the Europeans.

Aboriginal people see opportunities for their cultures to be further developed, extended and refined through education. This will be achieved through participation in Australian life for Aboriginal people, not separation and degradation. This requires Aboriginal identity to be affirmed and recognised by all Australians.

The shapes of Aboriginality

What, then, are some of the shapes of Aboriginality?

> Aboriginal culture cannot be separated from the land. On the land are stories — Aboriginal stories that explain why people, rockholes, the hills and the trees came to be there. The land is full of stories. Every square mile is just like a book, a book with a lot of pages, and it's all a story for the children to learn. [Yami Lester in Mattingley and Hampton, 1983: 73]

An Aboriginal social identity is no longer simply an aspiration. It is now a reality, relevant to virtually all persons of Aboriginal descent. Even though the content varies, there are a sufficient number of elements held in common by Aboriginal people to distinguish it.

> To me as a black theologian, God is black as much as white. Why? Because God speaks our language, knows our culture and made this land we now live in and enjoy. If I am to have my true identity before God, you cannot lock me into white ways. You must give me freedom to be me. God has the same concern for the Aboriginal as for the white. [Gondarra, 1986: 13]

Some academics are claiming that Aboriginal identity is largely a response to European invasion and domination of the land. Von Sturmer, for example, argues that Aboriginality simply does not exist:

> "Aboriginality" is a fiction which takes on a meaning only in terms of white ethnocentrism ... [Von Sturmer and Tonkinson, 1992: 199]

To some Aboriginal people, this would parallel a claim that European Jewish identity is a result of its reaction to Nazi Germany.

This is not to refute that Aboriginal people and their culture today are affected by all factors prevailing in Australian society. Legal, health, education, technological and economic factors all affect the Aboriginal population. They place pressure on Aboriginal cultures, identity and spirituality and it is hard for some to remain Aboriginal today.

Aboriginal people have formed organisational structures to meet their needs and serve as cultural symbols and, in at least one instance, to serve as proof of Aboriginal cultural continuity in the modern sense. In 1976, when Justice Lush had to rule in a Victorian Supreme Court case whether or not Aboriginal people still existed in Victoria, he said that "Aborigine" was a word probably used much more widely in Australia than in other English speaking countries. He said that "the Aborigines" was used to describe persons in groups or societies irrespective of mixture of blood. In the case of Bryning Re, he found that Aboriginal people and their descendants continued to exist in Victoria and cited the existence of the Australian Aborigines' League from the 1920s as evidence.

However, Aboriginal culture and identity continue to come under increasing pressure. Aborigines are flooded with mass media and are themselves using and participating in Western media forms. The dominance of English and the loss of Aboriginal languages provide just one indicator of how Aboriginal culture can be diminished. Aboriginal arts and crafts are popular commercially, but this commercialism may pose a threat to their traditional purposes and meanings. The way in which Aboriginal Australians will choose to deal with these and other aspects of Aboriginal culture will serve to further shape modern Aboriginal identity.

Most non-Aboriginal commentators today fail to understand that, though many Aboriginal people may have experienced traumas fitting into modern Australian life, many retain Aboriginal knowledge within themselves. This locates them in a particular world unknown to non-Aboriginals and, indeed, to other Aboriginal people outside their immediate group. Hence Neville Bonner's comment from his maiden speech in the Senate in 1979:

> All persons who desire to be classified as indigenous, regardless of hue of skin and who have flowing in their veins any portion, however small, of Aboriginal or Torres Strait Island blood are indigenous people. It does not necessarily follow that the degree of one's emotional scars matches the darkness of personal pigmentation or that the lightness of one's skin necessarily indicates a lessening of knowledge of, and belief in, Aboriginal or Torres Strait Island culture and tradition. [Burger, 1979: 89]

all within ... that is Aboriginal yearns to be heard ... as the voice of the indigenous people of Australia ... [Burger, 1979: 88]

The term "Aboriginalism", then, might be said to give due recognition to the existence of Aboriginal people and their prior occupation of Australia. Therefore, Aboriginality is the quality of being Aboriginal and all it encompasses. Herein lies the key to some of the discourse. Many non-Aboriginal academics see only a response, mostly in the negative, by Aboriginal people to their unequal status in Australian society. This arises from attempts to place Aboriginal history into a post-colonial context only and to fit Aboriginality into theories of racism. As Mudrooroo has said:

It is the Aboriginal "essence" which makes an Aborigine and it is this essence which states, restates, informs and reforms his/her and our culture and social reality. [Nyoongah, 1992: 157]

References

Alcoze, T. (1992). "The response and fate of the first nations (the Amerindians) to the discovery of the Americas". *Geojournal*, vol. 24, no. 4, April, pp. 473–76.

Berndt, C.H. and R.M. (1978). *The World of the First Australians*. Canberra: Aboriginal Studies Press.

Bourke, C. (1978). "Aboriginal culture and schools". *Polycom*, vol. 14, p. 3.

Brunton, R. (1993). *Black Suffering, White Guilt?* Victoria: Institute of Public Affairs Ltd.

Burger, A. (1979). *Neville Bonner*. Melbourne: Macmillan.

Butlin, N. (1983). *Original Aggression: Aboriginal Population of South Australia 1788–1850*. Sydney: Allen & Unwin.

Eyre, Edward John (1845). *Journals of Expeditions into Central Australia,* Vol. 2 (Facsimile). London: T & W Boone.

Gondarra, Djiniyini (1986). *Series of Reflections of Aboriginal Theology*. Darwin: Bethel Presbytery, Northern Synod of the Uniting Church.

Hollinsworth, David (1992). "Discourses on Aboriginality and the politics of identity in urban Australia". *Oceania*, vol. 63, no. 2, December, pp. 137–55.

Historical Records of Victoria 2A (1982). *The Aborigines of Port Phillip 1835–1839*. Melbourne: Victorian Government Printer.

Horner, J. (1974). *Vote Ferguson for Aboriginal Freedom*. Sydney: ANZ Book Co.

Jordan, D. (1985). *Census Categories: Enumeration of Aboriginal People or Construction of Identity.* Adelaide: University of Adelaide Paper

Keen, I. (ed.) (1988). *Being Black*. Canberra: Australian Studies Press.

Markus, A. (ed.)(1988). *Blood from a Stone*. Australia: Allen & Unwin.

McCorquodale, J. (1987). *Aborigines and the Law: A Digest*. Canberra: Australian Studies Press.

Mattingley, C. and Hampton, K. (1988). *Survival in Our Own Land*. Adelaide: Wakefield Press.

Nyoongah, M. (1992). "Self-determining our Aboriginality, a response to Discourses on Aboriginality and the politics of identity in urban Australia". *Oceania*, vol. 63, no. 2, pp. 156-57.

Oceania (1992), vol. 63, no. 2, December pp. 137-171.

Royal Commission for Aboriginal Deaths in Custody (1991). *National report*. Canberra: AGPS.

Tonkinson, Myrna (1990). "Is it in the blood? Australian Aboriginal identity". In *Cultural Identity and Ethnicity in the Pacific*, edited by J. Linnekin and L. Poyer. Honolulu: University of Hawaii.

Tylor, E.B. (1871). *Primitive Culture*. London: [publisher unknown].

UN Working Group on Indigenous Populations 10th Session — 1992. Switzerland: The Australian Contribution.

Chapter 4

Two Laws: One Land

Colin Bourke and Helen Cox

Introduction

The Aboriginal peoples of this country had well-developed systems of law long before the arrival of the First Fleet from England in 1788. Underpinning these systems was the relationship of the people to the land. (This relationship remains an important source of spirituality for many people today.)

This chapter describes the main features of traditional Aboriginal legal systems. The impact of European "settlement" and the imposition of English law are described and analysed from a legal viewpoint. The imposed criminal justice system has incarcerated Aborigines at a disproportionate rate.

The relationship between Aboriginal and European law is examined with reference to the denial of human rights and failure to recognise native title to land. This leads to the contemporary situation with a discussion of the decision of the High Court in the Mabo case. A focus on the traditional relationship between Aboriginal people and the land cannot be avoided in any discussion of the law.

Traditional Aboriginal law

The Aboriginal ancestors travelled the country during The Dreaming, the creative period from the time immemorial. They established the code of life which today is called The Dreaming or The Law. The Law has been passed on for countless generations of people through the remembrance and celebration of the sites which were the scenes of the ancestral exploits. Song, dance, body, rock and sand painting, special languages and the oral explanations of the myths encoded in these essentially religious art forms have been the media of The Law to the present day (statement of Marcia Langton, World Council of Churches, 1981: 13).

Traditional Aboriginal law is often referred to as *customary law*. It is difficult to define in non-Aboriginal terms because it covers the rules for living and is backed by religious sanctions. It also prescribes daily behaviour. Through The Dreaming, the law is prescribed for the land and its inhabitants.

Aborigines had occupied all of Australia before 1788, but they had no *lingua franca*. No shared language spanned the continent. There were also variations in the laws from one group to another and one region to another. However, in all regions, law and spirituality were intermingled and common features can be identified. The broad roles and responsibilities of men and women in sacred ritual, economic affairs, marriage and other aspects of daily life had been laid down in The Dreaming. The ancestors were the source of Aboriginal life and there were religious sanctions for the traditional dictates of right and wrong.

Aboriginal government was very decentralised and it was largely informal and loosely organised. This had a direct bearing on the maintenance of law and order. Within each group there were recognised forms of behaviour with which its members were in fundamental agreement. Children were enculturated into the correct forms of behaviour by their own families (Edwards, 1988: 6; Berndt and Berndt, 1967: 102).

The people most conversant with all the features of their own culture are those who are fully initiated and no longer young — usually the elders. They have the most wisdom and knowledge and their opinions carry the most weight when it comes to a debatable point or upholding the Law (Berndt and Berndt, 1967: 102).

In Aboriginal Australia there were no formal courts of law with specially designated persons vested with authority and power to deal with cases, to judge and to punish. Instead most problems were handled informally within the group by a council of elders. Intra-group difficulties would be settled when the opportunity arose, such as when groups came together for ceremonies or when particular food supplies, such as yabbies, Bunya pine nuts or Bogong moths, were in abundance (Berndt and Berndt, 1967: 103–4).

Traditional law can be compared with the Ten Commandments. It covered homicide, sacrilege, sorcery, incest, abduction of women, adultery, physical assault, theft, insult, including swearing, and the usurpation of ritual privileges and duties — a reasonable comparison. However, Aboriginal traditional laws also included offences of omission towards other people, such as failure to share food, to avoid particular relations, perform rituals or ceremonies or to educate nominated group members (Edwards, 1988: 61; Meggitt, 1962).

In 1962 Meggitt published his study of Walbiri society, which had had minimal European contact. He produced a summary of the rules of customary law which categorised a number of offences which the Walbiri recognised as unlawful. The Law covered ritual, economic, residential and kinship rules and conventions. It also covered the care of sacred objects, the division of labour by gender, the avoidance of mothers-in-law and even the rising of the sun. Meggitt believed that in pre-contact times rules of law and norms of politically appropriate behaviour were probably not distinguished (Meggitt, 1962).

Most social behaviour was public. It was nearly impossible to offend without others knowing. It was rare for any discussion to occur in the group as to the question of guilt. There was almost no privacy in any camp, so everyone knew what had occurred. Punishment was meted out in public. This would certainly have been a deterrent to breaking the more important rules.

The range of penalties included death, wounding, fear of sorcery, corporal punishment and abuse or ridicule to shame people into compliance (Berndt and Berndt, 1967: 103; Edwards, 1988: 62–64). There were no gaols or fines. Close relatives could plead for leniency, but they could also seek the heaviest penalty.

European impact, post-1788

Much of Aboriginal law did not openly conflict with British law, but those aspects which required secrecy or inflicted punishment directly by the group raised considerable difficulties as whites spread across Australia. Most problems were, however, caused by colonists breaking Aboriginal law, especially land seizure and the treatment of Aboriginal women by Europeans.

Many of the Aboriginal groups tried to incorporate the newcomers into their system of law by extending kinship rules and networks and sharing resources. However, many of the intruders failed to conform to the traditional laws. In particular, they were ignorant about the principle of *reciprocity*. Sharing was expected. The European settlers appeared greedy and selfish, as they rarely shared their resources, even when they were granted favours by Aboriginal people (Reynolds, 1981: 68–70; Edwards, 1988: 61).

Many Aboriginal people strongly resisted the invading Europeans. Pemulwuy led the Eora resistance to the establishment of Sydney, while the Kalkadoons in north Queensland struggled for many years to protect their physical and spiritual life against the invading colonists.

British response: application of **terra nullius**

The British sought to extend their laws to the land now called Australia and its Aboriginal inhabitants. The laws of England were imported to the new colony of New South Wales to the extent that they were applicable to those times and conditions (Australian Law Reform Commission [ALRC] 1986: 34).

Despite Aboriginal resistance, England declared itself the sovereign or ruler of Australia. The established legal doctrine that enabled it to do this is known as *terra nullius*. The European legal view at the time was that the Crown had absolute title to all land. Under the doctrine, colonising powers such as England could apply their own law to land which they peacefully occupied, if the land was uninhabited, or was occupied by a people without settled laws or customs. In conquered or ceded (surrendered) countries, the pre-existing laws of that country were applied until they were displaced or altered by the new sovereign (Hanks, 1991: 1).

Australia was declared to be a land that was not occupied by a people with settled laws. In legal effect, it was *terra nullius*. This was upheld in the case of *Cooper v Stuart* (1889) 14 Appeal Case 286. The legal order of the Aboriginal peoples was not seen as sufficiently organised to be recognised. This view was not supported by Justice Blackburn in *Milirrpum v Nabalco* (1971); however, his judgment followed the precedent set in the previous cases:

> They [previous cases] all affirm on the principle, fundamental to the English law of real property, that the Crown is the source of all title to land.

Generally Aboriginal people were expected to abide by these imported laws, even though they were largely ignorant of them and had never agreed to be bound by them. Some attempts were made to educate Aborigines about the new system of law. For example, in Tasmania in 1828, Governor Arthur ordered picture boards to be nailed to trees in the bush depicting a black man spearing a white man and then being hanged as well as a white man shooting a black man and meeting the same fate (although this may have been done in an attempt to encourage peaceful relations rather than to educate *per se* (Ryan, 1981: 96–97). Aboriginal people were officially regarded as British subjects and, in theory, were entitled to the protection of the British system (ALRC Report 31: 19).

Although the existence of the many Aboriginal groups was recognised by the early European explorers and settlers, their laws, customs and rights under British law were not acknowledged. Resistance, massacres and genocide were also ignored in the application of the doctrine of *terra nullius*, which justified the acquisition of land. Aboriginal resistance was far from insignificant, as many documented examples show.

Some non-Aborigines were horrified by what was happening and wrote to England deploring the situation. This was largely to no avail. In 1828 the Governor of Tasmania (Arthur) proclaimed martial law, which was tantamount to a declaration of war against Aborigines. During the three years in which martial law remained in force, the military were entitled to shoot on sight any Aboriginal person in the settled districts (Ryan, 1981: 99; Plomley, 1966: 29; ALRC Report 31).

Yet the legal fiction that the islands and the mainland were settled peacefully was maintained. By ignoring Aboriginal customs and law and the resistance to white settlement, English law was applied to Aboriginal Australians. To do otherwise would have meant that not only would Aboriginal law have to be acknowledged, but so too would Aboriginal sovereignty and rights to the land. So long as Australia was seen to be settled under the doctrine of *terra nullius* there need be no common law recognition of Aboriginal land rights — or, indeed, any Aboriginal law.

Relationship between Aborigines and European law

Not only were Aboriginal people denied recognition of their own laws; in reality they were also deprived of the protection of the new system. Edward John Eyre made the following report when he was resident magistrate at Moorunde on the River Murray:

> In declaring the natives British subjects and making them responsible to British laws, indigenous people were placed in an anomalous position of being made amenable to laws of which they are quite ignorant, and which, at the same time did not afford them the slightest redress from any injuries they may receive at the hands of Europeans. This arose from their being

unable legally to give evidence in a Court of Justice, and from its rarely happening that any aggressions upon them take place in the presence of other Europeans who might appear as witnesses for them ...

It is impossible to explain to the natives the reason of their being unable to give evidence; they only see that their own people are always punished for offences, that the Europeans almost always escape (?). [E.J. Eyre, Resident Magistrate at Moorunde, Report SA GG, 9 February 1843: 44]

Aboriginal people could not give evidence in court because they were not Christians. Thus it was very difficult for them to defend serious charges or to have European offenders brought to justice (Ryan, 1981: 88). In practice, Aborigines were not accorded the same rights as British subjects in judicial proceedings (Ryan, 1981: 39).

The legal system of Australia was used to deny Aboriginal people fundamental human rights and it continued to do so. Under the rhetoric of protection, children were removed from parents, the right to marry was limited, freedom of movement was restricted and special laws regulated Aboriginal employment. Aborigines were forced to live on reserves, settlements and missions (ALRC Report 31: 21). Those Aborigines who demanded their rights were oppressed. As late as 1962, the Council for Aboriginal Rights found that the Director of Native Affairs in Queensland may cause any Aborigine to "be removed from any district to a reserve and kept there. He may also cause any Aboriginal on a reserve to be removed to another reserve and kept there." (Murray, 1962: 17)

The law also provided that the Director of Native Affairs and not the parents "shall be the legal guardian of every Aboriginal child in the State while such a child is under the age of twenty one years". The government controlled marriage, property and employment. Even wages were not paid in full. All or most were put into a bank account controlled by the Director.

In Western Australia, the Commissioner of Native Welfare had control over all Aboriginal children and the property of Aboriginal people and could restrict the movements of Aboriginal people and censor the mail of those in institutions. Regulation 28 of the *Native Welfare Act* included the undefined offence of "insubordination" (Murray, 1962: 41). Particular offences were created to control Aborigines.

The 1957–58 Annual Report of the Northern Territory disclosed that 8,000 people, or about 48 per cent of the Aboriginal population, were

residents in institutions. They were controlled, submissive and isolated. Their legal rights were compromised. Aboriginal people were
forcibly removed from their lands and families were separated (Murray, 1962: 31).

The Melbourne *Herald* on 19 March 1958 carried a report from
Douglas Lockwood:

> Aboriginal prisoners are chained by the ankle to a verandah post at Halls
> Creek police station while awaiting trial and serving their sentences ... It
> is done here because the 80 year old building has only one cell. A few
> months ago 12 prisoners were on the chain at the same time. When one
> wanted to move, the other 11 had to move with him.

Aboriginal people were subject to the law but unable to have a
legitimate input into the content of the laws or choice of parliamentary
representative. Aboriginal people did not have the right to vote in
federal elections until 1962. The movement for full citizenship rights
gathered momentum, and in 1967, 90 per cent of Australians voted
"yes" to a referendum removing the constitutional provision excluding
"Aboriginal natives" from being counted in the national census (s 127)
and giving the commonwealth government (s 51 [XXVI]) power to
legislate in relation to Aboriginal Affairs (ALRC Report 31: 22). The
injustices, however, continued.

The lack of justice for Aboriginal people led to the establishment of
Aboriginal legal services in all states during the 1970s. The legal
services have endeavoured to have the legal system give justice to
Aborigines. Despite this, Walker found in 1987 that "overall, in
Australia, an Aboriginal is over sixteen times more likely to be in prison
than a non-Aboriginal" (Hazelhurst, 1987: 107). Walker raised the
distinct possibility that Australia, in a more subtle way, is as racist as
South Africa in its treatment of the indigenous people.

In October 1987 the Royal Commission into Aboriginal Deaths in
Custody was established. If non-Aborigines had died at the same rate,
it has been estimated there would have been up to 9,000 deaths during
the period 1980–89 investigated by the Royal Commission (RCIADIC,
1991: 3). However, the primary reason for the high number of deaths
(ninety-nine) was found to relate to "the disproportionate rate at which
Aboriginal people are detained in this country" (RCIADIC, 1991, vol.
4: 1).

In 1991 the *National Report: Overview and Recommendations* was delivered by Commissioner Elliot Johnson, QC. This report documented the institutionalised racism rampant in Australian society. The socioeconomic problems faced by many Aboriginal and Torres Strait Islander people were linked to the limited access to land and failure to protect sacred sites. The Commissioner recommended:

> That in all jurisdictions legislation should be introduced, where this has not already occurred, to provide a comprehensive means to address land needs of Aboriginal people. Such legislation should encompass a process for restoring unalienated Crown land to those Aboriginal people who claim such land on the basis of cultural, historical and/or traditional association. [RCIADIC, vol. 5: 37, recommendation 334]

Legal responses to native title

Although the British common law failed to recognise Aboriginal rights to land, many Aboriginal and Torres Strait Islander people have maintained their claim to and connection with their land.

Over time it has also become clear to more and more white Australians that many Aboriginal and Torres Strait Islander peoples lived by sophisticated sets of traditional rules. ALRC Report 31 acknowledged that "there are many indications that Aboriginal customary laws and traditions continue as a real controlling force in the lives of many Aborigines" (1986: 33).

Some of these rules included mechanisms for "ownership" of land. Legal cases were mounted but lost on the basis that Australia was *terra nullius* — land belonging to no one. (Although these issues were raised in *Coe v Commonwealth* (1979) at 403, the case did not proceed to a full hearing.)

In the case of *Milirrpum v Nabalco Pty Ltd* (1971) 17 FLR 141, the Yolgnu (Aboriginal) people from Yirrkala on the Gove Peninsula tried to protect their native title by asserting their rights in the Supreme Court of the Northern Territory. After the discovery of bauxite in 1953, a mining lease was granted by the federal government and mining activity commenced. Sacred sites were threatened and destroyed. In 1963 the Yolgnu people presented a bark petition to the House of Representatives. A Committee of Inquiry was held and a report produced, but no action was taken. In 1968 the federal government granted a forty-two-year lease to the mining company Nabalco, which included an agreement for the establishment of a town. No consultation occurred. The Yolgnu brought proceedings in the Northern Territory Supreme Court. This attempt failed as Justice Blackburn felt bound by the established precedent that Australia was *terra nullius*, even though he found that:

> The evidence shows a subtle and elaborate system highly adapted to the country in which the people led their lives, which provided a stable order of society and was remarkably free from the vagaries of personal whim or influence. If ever a system could be called "a government of laws, and not of men", it is that shown in the evidence before me. [*Milirrpum v Nabalco Pty Ltd* (1971) at 267]

Land rights

As the common law refused to recognise native title, Aborigines, Torres Strait Islanders and other Australians fought for land rights through legislative reform. In 1972 an Aboriginal Tent Embassy was set up on the lawns of Parliament House, Canberra.

In the 1970s and 1980s, numerous land rights marches were held. In many ways they were successful. Although Australia has lagged behind other comparable countries in the recognition of common law native title, it has been at the forefront of land rights legislation.

In 1966 South Australia passed the first Australian land rights legislation. The *Aboriginal Lands Trust Act* (SA) set up an Aboriginal body to which the Governor might transfer Crown lands or Aboriginal reserves. In 1970 Victoria was the first state to pass an act granting land. It gave full title of the Lake Tyers and Framlingham reserves to their residents in trust. Since then, all state parliaments except Tasmania have adopted some form of land rights legislation. However, most of this legislation is limited in its application. It is land granted by an act of parliament rather than land gained as of right. For Aboriginal people holding the view that "the land is our mother", land rights legislation is an important aspect of self-determination.

Native title and Mabo

In the past Australian courts were not sympathetic to the notion of a common law native title, but Australian indigenous people refused to acquiesce. The term "native title" refers to the interests in land held by indigenous inhabitants by virtue of their prior occupation. It is necessary to go to customary law to establish what these rights and interests are and they will vary on a case-by-case basis. In Australia, acknowledgment of native title was precluded by the application of the doctrine of *terra nullius*.

In May 1982, Eddie Mabo and four other Meriam people from the Murray Islands in the Torres Strait began an action seeking legal recognition of their family's common law title in the land. This action apparently commenced because Mr Mabo was refused permission by the Department of Aboriginal and Islander Affairs to visit his family on Murray Island. The Meriam people were actually asking the courts to review the doctrine of *terra nullius*. The Queensland government tried to head off this claim by developing legislation extinguishing any native title that may have existed. This was found to be contravening the *Racial Discrimination Act* 1975, so the claim proceeded.

In what is now known as the Mabo case, the Australian High Court reviewed the law in the light of established facts: that Torres Strait Islander people had settled laws, that these laws covered relationships with land and that some people continue to maintain a connection with their land in accordance with their native laws and customs. The case had been in the courts for ten years before the High Court gave its decision in June 1992 (Reynolds, 1991).

The High Court stated that, at the time of occupation, Australia was **not** *terra nullius* and rejected the application of this doctrine and its consequences for native title.

In their joint judgment, Justices Deane and Gaudron went so far as to say:

> The acts and events by which that dispossession in legal theory was carried into practical effect constitute the darkest aspect of the history of this nation. The nation as a whole must remain diminished unless and until there is an acknowledgment of, and retreat from, those past injustices ... The lands of this continent were not *terra nullius* or "practically unoccupied in 1788". [Mabo and Orr, 1992: 100]

Justice Brennan also dismissed the legal fiction that Australia was *terra nullius*. Brennan stated (Mabo and Orr, 1992: 47):

> The common law of this country would perpetuate injustice if it were to continue to embrace the enlarged notion of *terra nullius* and to persist in characterising the indigenous inhabitants of the Australian colonies as

people too low in the scale of social organisation to be acknowledged as possessing rights and interests in land.

Justice Brennan (Mabo and Orr, 1992: 46) said:

If native title survives the Crown's acquisition of sovereignty as in my view, it does, it is unnecessary to examine the alternative arguments advanced and ... the common law of Australia rejects the notion that, when the Crown acquired sovereignty over territory which is now part of Australia it thereby acquired the absolute beneficial ownership of the land therein and accepts that the antecedent rights and interests in land by the indigenous inhabitants of the territory survived the change in sovereignty. Those antecedent rights and interests thus constitute a binder on the radical title of the Crown.

Under native title the Crown is the ultimate owner of the land (as is the case with all land in Australia) but this ownership is subject to the rights of the indigenous people using the land. Native title supports rights to use and occupy the land but may not be full ownership. The extent and content of the rights are determined by the traditional laws.

Justice Brennan (at page 47 of the Mabo case) described it in the following way:

Native title has its origins in and is given its content by the traditional laws acknowledged by and the traditional customs observed by the indigenous inhabitants of a territory. The nature and incidents of native title must be ascertained as a matter of fact by reference to those laws and customs.

Thus, for non-Aborigines, native title is a very unclear and imprecise concept as it requires an understanding and knowledge of traditional Aboriginal culture.

Limitations

Mabo is an important High Court decision, but it may not lead the way to many successful claims or compensation as the court laid down several limiting factors. Native title is easily extinguished and many groups may have lost it over the last 205 years. If the people have left the land either voluntarily or forcibly and lost connection with their land, then the title is lost. If the government has dealt with the land in a way that is inconsistent with traditional native title, then that title is extinguished. Once the title is extinguished in any way, it cannot be revived. Any land that is held freehold cannot be subject to a Mabo style claim. This effectively rules out any common law claims over cities, towns or developed areas.

Aboriginal claimants for native title will need to establish a continuous connection with the land. Native title claims have to be based on traditional laws and customs. Native title is defined as the rights and interests possessed under the traditional laws acknowledged, and the traditional customs observed by, Aboriginal and Torres Strait Islander peoples. Native title is not freehold title. It consists of the exclusive or beneficial use of the land by the groups and it is inalienable.

Aboriginal title to land may be extinguished by Aboriginal dealing with it in a manner which is inconsistent with Aboriginal title. The land cannot be sold or transferred outside its traditional groups. This restriction arises because native title is not a proprietary right, but a personal and usufructuary right.

There are also evidentiary problems with native title. How does one prove native title? What if it involves revealing information that may be secret? Native title is based on traditional laws and involves evidence based on oral histories. The issues relating to establishing the proof of Aboriginal customary laws and the taking of Aboriginal evidence in Australian courts are discussed in ALRC Report 31 (chapters 24–25).

The majority of the High Court decided that compensation for dispossession was unlikely and in most cases impossible. However, this was not a final determination by the court. There are many bars to compensation, although the *Racial Discrimination Act* 1975 may ensure that native title destroyed since the introduction of this Act will require compensation. Issues are also raised by section 51 (XXXI) of the commonwealth Constitution, which speaks of "just acquisition". If the commonwealth compulsorily acquires property it is required to do so on "just terms". However, this only binds the commonwealth and not the states. Native titles extinguished by the states will not be caught by this provision, but state destruction of titles post-1975 may run foul of the *Racial Discrimination Act*.

Implications

The relevance of Mabo for many urban Aborigines must be explored. How substantial must the connections to the land be? For many, while the decision sets the record straight, it doesn't change what happened. This sentiment is echoed by Frank Brennan: "The court did not undo the injustices of the past: it has set the foundations for just land dealings in the future" (*The Australian*, 4 November 1992: 11).

Other aspects of Mabo and the legislation are still uncertain, such as its impact on exploration or mining leases, pastoral leases and reservations of land for parks and offshore areas. This has resulted in great concern being expressed by powerful interest groups. (Howard, 1993: 8–9).

Uncertainties also exist for Aboriginal communities which must make decisions about taking legal action, including who pays and who benefits. Little has been said about the costs to the Murray Islanders of taking legal action. It has not been a victory without its costs. Only two of the original five plaintiffs survived to hear the decision.

There are other implications of the judgment. Recognition of native title is a recognition and protection of some customary law by the wider Australian legal system. The *Australian Law Reform Commission Report* 1986 noted that although there had been some recognition of customary laws and traditions by some courts and some legislation, generally such recognition has been "exceptional, uncoordinated and incomplete" (p. 82). However, the *Summary Report* also stated that:

> A reclassification of Australia as a "conquered colony", were it to occur, would not as such bring about appropriate forms of recognition of Aboriginal customary laws and traditions as these exist now. [ALRC 1986: *Summary Report*: 82]

Sovereignty/self-determination

The Mabo case, then, begs the question "if Australia was not acquired by settlement then how did the British assume sovereignty?" It is a question that the court refused to examine.

Throughout all the cases, the courts have clearly agreed on one thing — the issue of sovereignty.[1] The courts have consistently refused to entertain any concept of Aboriginal sovereignty as it is against their powers to question the legitimacy of Australian sovereignty.

Although the Mabo case creates many uncertainties, one thing is certain: it has put the issue of Aboriginal and Islander self-determination back on the political agenda. It is not only native title or land rights that are being discussed, but the nature of the future relationship between indigenous and other Australians. Reconciliation is high on the federal government's agenda. Dodson (1993: 6) says: "The Mabo decision, which is a win, gives impetus to Aboriginal and Torres Strait Islander calls for a new deal."

The fear of Mabo is bringing groups to the negotiating table. But the fear may also lead to hasty deals made behind closed doors without appropriate consultation. It has also resulted in a mass of anti-Mabo propaganda by groups seeking to protect their current position. The cost of Mabo is uncertainty, but the gain is the promise of justice. Frank Brennan writes:

> The law of the land is now more complex because it reflects more justly the history of land use and extends the rule of law to all citizens whose country it is. [*The Australian*, 4 November 1992: 4]

Conclusion

As Australian government cases followed English precedents, it was obvious that Aboriginal rights would receive inadequate recognition. They were not part of English law and had not been developed in English law. Legislation was very much enacted to support the foundation of a colony, not to protect indigenous people.

European settlement produced a conflict between two systems of law and two cultures. This was not officially acknowledged for nearly 200 years. The introduced British legal system has assumed that Aborigines are subject to its rule. The existence of traditional laws has been ignored.

The British invasion was the beginning of the modern Aboriginal movement in Australia. The issues of land ownership, culture, development, progress and law were at the centre of Aboriginal and non-Aboriginal relations from the first days of the colony. They are still the habit of relations between Aborigines and other Australians today.

Non-Aboriginal Australians are prone to argue that they should not have to be guilty for the sins of their forefathers. They wish to forget what happened to Aborigines, but, as Henry Reynolds (1981: 201) says:

> Forgetfulness is a strange perception coming from a community which has revered the fallen warrior and emblazoned the phrase "Lest we Forget" in monuments throughout the land.

Aborigines cannot forget. Too many warriors have fallen. Black memories are scarred. Aboriginal people have fought long and hard for justice, for their land, preservation of culture and development on their own terms. Perhaps the High Court decision on Mabo will enable the indigenous Australians to at last be given justice through the Australian legal system, and a true process of reconciliation can be commenced.

Note

1. The sovereign is the supreme power over the land and the people.

References

Australian Law Reform Commission (1986). *Aboriginal Customary Law*. Canberra: AGPS.

Berndt, R.M. and Berndt, C.H. (1967). *The First Australians*. 2nd edn. Sydney: Ure Smith.

Bird, Greta (1988). *The Process of Law in Australia: Intercultural Perspectives*. Sydney: Butterworths.

Dodson, Patrick (1993). "Reconciliation and the High Court's decision on native title". *Aboriginal Law Bulletin*, vol. 3, no. 61, April.

Edwards, W.H. (1988). *An Introduction to Aboriginal Societies*. Wentworth Falls: Social Science Press.

Hanks, J. (1991). *Constitutional Law in Australia*. Sydney: Butterworths.

Hazelhurst, K.M. (1987). *Ivory Scales*. Kensington: NSW University Press.

Howard, Colin (1993). "The Mabo case". *Adelaide Review*, February, pp. 8–9.

Mattingley, C. and Hampton, K. (1988). *Survival in Our Own Land*. Adelaide: Wakefield Press.

McRae, H., Nellheim, G. and Beacroft, L. (1991). *Aboriginal Legal Issues*. Sydney: Law Book Co.

Meggitt, M.J. (1962). *Desert People: A Study of the Walbiri Aborigines of Central Australia*. Chicago: The University of Chicago Press.

Murray, William M. (ed.) (1962). *The Struggle for Dignity*. Melbourne: Council for Aboriginal Rights.

Plomley, N.J.B. (ed.) (1962). *Friendly Mission*. Tasmania: Tasmanian Historical Research Association.

Reynolds, Henry (1981). *The Other Side of the Frontier*. Ringwood: Penguin.

―――― (1991). "For seven judges two hundred years of questions". *Australian Society*, vol. 10, nos 11 and 12.

Royal Commission into Aboriginal Deaths in Custody (1991). *National Report*. Canberra: AGPS.

Ryan, Lyndall (1981). *The Aboriginal Tasmanians*. St Lucia: University of Queensland Press.

Cases

Coe v Commonwealth (1979) 53 ALJR 403.

Cooper v Stuart (1889) 14 App Cas 286.

Mabo and Orr v Queensland (1992) High Court of Australia CLR

Milirrpum v. Nabalco (1971) 17 FLR 141
State Government Insurance Commission v Trigwell (1979) 142 CLR 617 at
    625–34

Chapter 5

Living the Dreaming

Bill Edwards

Introduction

The roots of contemporary Aboriginal spirituality lie in a variety of traditions and experiences. First and foremost are the various stories, ceremonies, values and structures which sustained Aboriginal peoples throughout their long period of relatively unchallenged occupation of the continent. Colonisation was accompanied by the introduction of Christianity, and many Aboriginal people have been influenced by Christian teachings and values. Other introduced religions, such as the Baha'i faith and the Rastafarian movement, have had some impact. The responses of Aboriginal people to two centuries of invasion, dispossession, suffering and racism have shaped further their understandings about life and purpose, fusing with the other traditions to shape their contemporary religious ideas and feelings.

In recent decades, Aboriginal land rights, and now the High Court decision in Mabo, have focused attention on Aboriginal understandings about the world and their place and purpose in it. Earlier misconceptions and prejudices have been exposed as researchers have sought to discover Aboriginal viewpoints and Aboriginal people themselves have revealed more about their relationships to the world in order to substantiate their claims to land. Appearing before the Ranger Uranium Inquiry in 1975, the late Silas Roberts, as Chairman of the Northern Land Council, stated that "Our connection to all things natural is spiritual." (Cole, 1979:162) This assertion of the centrality of spiritual beliefs to Aboriginal life contrasts with some of the statements made by early colonial observers in which the existence of any kind of spiritual understandings was denied.

The nineteenth century Presbyterian leader in New South Wales, the Rev. John Dunmore Lang, allowed Aborigines

> nothing whatever of the character of religion, or of religious observance, to distinguish them from the beasts of the field. [Harris 1990: 542]

Writing in Victoria in 1978, A. Le Souef asserted that:

I never could discover among them anything amounting to religion … My opinion is that they have no religious notions or ideas whatever. [Stanner, 1984: 139]

Recent archaeological discoveries suggest that, in fact, Aboriginal people are inheritors of the longest surviving tradition of religious beliefs and practices in the world. Radio-carbon dating of skeletal remains has provided evidence of human occupation of sites 40,000 years ago, and shown that cultural practices, including belief and ritual systems, have been maintained over this long span of time — for example, the use of red ochre, and the arrangement and adornment of bodies in ancient burial sites (Edwards, 1988: 7).

The early European observers of Aboriginal life came with preconceived ideas about what religion and spiritual existence represented, based on their experience in Western Europe of Christianity, church buildings, forms of worship, the roles of priests and ministers, belief in one God and the importance of scriptures. When they observed similar phenomena of rites, holy men, shrines or temples and sacred books in Africa and Asia they acknowledged the presence of religious systems. However, as the forms of religious expression in Australia were so different and subtle, their very existence was denied.

In contrast to those early views, recent observers have emphasised the centrality of beliefs in spiritual powers in Aboriginal cosmology. Tonkinson, who studied the Mardudjara people of Western Australia, wrote of the "profoundly religious view of life that characterises the Aborigines" (Tonkinson, 1978: 15). Rose, who researched in the Victoria River region of the Northern Territory, wrote that:

We are talking about a profoundly moving representation of humanity's search for religious meaning. [Rose, 1987: 266]

Since the earlier pejorative comments were made, the definitions of religion have broadened and more detailed study of Aboriginal societies has revealed the variety, complexity and depth of the belief and ritual systems. These studies have shown that Aboriginal systems of beliefs provided answers to the great universal religious questions of humankind, the questions about origins, meaning, purpose and destiny.

The Dreaming

The term "The Dreaming" is used commonly to describe the Aboriginal creative epoch. Each language group had its own term to refer to this epoch and all associated with it. Ngarinyin people in the north-west of Western Australia refer to it as Ungud, the Aranda of Central Australia as Aldjerinya, the Pitjantjatjara of north-west South Australia as Tjukurpa, the Yolngu of north-east Arnhem Land as Wongar, while in the Broome region it is referred to as Bugari. While the term used in some of the languages is related to the word for Dreaming, this does not apply to all of them. The use of the English word Dreaming should not suggest that it refers to some vague reflection of the real world. Rather, Aboriginal people see the world of The Dreaming as the fundamental reality. The indigenous terms have a meaning of story and they refer to each group's stories which enshrine their understandings about their origins.

Previously referred to as the Dreamtime, the term was changed to The Dreaming by Professor Stanner in a paper first published in 1956 (Stanner, 1987), in acknowledgment of the fact that the Aboriginal creative epoch cannot be understood within a Western framework of linear time. Western concepts of linear time with the separation of past and present make it difficult to describe The Dreaming as it is conceived in Aboriginal thought. While there is a sense in which The Dreaming activities occurred at the beginning of the world, and are past, there is a sense also in which they are still present. Through ritual, humans are able to enter into a direct relationship with The Dreaming. The Aboriginal concept of time is therefore cyclic, rather than linear, but in the sense that each generation is able to experience the present reality of The Dreaming. Rose refers to it as the "heroic time which existed in the past and still exists today" (Rose, 1988: 260). Stanner coined the term "everywhen" in an attempt to convey this idea. "One cannot 'fix' The Dreaming in time: it was, and is everywhen." (Stanner, 1987: 225)

In a recent study of Australian Aboriginal being, Swain suggests that the attention given to time in relation to The Dream events has diverted attention from the significance of place.

> Were we to cling to the dream-root, this would be best rendered as "Dreaming-event" (a qualitative rather than temporal distinction) or Dream-place. [Swain, 1993: 24]

The concept of The Dreaming does not assume the creation of the world from nothing, a *creatio ex nihilo*. It assumes a pre-existent substance, often described as a watery expanse or a featureless plain. Spirit Beings lay dormant under the surface of this substance. According to The Dreaming stories, the Spirit Beings emerged from the formless earth and assumed forms and identities which combined, in many instances, features of humans and the various animal and plant species which now inhabit the cosmos. They appeared as kangaroo-men, shark-men, serpent-women, brolga-women, mulga seed-women and bush fig-men. The stories of each area reflected the faunal and floral species of the various environments. Some of The Dreaming beings were humans — for example, the Two Youths — while other stories ranged over objects and incidents of the Aboriginal environment — for example, grind stones, wind, coughing and diarrhoea.

The Spirit Beings, on emerging from the formless substance, moved over the surface of the earth, performing the everyday activities of the humans and other species they represented. They hunted, ate, fought, cheated, made tools, sang, danced, gathered foods, dug for water and died. At times they are said to have performed human type activities such as hunting, making tools or dancing. At other times they performed the activities of the other species they represented, such as munching grass or hopping over a sandhill. As they travelled, they and their tracks, artefacts and activities were transformed into the rocks, mountains, waterholes, caves, sandhills, trees, watercourses, stars and the other phenomena of the environment. For example, a kangaroo-man sitting up to view the country became a rocky ridge, the winding track of a serpent became a watercourse, bush tomatoes gathered by some women became small stones, a bush shelter built by a group of sisters became a cave and these sisters eventually went into the sky to become the star constellation known as the Pleiades. For more examples, see Edwards (1988: 16–18) and Isaacs (1980).

The land

This brief outline of The Dreaming illustrates the significance of land in Aboriginal thought. The whole of the landscape is conceived as having been formed through the activities of the Spirit Beings. The whole environment is viewed as the arena in which the dramatic events of The Dreaming were and are enacted. The continent is dotted with significant sites associated with the stories — for example, places where the Spirit Beings first emerged, where they performed a ceremony or where they died and re-entered the earth. It is criss-crossed with the tracks of the Spirit Beings as they travelled from site to site. Aboriginal people today do not invent sacred sites as is sometimes suggested by opponents of land rights. In one sense, all the land is a sacred site. The Spirit Beings are said to be present continually in the forms of the landscape which were created through their activities.

The Ancestral Spirit Beings of The Dreaming are believed to be the ancestors of both the Aboriginal groups which live in the areas of the various stories and of the species associated with them. For example, one group of people is said to be descended from the Kangaroo-man who is also progenitor of the kangaroos. People derive their spiritual essence from the Ancestral Spirit Beings and share the same spiritual essence which inhabits the land and other species.

In contrast, Western ideas about reality and religion are based largely on the general acceptance of dichotomies between natural and cultural, material and spiritual, past and present, secular and sacred, subject and object. Reference has been made earlier to the different concept of time in Aboriginal thought. Just as the clear demarcation between past and present is lacking in Aboriginal conceptualisation, the other dichotomies are not present. In Western thought, culture as human achievement is distinguished from the natural world. Aborigines envisage other species taking part in cultural activities (Rose, 1987: 264). Sutton comments that:

In traditional Aboriginal thought, there is no nature without culture. [Sutton, 1988: 18]

The distinction between subject and object breaks down as people identify rocks, trees or birds as representations of their own beings, and not as things solely objective and external to them. Rose sees a difference between Aboriginal and other forms of mysticism which tend to focus on the transcendent and supernatural:

Aboriginal religion leads people into this world and towards an immanent experience of unity in the here and now. [Rose, 1987: 268]

The realm of spiritual existence is not divorced from the material world, but is embedded in it. The various languages have terms which are similar to the English concept of spirit. For example, the Pitjantjatjara people refer to *kurunpa. Kurunpa* is present in all aspects of the world. The Ancestral Beings left their spiritual essence in the rocks, the trees, the animal and other species. People walk with care over the earth in an awareness that spiritual forces surround them and that they must heed the laws and taboos which dictate relationships to them. For example, a person nearing a waterhole may throw a stone into the water to alert the water serpent spirit of his or her approach to avoid the danger of being bitten.

Animism and totemism

These beliefs led to the application of two terms in early studies of Aboriginal religion. An anthropologist at Oxford University, Edward Tylor, introduced the term "animism" (from the Latin, *anima*, for soul or spirit) to describe these Aboriginal beliefs because of this attribution of possession of spirit to a wide range of inanimate objects as well as to animate beings. The term "totemism" has been applied to describe the association existing between a local descent group of people and the animal or plant species with which they are thought to share descent. This shared descent bestows on the local groups the rights to utilise the resources in the area and the obligations to care for sites and carry out the associated rituals designed to ensure the continued existence of the related species. (For a detailed description of totemism, see Berndt and Berndt, 1981: 231–40.)

While the terms "animism" and "totemism" point to important aspects of Aboriginal understandings about the presence of spiritual essence in the world and the relationship of people to other parts of the world, they were reductionist terms introduced by theorists who viewed Aboriginal religion as a primitive expression of the human search for meaning. Neither term adequately conveys the complexity, and varieties, of Aboriginal religious systems.

Another of the dichotomies underlying Western thought is that between the secular and the sacred. Aboriginal thought had contained no such distinction. Because all life was conceived as originating from the activities of the Ancestral Spirit Beings, all parts of the cosmos partook of their spiritual essence and were sacred. There are, however, places, objects and ceremonies which are believed to have associated with them a special quality of power, sacredness and danger. Access to, use of and participation in them is restricted to those who are thought to have the prerequisite knowledge and experience. Differences in age and sex are basic factors related to the knowledge and experience.

The passing on of the Dreaming stories from one generation to the next was a most important aspect of education. Knowledge of the story was the most prized possession of senior Aboriginal people. Males and females knew differing and complementary parts of stories. This knowledge was not passed on indiscriminately, but only as recipients were seen to be ready to accept the obligations which accompanied the knowledge. The stories record that the Ancestral Spirit Beings gave their first descendants the various languages in which the stories have been related. For example, the kangaroo-men left the dialects of the Western Desert groups and the first Mother, Waramurungundji, emerged from the sea and, as she gave birth to the first children of Arnhem Land, gave them the languages they were to speak.

The Ancestral Spirit Beings left as a legacy the other forms of symbolism — song cycles, paintings and rituals — through which their exploits were recorded and passed on. The correct narration of the stories, painting of the symbols, singing of the songs and performance of the rituals is designed to ensure the maintenance of the cosmos and society. The well-known Wandjina paintings in the caves of the Kimberley region of north-west Western Australia are believed to have been first painted by the Wandjina Spirit Beings. As the paintings are touched up, the spirit powers are renewed and released for appropriation by the descendants of the Ancestral Beings.

A pattern for life

The Dreaming ancestors provided the model for life. They established a pattern for the daily round of economic, social, political, cultural and ritual activities. People hunt and share food, make tools, punish offenders, draw designs and relate to each in certain ways because the ancestors are believed to have acted in these ways, and to have left examples to be followed. The stories reflect the daily events in the lives of the people of the particular region. Just as Aboriginal people depended on hunting, fishing and gathering for daily sustenance, the ancestors are portrayed as engaging in these pursuits in The Dreaming. Strehlow commented that in the stories we see the Aborigine:

at his daily task of hunting, fishing, gathering vegetable food, cooking and fashioning his implements. All occupations originated with the totemic ancestors. [Strehlow, 1947: 35]

The particular roles of males and females in hunting and gathering, the ways in which foods were prepared, cooked and shared, and the use of implements were all pre-ordained by the ancestors. Even in the most mundane tasks, people re-live the events of The Dreaming. All living is in a sense sanctified. For an attempt to illustrate the unity of all aspects of Aboriginal life, as centred on the principle of The Dreaming, see the design in Edwards (1988: 13).

Yami Lester, a Yankunytjatjara man from the north-west of South Australia, recalls learning about the land, people and culture as a child, when his parents:

> just talked about the country. And I believed what they said. You couldn't doubt, it was just something real. The country wasn't just hills or creeks or trees. And I didn't feel like it was fairy tales they told me. It was real, our *kuuti*, the force that gives us life. Somebody created it, and whoever created it did it for us, so we could live and hunt and have a good time. That's how we come to be here because that *malu* and *ngintaka* created this image for us to live and breathe: the plants, the language, the people. [Lester, 1993: 10]

Malu is the kangaroo, and *ngintaka* is the perentie.

The relatively limited technological development in Aboriginal societies was counter-balanced by the sophisticated elaboration of social relationships. The Pitjantjatjara word for relation, *walytja*, is a basic concept. This aspect of Aboriginal life is described in Chapter 6.

Relationships are of vital importance in Aboriginal societies. Members of the various groups can identify their relationships to all other members of the group. These relationships dictate much of the day-to-day behaviour of individuals. The same kinds of relationships and obligations which flow from them are accorded to the Ancestral Spirit Beings. The reciprocal obligations between individuals and groups dictated ways in which offenders against the rules and structures should be punished. The rules, taboos and punishments are enshrined also in The Dreaming stories. Thus Aboriginal people today commonly gloss their own terms for The Dreaming with the English word "Law".

Rituals

Religion and spirituality are concerned with access to spiritual powers. The Aboriginal belief that they share the same spiritual essence with all parts of the cosmos encourages them to seek contact with the Spirit Beings and access to spiritual powers through rituals. The Ancestral Spirit Beings had themselves performed ceremonies on their travels and left songs, dances and other rites to be followed to ensure the continual existence of the world and all its life forms. Rose wrote of "all those ceremonies through which cosmic life is regenerated" (Rose, 1987: 264). Some rituals were designed to ensure the continued supply of the species whose Dreaming exploits they re-enacted. Others marked the passage of individuals through significant stages of life, such as puberty, marriage and death. Some rituals belong to the domain of males; others to that of females. In some, both sexes have complementary roles. Each group is responsible for preserving the stories, maintaining the sites and ensuring the performance of the rituals related to its totemic species. As all groups undertake their responsibilities, all species and the whole world are nurtured and regenerated.

Ritual linked the performers with The Dreaming. They were not just re-enacting the creative deeds of the Ancestor Spirit Beings but as they were painted with the symbols of the stories, sang the songs and danced the steps, they entered into the very being of those ancestors. Eliade wrote that for Aboriginal people:

> The communication with the Dream Time, regenerates life, and assures its continuation. In short, the ritual "re-creates" the world. [Eliade, 1973: 61]

He quotes Strehlow's comment that the performer as the reincarnation of one of the ancestors "himself has played a part in that first glorious adventure" (Eliade, 1973: 57).

In inland regions, the most significant rituals relating to the passage of individuals through stages of life were the male initiation ceremonies. Less attention was given to mortuary rituals. As people were scattered in arid regions, there were few people on hand on most occasions when a person died, and burial took place as soon as possible. It was believed that the spirit of the person left the body after death, wandered around the area for a short while and returned to the realm of spiritual existence, adding to the store of spirit essence from which spirits entered women to cause conception and generate further births.

In northern tropical areas, mortuary ceremonies are more significant. More fertile ecological conditions allow for larger population clusters, enabling more people to be involved. The mortuary ceremonies of some groups in Arnhem Land have three stages, concluding with the placing of the bones in a hollow log coffin. Clan symbols painted on the coffin are designed to be recognised by the ancestors who receive the spirit of the dead person (Morphy, 1987: 22).

Reference has been made to the idea that The Dreaming provides a pattern for the way life is to be lived now. There are problems associated with this interpretation of The Dreaming. It is not a pattern of an idealised perfect state. All the affairs of human life, good and evil, are included in the stories. Sutton writes that the Ancestral Beings exhibit all the faces of human virtue, vice, pleasure and suffering (Sutton, 1988:15). The stories enable people to reflect on all the vicissitudes of life.

> The key characters of the more important myths are hardly models of approved behaviour. Liberal misdemeanours by mythic ancestors are frequently unjustified and go unpunished, or if punished, then to an extent that often goes beyond any conceivable justice. Explicit moral comment is rarely a feature of traditional Aboriginal narratives, or even of historical reminiscences. Listeners must make their own judgments, if any. [Sutton, 1988: 18]

Another problem associated with the above description of The Dreaming is that it gives an impression of a fixed, static and unchanging pattern of culture, whereas change is inevitable in any society as groups adapt to changing environmental conditions, external contacts and internal pressures for change. While in Aboriginal societies there is a rhetoric of the unchangeableness and immutability of The Dreaming and of the social life lived in its image, referred to by Stanner as "a metaphysical emphasis on abidingness", (Stanner, 1987: 234), change and innovation were present, albeit very gradual, and the changes in the material and social conditions of life were reflected in changes to The Dreaming stories.

The impact of colonisation

Aboriginal societies which had known only gradual and minimal change over their long histories suffered sudden and momentous changes with the advent of English colonial settlement, or invasion, from 1788. Many of the groups subject to the initial impact of settlement were wiped from the face of the land by killings, the introduction of new diseases and the loss of will as they were driven from lands which had been central to their way of life (Broome, 1982: 62). The dispossession of the land was justified by emerging Western theories culminating in Social Darwinism, which assumed that earlier forms of social organisation would be replaced inevitably by more progressive and more highly developed forms.

Other groups in remote regions had more time to adjust to this impact and did not face the same pressure of invasion. They were able to survive despite a severe decline in population. Colonial authorities revised their policies for administering the surviving groups according to changing ideologies, the demands of the dominant population and the resistance of the groups to the policies. Broome refers to the twin objectives in early policies of civilising and Christianising the Aborigines (Broome, 1982: 31). As adherence to traditional beliefs and practices were seen as inimical to the process of civilising, there was pressure to discard them.

The objective of Christianising was instituted by the establishment of missions. Mission work in Australia among Aboriginal and Torres Strait Islander people was part of a worldwide movement. Influenced by Evangelical revivals and concerns for indigenous peoples, who were suffering as a result of slavery and colonial expansion, churches in Europe and America in the late eighteenth and nineteenth centuries sought to obey the command of Jesus to make "disciples of all nations" (Gospel of St Matthew, 28: 19). While missions in Australia provided a refuge which in many regions enabled Aboriginal groups to survive, the failure on the part of many missionaries to recognise and appreciate the values of Aboriginal societies and the tendency to regard all aspects of these societies as pagan and immoral led to suspicion, antipathy and despair. The first missionary in New South Wales, Walker, expressed a common theme that no good could be done with the adults of the "scattered, uncivilised, unsocial and cannibal tribes" (quoted in Harris, 1990: 47), but that the work must be commenced with the young men and children. Some early missionaries did, however, draw attention to the frontier brutality and the atrocities inflicted on Aboriginal groups by settlers. Threlkeld saw the cruelty associated with the convict system as degrading "the white to a lower degree than that of the despised aborigine of New South Wales" (Gunson, 1974: 48).

An itinerant Presbyterian missionary in New South Wales, William Ridley, recognised the worth of Aboriginal culture and inconsistency between the white people's profession of religion and their stealing of Aboriginal women and dispossessing Aborigines of their land. He wrote in 1861:

> One poor fellow on the Mooni addressed me in a long and pathetic harangue on the wrongs which his people have suffered at the hands of the white men. [Harris, 1990: 234]

Since the commencement of missionary activity in 1824, the Christian mission enterprise amongst Aborigines has been persistent and widespread. The work has been sponsored by a variety of denominational and interdenominational mission societies and basic philosophies and approaches have varied. In many early — and some recent — missions, no value was seen in traditional Aboriginal cultures and attempts were made to eradicate languages, rituals and other practices. Other missionaries, such as the Rev. J.R.B. Love, who worked at Kunmunya in the north-west of Western Australia in 1915 and from 1927 to 1940, respected the structures and values of the societies in which they worked and sought to graft the Christian message on to existing cultures. Love wrote of his experience of a Worora ceremony:

> As I looked at these rites the amazing realisation flashed upon me that here, among one of the most primitive tribes … I had been witnessing rites akin to the most sacred observances of the Christian faith. I had been witnessing, in all their primitiveness and crudeness of administration, the rites of the Laying-on of hands, of Baptism, and of a sacred meal that could without irreverence be called a Communion. [Love, 1936: 219]

It is not the purpose of this chapter to attempt to provide a history of the Aboriginal–Mission encounter and to evaluate the effectiveness of the missionary endeavour. Rather, an outline is given of some of the contemporary Aboriginal movements which have their roots in this missionary enterprise. Aboriginal responses to missions have been varied. Some groups have reacted to the challenge presented by new stories and ceremonies by incorporating elements of them into the former systems but seeking to retain the traditional systems as paramount. Others have responded positively to Christian evangelism and have themselves become active in, and expressed their spirituality through, the life and mission of Christian churches. Still others have rejected the Christian message because of the paternalism and severity of much of the missionary practice, and the involvement of missions in the break-up of families and the loss of traditions.

In the Torres Strait Islands, the annual celebration of the Coming of the Light suggests that the mission enterprise gained wider acceptance. According to Beckett, the available sources enable us to form only a vague impression of island life in pre-colonial times (Beckett, 1987: 30). The traditions suggest that the fear of violent death was ever-present, warfare was common, and sorcery was feared as men sought supernatural power. The London Missionary Society established work in the Islands in 1871 and teachers from the South Pacific played important roles in the building of local churches. They encouraged the cessation of many traditional practices. The protection afforded by the warfare and sorcery encouraged the Islanders to accept their authority and influence (Beckett, 1987: 40). As local church leaders were trained, they became mediators between Europeans and Islanders. The London Missionary Society withdrew from the Islands in 1914, having passed on its role to the Anglican Diocese of Carpentaria.

Syncretic movements

Syncretism, or the merging of elements from different, even seemingly irreconcilable, world views, is a feature of all religious systems as they seek to adapt to their environments. Some syncretic movements have been referred to as revitalisation or nativistic movements as through them leaders have sought to revive elements of traditional authority and practice in the face of the challenge of introduced ideas, influences and authorities. Syncretic movements range from those in which reaction is strong and the external pressures are resisted strongly, to those where syncretic elements may be present in movements which are more accepting of the introduced systems. The former tend to be secretive and closed, with knowledge of them by outsiders limited. Cultic movements present in Western Australia from the 1930s to the 1970s appear to have characteristics of such movements.

The *Woagaia* movement emerged from traditional complexes in Central Australia and took on nativistic features at Lagrange on the north-west coast in the 1960s. Another movement in that region during the 1960s focused on a black Jesus, known as *Jinimin*, with a mixture of traditional and Christian forms in the ceremonies. For example, in some ceremonies the distribution of food appears to have copied Christian eucharistic practices. A syncretic movement observed by Ronald Berndt at Elcho Island, off the north coast of Arnhem Land, in the late 1950s was linked more openly to both church and traditional systems, with traditional sacred objects, *rannga*, and the Christian cross featured in public displays. Kolig (1988) provides a brief description of some syncretic movements.

Aboriginal Christian movements

The control of Christian missions by white missionaries and mission boards tended to inhibit the emergence of Aboriginal leadership and Aboriginal forms of worship. Even when Aboriginal Christians were encouraged to incorporate indigenous elements of music or ritual, they were diffident in their response. Because of the close association of form and meaning in Aboriginal rituals, it was difficult for them to take the forms and give them new meaning. There was a tendency to accept the ways in which the Christian message was introduced to them as the correct way, the given Christian Dreaming way. Changes in Aboriginal policy and political arenas over the past two decades have been accompanied by the emergence of new Christian movements. Former missions have come under the control of local community councils. Because the missions had provided education and some opportunities for leadership, Aboriginal Christians emerged as leaders in their communities and organisations as policies of self-management were implemented. They were encouraged in turn to seek more responsibilities in their churches. Increasing mobility has brought together Aboriginal Christians from widespread groups.

An early movement in the modern era was a Pentecostal movement amongst the Bandjalang people of north-east New South Wales in the 1950s. Some traditional elements were incorporated with characteristic features of Pentecostalism. The movement, which had anti-white overtones, brought purpose and pride to a group which had suffered severe breakdown and anomie. The Bandjalang had been evangelised by the interdenominational United Aborigines Mission. This mission society and another fundamentalist society, the Aborigines Inland Mission, established several mission stations, children's homes and other institutions throughout Australia. These included Warburton Ranges Mission and Mount Margaret Mission in Western Australia, Nepabunna and Colebrook Home in South Australia, and the Retta Dixon Homes in Darwin. Aboriginal people influenced by these societies were encouraged to forsake any association with traditional belief and ceremonial systems, with even the use of Aboriginal languages being discouraged, as they were viewed as pagan. It should be acknowledged that these views were modified by some later missionaries in these organisations and some engaged in language study and translation. Also, the popularity of hymns, such as "The Old Rugged Cross", at many funeral services of Aboriginal people indicates the continuing influence of this tradition on contemporary Aboriginal spirituality.

Aboriginal leaders who were trained within these and similar contexts established the Aboriginal Evangelical Fellowship in 1971. A fellowship had been formed in Western Australia in 1967 and a meeting with leaders from eastern states in 1968 led to a conference of seventy leaders at Port Augusta over the Christmas/New Year period of 1970–71. Conventions held at Port Augusta annually have attracted Aboriginal people from all over Australia and attendances reached 2,000 in the late 1970s. A leader in this movement, Pastor Jack Braeside, commented that:

> The value of the convention is that people come into a deeper experience of God and go back to their own places contributing to their churches and fellowships. Others are being inspired to start churches of their own and become an asset to their community churches. People are being educated as Christians in organising things in the convention, contributing choir items, preaching and attending council meetings. Doing this ourselves has been an educational exercise. [Hart, 1988: 8]

The Aboriginal Evangelical Fellowship was formed by Aboriginal people and remained under their control. A significant movement in its early years, when it provided leaders for other Aboriginal movements (e.g. see Gilbert, 1978: 60), its influence has declined in recent years, partly because of the narrowness of the tradition which gave it birth. Differing attitudes to traditional culture, disputes over doctrine and varying responses to the charismatic movement have caused divisions and a decline in membership. Harris (1990) provides a brief history of the movement.

From mission traditions where Aboriginal cultures and values were accorded more respect, such as at Ernabella in South Australia and Elcho Island and Yirrkala in Arnhem Land, have emerged Aboriginal Christian leaders who are at the same time upholders of many aspects of their traditional cultures and active participants in Church life. A significant movement which originated on a denominational mission and spread to many Aboriginal communities in widespread regions of Australia was the Elcho Island revival which commenced in 1979. Elcho Island had been a Methodist Mission until control passed to a local council in the early 1970s. As with the Bandjalang movement, this revival brought a new spirit to a community suffering from severe social problems. Leaders in the movement were sons of men who had been involved in the movement referred to earlier which Berndt had observed at Elcho Island in the 1950s.

Most members of the community were caught up in this charismatic movement which featured well attended nightly services with singing, prayer and healing. The movement spread throughout Arnhem Land and to communities as far distant as Wiluna in Western Australia and Yalata in South Australia. While the initial enthusiasm waned, the movement has left a lasting impact on many Aboriginal people and on styles of Aboriginal Christian worship in many regions. The leaders of the movement saw it as offering a model for other churches and Christians in Australia. The Rev. Djiniyini Gondarra, a past Moderator of the Northern Synod of The Uniting Church, has written:

> The Christian churches in Australia need to be more open to recovering joyfully the blessings and insights offered through Aboriginal culture and spirituality. [Gondarra, 1988: 6]

Djiniyini Gondarra is a leader of the Uniting Aboriginal and Islander Christian Congress, formed under the inspiration of a former Assemblies of God pastor, Charles Harris, who had called Aboriginal Christian leaders from several traditions to meet at a conference in 1982. Constituted in 1983, the Congress had its charter adopted by the National Assembly of The Uniting Church in Australia in 1985 (Edwards and Clarke, 1988: 198). The Congress has challenged Australian churches through a Manifesto which includes the following:

> Aboriginal culture has never understood life in this divided way. All parts of life belong together as they do in the Bible. Our people have always lived

their spiritual lives in the political processes of our community life. [UAICC, n.d.: 6].

The Congress played an important role during the 1988 Australian Bicentennial year by organising an Aboriginal march in Sydney through its Justice, Freedom and Hope Committee.

Aboriginal Christians in churches where traditional belief systems are still strong have tended to compartmentalise these systems with the Christian stories. They have been willing to accept the validity of Dreaming stories at the same time as acknowledging God as creator. Dreaming stories do not assume the logic of Western thought and they have seen no incongruity in affirming both belief systems. Through the Congress and other movements, Aboriginal Christians are seeking to express their Christian faith through forms which are congruent with their own traditions. At the ordination of the first Aboriginal woman minister in The Uniting Church, Liyapidiny Marika, in 1991, her clan brought her forward in a traditional ceremony accompanied by clap sticks. She wore both the white ordination alb and a traditional feather headdress.

An Aboriginal Roman Catholic woman in the Northern Territory, Miriam-Rose Ungunmerr, is another who sees this combination of traditional Aboriginal and Aboriginal Christian forms and values offering hope to others in Australia. In 1984 she produced a series of paintings of the Stations of the Cross based on Aboriginal symbols.

Aboriginal Catholics have been encouraged to explore Aboriginal spirituality through the address to them by Pope John Paul II in Alice Springs in 1986:

> For thousands of years you have lived in this land and fashioned a culture that endures to this day. And during all this time, the Spirit of God has been with you. Your "Dreaming", which influences your lives so strongly that, no matter what happens, you remain for ever people of your culture, is your own way of touching the mystery of God's Spirit in you and in creation. [Hendricks and Hefferan, 1993: 90]

Around Australia, Aboriginal Catholic movements are revising liturgies to introduce elements from their own traditions. From this tradition, an Aboriginal deacon, Boniface Perdjert, has written:

> their traditional religion did give my people deep awareness of the spirit and things of the spirit. Their religion contained some elements that are on

a wave-length rather close to the Christian wave-length. It is up to the Christian apostle, with delicacy and skill, to tune these two wave-lengths together, so that the resultant harmony may be recognised by the Aborigines as truth, the truth that sets him free. [Hendriks and Hefferan, 1993: 39]

Contemporary Aboriginal spirituality

While many Aboriginal people have accepted the Christian message, either following it exclusively, or attempting to graft it on to their traditional beliefs, other Aborigines in contemporary Australia have rejected formal Christian structures and seek to express their spirituality by reaffirming Aboriginal beliefs and values. For some it has involved a process of relearning stories which had almost been lost to their parents' generation. Some have sought enlightenment from other religious systems, such as Islam, the Baha'i faith and the Rastafarian movement. Reacting to the dominant materialism of Australian society, many are turning again to the centrality of spiritual existence and values in their lives. Some see this emphasis on spirituality as central to their identity as Aborigines.

Aboriginal people are encouraged in the recovery, reaffirmation and sharing of their story about the world and life, through growing links with other indigenous peoples throughout the world. Early in 1993, Aboriginal delegates who met with other indigenous people in New Zealand at a World Conference on Spiritual Healing experienced this encouragement. Non-Aboriginal Australians are giving Aboriginal beliefs about land, relationships and spiritual existence greater respect as the world faces threats to the ecology of the land, to social and family life and to economic systems. Some sense that Aboriginal concepts of spirit and of peoples' relationship to land offer insights to all who are concerned about these problems.

Aboriginal writer, the late Kevin Gilbert, expressed an Aboriginal attitude which accords with the views of many environmentalists:

> The Aboriginal way is that everything created is equal and sacred; that the soil, the clay, the rocks are all sacred within, say, creation, and that all have a personality, a distinct personality. I had the strength of knowing my creator is not above me somewhere, but is always with me. [Jones, 1990: 56]

Gilbert saw no need for church or systems of religion.

There's no need to meditate distinctly; there's no need to go to any church; there's no need to think spiritual or religious thoughts. There's a constant flowing of life and we are very much a part of that life. [Jones, 1990: 57]

Contemporary Aboriginal songwriter/singer Kevin Carmody, although referring in his songs to Jesus and religious symbols, has no time for the formal structures of religious systems. Aboriginal people now, as they have always done, are expressing their fundamental ideas about reality through story, song and art.

As many people in the modern world are turning both from traditional religious systems and materialist interpretations of the world, there is renewed interest in a variety of spiritualities — Eastern, New-Age, Celtic, feminist and others. As part of this movement, Aboriginal beliefs and values, which sustained them for many thousands of years in environments which others have found alien and threatening, are attracting new interest and respect. In the Introduction to her book, *The Search for Meaning*, the broadcaster Caroline Jones, writes:

Aboriginal people gave meaning to my life by showing through their suffering, their courage, their unselfishness, their sense of family, their forgiveness, their survival and their sense of the sacred what it is truly like to be human. For me they are the steady beating heart at the centre of our Australian spirituality. [Jones, 1989: 17]

Her words reflect the comment of Miriam-Rose Ungunmerr, that Aboriginal spirituality is the gift for which Australia is thirsting (Ungunmerr, 1988: 9).

References

Beckett, Jeremy (1987). *Torres Strait Islanders: Custom and Colonialism*. Cambridge: Cambridge University Press.

Berndt, R.M. & C.H. (1981). *The World of the First Australians*. Sydney: Lansdowne Press.

Cole, Keith (1979). *The Aborigines of Arnhem Land*. Adelaide: Rigby.

Edwards, W.H. (1988). *An Introduction to Aboriginal Societies*. Wentworth Falls: Social Science Press.

_____ & Clarke, B.A. (1988). "From missions to Aboriginal churches: The Uniting Church in Australia and Aboriginal missions". In *Aboriginal Australians and Christian Missions*, edited by Tony Swain, Rose Swain and Deborah Bird. Bedford Park SA: Australian Association for the Study of Religions.

Eliade, Mercia (1973). *Australian Religions*. Ithaca: Cornell University Press.

Gilbert, Kevin (1978). *Living Black: Blacks Talk to Kevin Gilbert*. Ringwood: Penguin.

Gondarra, Djiniyini (1988). *Father You Gave Us The Dreaming*. Darwin: Bethel Presbytery.

Gunson, Niel (ed.) (1974). *Australian Reminiscences and Papers of L.E. Threlkeld, Missionary to the Aborigines 1824-1859*. Canberra: Australian Institute of Aboriginal Studies.

Harris, John (1990). *One Blood: 200 Years of Aboriginal Encounters with Christianity — A Story of Hope*. Sutherland: Albatross Books.

Hart, Max (1988). *A Story of Fire: Aboriginal Christianity*. Blackwood: New Creation Publications.

Hendriks, Joan and Hefferan, Gerry (eds) (1993). *A Spirituality of Catholic Aborigines and the Struggle for Justice*. Brisbane: Aboriginal and Torres Strait Islander Apostolate.

Jones, Caroline (1989). *The Search for Meaning*. Crows Nest: Australian Broadcasting Corporation.

—— (1990). *The Search for Meaning: Book Two*. Crows Nest: Australian Broadcasting Corporation.

Kolig, E (1988). "Religious movements". In *The Australian People: An Encyclopedia of the Nation, Its People and Their Origins*, edited by James Jupp. Sydney: Angus & Robertson.

Lester, Yami (1993). *Yami: The Autobiography of Yami Lester*. Alice Springs: Institute for Aboriginal Development Publications.

Love, J.R.B. (1936). *Stone-age Bushmen of To-day*. London: Blackie and Son Limited.

Morphy, Howard (1987). "The art of Northern Australia". In *Traditional Aboriginal Society: A Reader*, edited by W.H. Edwards. South Melbourne: Macmillan.

Rose, Deborah B. (1987). "Consciousness and responsibility in an Aboriginal religion". In *Traditional Aboriginal Religion: A Reader*, edited by W.H. Edwards. South Melbourne: Macmillan.

Stanner, W.H. (1984). "Religion, totemism and symbolism". In *Religion in Aboriginal Australia: An Anthology*, edited by Max Charlesworth et al. Brisbane: University of Queensland Press.

—— (1987). "The Dreaming". In *Traditional Aboriginal Religion: A Reader*, edited by W.H. Edwards. South Melbourne: Macmillan.

Strehlow, T.G.H. (1947). *Aranda Traditions*. Melbourne: Melbourne University Press.

Swain, Tony (1993). *A Place for Strangers: Towards a History of Australian Aboriginal Being*. Cambridge: Cambridge University Press.

Sutton, Peter (ed.) (1988). *Dreamings: The Art of Aboriginal Australia*. Ringwood: Viking–Penguin Books.

Tonkinson, R. (1978). *The Mardudjara Aborigines*. New York: Holt, Rinehart and Winston.

UAICC (n.d.). *Manifesto of The Uniting Aboriginal and Islander Christian Congress*. Sydney.

Ungunmerr, M.R. (1988). "Dadirri". *Compass*, vol. 22.

Chapter 6

Family and Kin

Colin Bourke and Bill Edwards

Background

All aspects of Aboriginal society have been directly affected by the arrival of British colonists. Land use, law, spiritual beliefs and ways of life have been traumatised. All aspects of Aboriginal society have felt the full force of the invasion, but it is arguable that traditional Aboriginal family life and the supporting kinship structures have taken the maximum disruptive impact, especially in areas of highest non-Aboriginal population density.

Aboriginal family life has been irreversibly changed in most of Australia. Many of the changes have come about merely by the presence of Europeans in this country; many others are attributable to the direct actions of the colonisers, actions which were deliberately aimed at destroying family life as it existed in Aboriginal society.

Aboriginal kinship and family structures are still cohesive forces which bind Aboriginal people together in all parts of Australia. They provide psychological and emotional support to Aboriginal people even though they create concern among non-Aboriginal people who would prefer Aborigines to follow European social preferences for nuclear families with few kinship responsibilities. Aboriginal family obligations are often seen as nepotism by other Australians, but they are cultural issues, involving longstanding kinship responsibilities.

Removal of children

Nearly all Aboriginal families know of relatives who were removed as children and put into European custody. Aboriginal people refer to them as "taken" or "stolen". The effects of such policies and practices are still reverberating in the Aboriginal community. Aboriginal adults who were taken away from their families as children experience difficulties adjusting without having an Aboriginal family-supported childhood. Though wanting to join their own people, some have a crisis of identity. They have been raised to think "white" and "be like white people". To gain acceptance in Aboriginal society, they have to learn new values and new rules and in many cases overcome negative views of their Aboriginal heritage.

The removal of Aboriginal children from their parents has been official policy in all states of Australia since the so-called "protection era". Missionaries established the practice in the early 1800s to instil Christian virtues of obedience, punctuality and religious observance. They wished to create an Aboriginal working class by developing marketable skills which would make Aborigines employable. The missionaries tried hard, but they failed and the Aboriginal people living near these early missions simply moved away.

The separation of Aboriginal children from their families began in earnest in 1883 when the New South Wales Aborigines Protection Board was established to control what non-Aborigines perceived to be a growing problem of Aboriginal populations congregating around towns (Reed, n.d.). It was argued that the children of these people could be turned into useful citizens if they were taken from their parents and socialised as Europeans. A policy of child removal began, based on the "idleness" of the parents from which the child should be "protected". It is ironic that the so-called protection policies era actually devastated Aboriginal life.

In New South Wales alone, official records show some 5,625 children, at least, had been removed from their parents between 1883 and 1969 (Reed, n.d.) and placed in Aboriginal Children's Homes. There are no records of Aboriginal children sent into other state or religious homes. Unofficial removals would also significantly inflate the figure. Similar situations prevailed in the rest of Australia. The passing of the *Child Welfare Act* in New South Wales in 1939 did not stop the practice. It was not until the 1950s that a reduction in the stream of enforced separations occurred. It was still believed, however, that non-Aboriginal parents could more quickly assimilate an Aboriginal child, so great pressure was placed on young Aboriginal mothers to have their children adopted by non-Aboriginal people. The number of Aboriginal children who were fostered increased in the 1950s. In 1957, the New South Wales Protection Board placed advertisements in newspapers seeking foster parents to look after Aboriginal children. Peter Reed (n.d.), in *The Stolen Generations*, noted that the response was extraordinary and within two years there were more Aboriginal children fostered out than there were in the homes.

Aboriginal families were often regarded as either homeless or as living in squalor by government officials, so Aboriginal children were never placed with black families. After being removed from their family and community support, most were subjected to racism, ignorance and prejudice. They grew up confused and unsure about their own identity. Peter Reed (n.d.) believes that in Australia today there may be 100,000 people of Aboriginal descent who do not know their families or the communities from whence they came.

These people have been institutionalised, fostered or adopted, loved, hated or ignored. They all share the mental torment of not belonging in the society into which European Australia had decided they belonged. Australian society accepted the young Aboriginal children into its institutions, but rejected them when they became adults.

Many of these adults have sought, and some are still seeking, to find their families. They know of their Aboriginal ancestry, but they need to know more about what it really means. They wish to be reunited with their families. They seek their Aboriginal identity. They need to know who they are and where their families are from. The psychological scars and damage to self-concepts are immeasurable for those removed from their families. The effects of being deprived of parent caring are still being felt in Aboriginal society.

Societies can place emphasis on either the individual or the social identity of a person. Western society places an emphasis on the individual. It values the rights and freedom of choice of the individual. Being strongly individualistic, there is less emphasis placed on group development.

Aboriginal society places greater emphasis on social identity, membership of a group and the obligations and responsibilities of individuals to conform to the expectations of others. It is a communal society where, even though the autonomy of each individual is respected, the individuality of each member receives less emphasis than their cooperative contribution. Being removed from such a society leaves the individual adrift without a point of reference and uncertain as to how to try to re-enter a society whose mores they do not know and whose kinship structure is not understood.

Kinship

In Western societies, the structures of social interaction and roles and obligations change as individuals move out from the immediate family circle to the wider society. In contrast to this, in Aboriginal societies the family structures and the sets of rights and obligations underlying them are extended to the whole society. As an individual moves out from the immediate family to the local group and to the total linguistic group, he or she is able to identify all other members of the groups by the same relationship terms which apply in the family. Terms usually applied to lineal relatives are used to refer also to collateral relatives. This is made possible by the application in Aboriginal societies of what is called the Classificatory System of Kinship.

A basic principle of this system is the *equivalence of same-sex siblings*. According to this principle, people who are of the same sex and belong to the same sibling line are viewed as essentially the same. Thus two brothers are considered to be equivalent. If one has a child, that child views not only his biological father as father but applies the same term to the father's brother. The same principle applies to two sisters with both being mothers to any child either one bears. As a father's brother is also identified as father, the latter's children will be brothers and sisters, rather than cousins. This system is known as the classificatory system of kinship because all members of the larger group are classified under the relationship terms. There is no need to expand the range of classifications or relationship terms. Several people are identified by an individual within each classification. Thus a person has several fathers, several mothers, and many brothers and sisters. A mother's brother, being on the same sibling line but of the other sex, is identified as an uncle. A father's sister is an aunt. (See Edwards, 1988: 48–49, for diagrams illustrating kinship terms.)

When speaking to, or about, another person in Aboriginal societies, the person's personal name is rarely used. A person is addressed by the appropriate relationship term, for example, father, aunt or older brother. Another person is referred to as so-and-so's son or mother. The personal names are seen as essentially part of the person and are used with discretion.

Because an individual is always interacting with others who are clearly identified by specific relationship terms, much of the behaviour in traditional societies is governed by the rights and obligations associated with the various relationships. According to the anthropologist, Robert Tonkinson,

> All over Australia, kinship is undeniably the most important single factor in restructuring Aboriginal social relationships. [Tonkinson, 1987: 210]

This applied in all spheres of life, in economic activities, social relationships, marriage, social control, ritual, education and politics. A person who brought in large game from the hunt, such as a kangaroo, was obliged to share a portion of it with specific relatives. Mothers, aunts and grandmothers had special roles in educating young children. In societies which did not have chiefs or designated leaders with wide powers, kinship was important in resolving conflict and restoring harmony. If a member of a group did something wrong, certain members of the group, according to the relationships, were responsible for punishing the offender.

Individuals are limited in the choice of marriage partners by their relationships. In most Aboriginal societies, a person married a person classified as a cross-cousin. Thus a man married either a mother's father's daughter or a father's sister's daughter, this varying according to the accepted rules in the group. This did not mean that marriage was between first cousins. People identified as uncles (mother's brothers) had special obligations related to the training, discipline and initiation of youths. In turn, in some groups, they promised one of their daughters to the young man as a prospective wife. In Aboriginal societies, marriages are significant, not only for the relationship between the two partners, but as forging alliances between groups.

Some relationships allow for great freedom in interaction, for example, between grandparents and grandchildren. In others, deference or restraint has to be shown at all times. One prominent type of relationship in Aboriginal societies is known as an avoidance relationship. These provide control over relationships which could give rise to extreme tensions in small groups. For example, a man may have to avoid all face-to-face contact with his mother-in-law. Brothers-in-law are also kept at a distance from one another. Brothers and sisters are expected to show some reserve in their relationship as they mature.

An important principle underlying all interaction is that of reciprocity. Pitjantjatjara people refer to this as *ngapartji-ngapartji*, or "in return". Between individuals, local groups and larger groups there are systems of rights, obligations and responsibilities based on this principle. If an individual or group gives food or a marriage partner to another individual or group, they expect to receive something or somebody in return. If a person or a group offends another person or group, they can expect retribution in return. These systems of checks and balances are designed to maintain equilibrium between individuals and groups. The kinship systems, with their sets of rights and obligations, provide individuals with a guide to their own behaviour and some security and confidence in predicting likely behaviours when meeting other people. Teaching about the relationships and associated behaviours is a major element in the traditional education of Aboriginal children.

The kinds of structures outlined above are identified as egocentric. From each individual's position, that person can specify his or her relationship, and the concomitant rights and obligations, to all other members of the group. The systems vary across the continent and books should be consulted for details of specific systems. All groups have complementary systems of social organisation which are identified as sociocentric. In these systems, all members of the group are viewed as members of social groups or categories.

Social categories

Whereas an individual is identified by various relationship terms according to the person who is applying them (e.g. a son calling him father, or another man calling him brother), people are placed into specific social categories according to their descent. In some societies this was determined by descent from the mother (matrilineal), in others by descent from the father (patrilineal). Membership of the categories is therefore ascribed by birth.

A basic division in Aboriginal societies is that between the moieties. Moiety means half and each group was divided into two groups or moieties. Membership of a moiety is significant in ritual, social interaction and marriage. In ceremonies, people sit in two circles according to moiety membership to sing the song cycles. Marriage in Aboriginal societies was normally exogamous in relationship to moieties — that is, a person married someone from the other moiety group. In northeast Arnhem Land, where children belong to the same moiety as their fathers, both their physical and their social environments are divided into two moieties, *Dhuwa* and *Yirritja*. A *Dhuwa* person must marry a

Yirritja person, and vice versa. Some areas of land are *Dhuwa*, and other areas are *Yirritja*. Animal, bird and plant species and implements are classified as either *Dhuwa* or *Yirritja* (Williams, 1981: 106). In Victoria, the Gunditjmara were divided into the *Krokitch* moiety, symbolised by the white cockatoo, and the *Kaputch* moiety, symbolised by the black cockatoo.

Many Aboriginal societies were further divided into systems of which there were four or eight categories. All members of the societies belong to one of these categories, according to descent and generation. The systems with four categories are known as sub-section systems. Each section or sub-section group is identified by a specific name. The use of these names enables strangers, when meeting, to work out their relationship and responsibilities without having to trace the precise relationship link. The systems are therefore interpreted by some as a shorthand way of identifying one's place in society. While the systems are often used to illustrate marriage arrangements, they served a much wider purpose in ordering social interaction. Maddock suggests that Aboriginal people viewed these systems as part of a cosmic order:

> The classifications made by Aborigines appear rather to manifest a passion for order that has driven them to try to apply to the whole world a single system. [Maddock, 1974: 95].

In section systems, all members of the society belong to one of four categories. For the purpose of illustration, these can be called A, B, C and D. Moiety membership and generation level are important constituents in these systems. A and B belong to the same generation level, C and D to the alternate generation level. A and C belong to the same moiety. Therefore, a man who is a member of section A must marry a woman who is a member of section B. A man who is a member of section C must marry a woman who is a member of section D. Children of A and B belong to either C or D, depending on whether descent is viewed as patrilineal or matrilineal.

Tonkinson observed amongst the Mardudjara of the desert areas of Western Australia that when strangers met they identified themselves by their section names, as this reduced the range of possible kin relationships. Once a person had decided on the basis of this information which kin term to give to one of the strangers, the relationship to all members of both groups could be worked out (Tonkinson, 1987: 214). See Figure 6.1 for the application of names from one Aboriginal society to sections. In some areas of Western Australia two of the sections in the four section system were divided into two sub-sections, to provide a variant of the section system.

Some groups, such as the Walpiri of Central Australia and the Yolgnu of north-east Arnhem Land, made a further division into eight categories, known as sub-sections. This can be illustrated by dividing each of the categories A, B, C and D into two, and symbolising them as A1, A2, B1, B2, C1, C2, D1 and D2. In the naming of these subsections, a further division is made by distinguishing the sex in each category. This refinement of the section system enables distinctions to be made between sets of relatives which are not made under the section system. For example, second cross-cousins, who are preferred as marriage partners, are distinguished from cross-cousins. See Figure 6.1 for the application of names from one Aboriginal society to sub-sections.

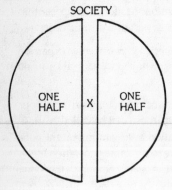

A   Moieties
In some regions people divide their whole world into two categories. Everyone, and almost everything, in that world belongs to one or the other. Where they are patrilineal in descent, you follow-your-father (and his father) directly and have the same moiety label as he does. Where they are matrilineal, you follow-your-mother (and her mother) directly and have the same moiety label as she does. Moieties are exogamous: you must not marry someone in the same moiety as yourself. (We could call this a kind of vertical stratification.)

B   Alternate generation levels
Here the division into two categories has a different basis. It depends on the classification of relatives into generation levels. These are endogamous: you should marry someone in the same generation level as yourself. (We could call this a kind of horizontal stratification.)

Figure 6.1 Categories, descent links and marriage patterns
Note: X indicates a marriage link.
Source: Berndt and Berndt (1978).

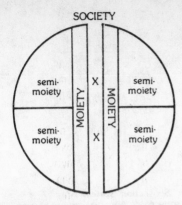

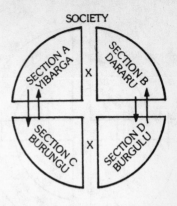

C   Semi-moieties

Here, each matrilineal moiety has two divisions. In this system you take the same semi-moiety and moiety labels as your mother. These divisions are exogamous: you must marry someone belonging to a different semi-moiety *and* to the opposite moiety.

D   Section system

In some regions there are four divisions, usually called sections. They are exogamous: you must marry outside your own section. Moieties and generation levels are actually built into this system but not always spelt out.

In the diagram, A and C together make up one *matrilineal* moiety, B and D the other. A and D together make up one *patrilineal* moiety, B and C the other. You must marry *outside* the moiety that includes your own section. A and B together represent one generation level, D and C the other. You marry *within* your own generation level.

In this system you belong to the same matrilineal moiety as your mother but not to the same section: your section is in the alternate generation level contrasted with hers in the same moiety. Where patrilineal descent is emphasised you belong to the same patrilineal moiety as your father, but your section is in the alternate generation level contrasted with his in that moiety.

Arrows in the diagram point from mother to child. The section names used came from Balgo, southern Kimberleys, Western Australia.

Figure 6.1 (cont.)

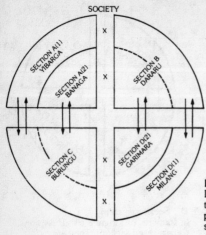

E   'Six-section' system

In some cases, Aboriginal groups coming together have had to adjust their partly-differing section systems, where some section names were the same but others were not. The result is often called a six-section system. The principles are the same as in a four-section system; and that is what it really is, because the labels not held in common are correlated with those that are. The section names here came from Ooldea, western South Australia.

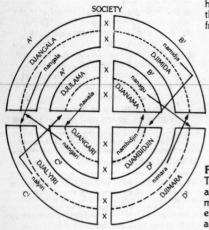

F   Subsection system

This combines some of the principles already noted: patrilineal and matrilineal moieties, and generation levels. There are eight subsections, with names differing according to region.

In the diagram the labels A¹, A² etc indicate that each section is divided into two subsections. In contrast to the section system, subsection names have male and female forms. Arrows in the diagram come from females, pointing to sons and daughters. The subsection names here came from Wave Hill, west-central Northern Territory.

Figure 6.1 (cont.)

Aboriginal kinship and social systems are complex and varied. They were incorporated in the mythology of The Dreaming and viewed as a legacy of the Ancestral Spirit Beings. They provide a sense of personal identity and social cohesion and are the co-ordinating force for all social interaction. They provide a code to enable people to live in relative harmony with one another.

Urban kinship and families

In the towns and cities of Australia today, Aboriginal families retain to varying degrees the kinship system of their ancestors. Many Aboriginal people have non-Aboriginal spouses and live in situations where they are embedded in non-Aboriginal society. Therefore, the family structures of rural and urban Aborigines are different from those of the more traditionally oriented groups. However, in the cities where most Aborigines are of mixed descent and have had long exposure to Europeans, they are an identifiable, separate cultural group. Aboriginal people, wherever they are, distinguish themselves from other Australians and are linked together by a sense of belonging to a locality and to an extended family.

Aboriginal families in urban and rural areas have developed a culture of their own through family, community and organisational structures. These structures give them psychological and physical support and provide security. Much of this security lies in the knowledge that urban Aborigines can continue to rely on group support and don't have to depend on non-Aborigines. Aboriginal people identify as a cultural group and have a growing pride in their Aboriginality. Today, depending on their location, they are known as Kooris, Murris, Nungas, Nyoongahs, Yolngu and Anangu, among other local names.

The battles for land rights, education and better living conditions, together with a growing interest in Aboriginal traditions, have led to the development of other social and political groupings not based wholly on kin. A heightened sense of cultural and political identity has developed a feeling of pan-Aboriginality. Aboriginal people from all parts of Australia are acknowledging a common cultural background of Aboriginality while maintaining a diverse range of lifestyles throughout Australia.

Non-Aboriginal anthropologists generally have not attached any significance of kin and country to the dispossessed mixed-race Aboriginal people. They tend to explain any such allegiances to kin or region as a matter of cultural survival and usually as a sub-culture of poverty.

This view is not supported by empirical evidence (Gale, 1972). Urban tertiary-educated Aboriginal professionals are still absorbed by geneaological ramifications, and kinship terms and courtesy titles are frequently used. Many people are referred to as aunty, uncle, sister, brother, cousin when there may be no blood relationship. This practice is often abhorred by some people, usually non-Aborigines, who believe that only traditionally oriented Aborigines should use such terms. At Aboriginal social gatherings, placing people in kinship terms in relation to those present is a most important part of the gathering.

The Aboriginal family is central to the survival of Aboriginal culture. The structure, values and practices can be based on the traditional complex kinship systems or the extended family, kinship ties and locality allegiances of rural and urban people. The values, beliefs and identity of Aboriginal culture can be best developed from within the family.

Fay Gale's study of urban Aborigines in 1972 described the phenomenon of urban Aboriginal people moving house within Adelaide to be near their kin. Aboriginal families are subjected to enormous acculturation pressures, as well as psychological, social and economic stresses. Non-Aboriginal programs and institutions continue to be destructive of Aboriginal urban, rural and traditionally oriented families as they were in the past. Aboriginal families will survive and thrive when Aboriginal people gain control of their own lives.

Children

Many Aboriginal people fear that their children may lose their cultural values and beliefs, and therefore not identify strongly with Aboriginal society. Traditionally oriented people are concerned their children are losing their language and increasing their use of English. At the same time, they are also adopting new values and traditional skills are being lost.

The Aboriginal Women's Taskforce Report 1986, *Women's Business*, noted:

> Children are the responsibility of the entire family rather than to the biological parents alone. Many Aboriginal people have been "grown up"

by members of the family other than their biological mother and father and this practice of growing up children is still very widespread today. Often it is the children's grandparents who carry out the growing up. They also are very important members of the family unit and are heavily relied upon to play a large part in child rearing. As a result of the children being encouraged to think and have responsibility at a very early age, they have a large degree of personal autonomy. [*Women's Business*, 1986: 27]

Women's Business also noted that, if a mother leaves the family for whatever reason, the children continue to grow up within the extended family. "Fostering", therefore, has a different meaning for Aboriginal people. Often there is no attempt to legalise the arrangements through the courts because it is the family which is involved. There is a reluctance to use the "white man's law" to give legal guardianship to members of a family to whom the children already belong. People are also reluctant to admit that the mother has left the child in someone else's care because of the long history of children being removed and placed into institutions by welfare officers. Another factor is that Aboriginal people have a different cultural view of child care. Such a mother would be seen by non-Aboriginal people as "no good" or "unworthy". In fact, she may be acting in a culturally acceptable way given the rights and obligations that Aboriginal families share.

The raising, care and discipline of children by the family is often extended to the wider Aboriginal community. Generally, there is the feeling that children belong to everybody and in a large gathering children are the responsibility of all, be they female or male, young or old. The movement of children between their relatives is a convenient and accepted practice that provides the children with the opportunity to learn many aspects of the traditional way of life.

Where Aboriginal people may not have members of their extended family living in close proximity, the traditional child-raising and care practices (in which grandparents and other extended family members play an important role) are not available. In a fragmented society, where Aboriginal people — through necessity, by persuasion or by force — have had to adopt a way of life which does not reflect their values, aspirations or expectations, the care of children becomes difficult (*Women's Business*, 1986). More recently, this has resulted in the establishment of Aboriginal child care and pre-school centres in the cities.

Women play many roles in the Aboriginal family. They are expected to play several roles — for example, wife, mother, grandmother, aunt, niece, daughter — each day of their adult lives. With Aboriginal family life under increasing pressure, the role of Aboriginal women has increased. In many urban situations, Aboriginal women are not only the base foundation of the family; they are also the strength of the Aboriginal community. As Fay Gale noted:

> It is not uncommon to find an Aboriginal household in Adelaide consisting of an extended family. The dominating character in such a household is often a grandmother. Her establishment may consist of daughters with their children and with or without spouses. Very often one or more single male relatives, sons, brothers and cousins may be attached to, rather than part of the household. [Gale, 1972: 165]

Similar situations are to be found with respect to Aboriginal families throughout urban Australia.

Aboriginal identification

Aboriginal people are invariably interested in finding out where a person is from as a first step toward placing a person whom they do not know correctly into their own universe. Quite often, when Aborigines meet for the first time, the situation is characterised by a high degree of diffidence. In 1981 John Von Sturmer recorded his account of two Aboriginal people meeting for the first time:

> I recall travelling with an Aboriginal man, Mickey, from Edward River. We stopped at Mareeba to buy some food. Mickey remained in the vehicle. I observed an Aboriginal man walk past him along the footpath. He was clearly intrigued to find out who Mickey was, and Mickey was equally curious. The man walked backwards and forwards several times. Finally he came up to the vehicle and the conversation went something like this:
> *Mareeba man:* Where are you from?
> *Mickey:* I'm Edward River man. Where you from?
> *Mareeba man:* I'm Lama Lama man … do you know X?
> *Mickey:* No. Do you know Y?
> *Mareeba man:* No. Do you know Z?
> *Mickey:* Yes. She's my aunty.
> *Mareeba man:* That old lady's my granny. I must call you daddy.
> *Mickey:* I must call you boy. You give me cigarette. [Von Stumer, 1981: 13]

Of course, this type of approach is possible even between Europeans and Aborigines, especially if the European already knows a number of Aborigines who have fitted him/her into the kinship system. People can search for relations whom they share and then establish their relationship on that basis. Presentation of a cigarette — an almost standard device — or another small gift may seal this preliminary transaction as it did on the occasion in Mareeba.

Aboriginal people often express the view that history gives them something to identify themselves by and to know that they do have a family. When they are with fellow Aborigines they feel a certain bond, a certain magic; they feel part of their family. It is a wonderful feeling, actually — a feeling of joy, a feeling of pride.

The younger generation of Aborigines are keen to find out to whom they are related. They use their family tree to see how the whole family is related. Some are worried about who they may marry. They are interested in identifying their different cousins on the tree and determining how they are related. Many others feel they need to know to be sure of their identity. For those who were removed from their family at birth or soon after, being given access to their geneaology gives them a feeling for their historical place in Aboriginal society. it is difficult to be proud of your Aboriginal heritage if you do not know your ancestry.

Aboriginal people have, since 1973, been required by the federal government to meet its definition of Aboriginality. It has three conditions, all of which must be met to participate in specific government initiatives for Aborigines and Torres Strait Islanders. An individual must:

- be of Aboriginal or Torres Strait Islander descent;
- identify as being of Aboriginal or Torres Strait Islander descent;
- be recognised by the community as being a person of Aboriginal or Torres Strait Islander descent.

For an Aboriginal person who cannot identify/describe their genealogy there is some insecurity as to whether they meet the government definition. A knowledge of their genealogy makes an Aboriginal person feel more secure, while also enabling a person to know the location of their ancestral lands and the history of their people.

Conclusion

Some Aboriginal people can draw strength from their traditional culture. They still practise their ceremonies, songs and dances and speak the language of the group to which they belong. Others do not have such ready access. Often they do not know their language group, cultural traditions or family history and, consequently, many of the traditional practices have been lost or severely modified.

Generally, the more urbanised Aborigines have not lost their sense of Aboriginality; they feel themselves to be, and identify themselves as, Aboriginal Australians. Nor does their identification necessarily depend upon physical features or skin colour. Rather, it has to do with shared experiences, sharing the same relatives (even on a national basis), stories, background, history, oppression, discrimination and a host of other factors. For most it provides a comfortable feeling of belonging and pride based on a knowledge of an ancient cultural heritage.

Some Aboriginal people who do not have dark skin, hair or eyes face a dual problem — acceptance of their Aboriginality by some Aboriginal and non-Aboriginal people alike. A Tasmanian woman who spoke to the 1986 Aboriginal Women's Task Force on this issue said that:

> the battle is made even harder when state governments — past and present — maintain there are no Aboriginal people in the State.

Social and economic conditions today may also put many Aboriginal people under stress. Thus, mixed marriage partnerships sometimes place pressures on women to conform to non-Aboriginal values and way of life and to reject their Aboriginal identity.

When Aborigines refer to their family, they invariably mean their extended family, which might include parents, several children, numerous aunts, uncles and cousins, and grandparents. These family members can be both genetic and classifactory. It is the kinship ties which determine a person's rights, responsibilities and behaviour.

Aboriginal kinship ties, values, beliefs, identity and language are maintained by the family. The continuance of Aboriginal society is dependent on keeping Aboriginal families strong and healthy, both physically and culturally.

References

Aboriginal Women's Task Force (1986). *Women's Business*. Canberra: AGPS.

Barwick, D. (1974). "The Aboriginal family in South-Eastern Australia and the family in Australia". In *Australian Families*, edited by J. Krupinska and A. Stoller. Sydney: Pergamon.

Berndt, C.H. and R.M. (1978). *Pioneers and Settlers*. Carlton: Pitman.

——— (1988). *The World of the First Australians*. Canberra: Australian Studies Press.

Edwards, W.H. (1988). *An Introduction to Aboriginal Societies*. Wentworth Falls: Social Science Press.

Gale, Fay (1972). *Urban Aborigines*. Canberra: ANU.

Maddock, Kenneth (1974). *The Australian Aborigines: A Portrait of their Society*. London: Allan Lane, The Penguin Press.

Mattingley, C. and Hampton, K. (1988). *Survival in Our Own Land*. Adelaide: Wakefield Press.

Radcliffe-Brown, A.R. (1952). *Structure and Function in Primitive Society*. London: Cohen and West.

Reed, Peter (n.d.). *The Stolen Generation* (Occasional paper number 1). Sydney: Ministry of Aboriginal Affairs.

Tonkinson, R. (1987). "Mardudjara Kinship". In *Australians to 1988*, edited by D.J. Mulvaney and J.P. White. Sydney: Fairfax, Syme and Weldon Associates.

Von Sturmer, J. (1981). *Talking with Aborigines: AIAS newsletter number 15*. Canberra: AIAS, pp. 13–30.

Wafer, J. (1982). *A Simple Introduction to Central Australia Kinship Systems*. Alice Springs: Institute for Aboriginal Development.

Williams, Don (1981). *Exploring Aboriginal Kinship*. Canberra: Curriculum Development Centre.

Chapter 7

Australian Languages: Our Heritage

Rob Amery and Colin Bourke

Australian languages

Aboriginal and Torres Strait Islander languages are the indigenous languages of Australia. Accordingly, they are correctly referred to as Australian languages (Dixon, 1980). Australian languages share certain typological features and are distinguished from other languages spoken outside Australia by virtue of their sound systems and grammars. They constitute Australia's unique linguistic heritage.

English is *not* an Australian language, even though it is Australia's national language and is used as a *lingua franca*, or common language, by speakers of Aboriginal and Torres Strait Islander languages from different parts of the country.

Multilingualism (defined as the use of a number of different languages within the same speech community) was widespread in the pre-contact period, as there was no common Aboriginal language which was understood across all the country. Some 600 dialects belonging to in excess of 270 different languages were spoken throughout the continent at the time of the invasion (House of Representatives Standing Committee, 1992: 1). However, non-Aborigines are generally ignorant of the linguistic richness of the indigenous Australians. This ignorance is reflected in questions like Can you speak Aboriginal? or What's the Aboriginal word for ———? Some books, written as late as the 1990s, still contain words drawn from Australian languages where the words are glossed simply as an Aboriginal word for ——— even though the source language is known and the information is readily available. Census statistics and language policy often lump all Aboriginal languages together, even though the same documents distinguish between other minority languages.

The current status and distribution of Australian languages

Only a small proportion of the 270 or so languages once spoken in Australia remain as fully viable languages — that is, they are still being acquired by children and spoken "right through", and used in all areas of contemporary life. Some twenty languages, including Pitjantjatjara, spoken in the northwest of South Australia, are in this category (Schmidt, 1990: 1). Map 7.1 is a guide to the distribution of strong Aboriginal languages.

It is reasonable to speculate that all of Australia's languages are threatened. In fact, one linguist warns that:

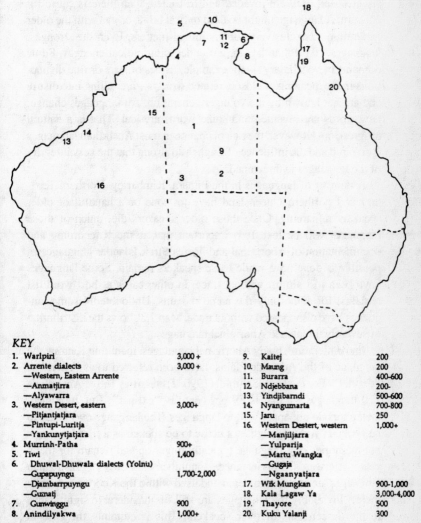

KEY

1.	Warlpiri	3,000 +	9.	Kaitej	200
2.	Arrente dialects	3,000 +	10.	Maung	200
	—Western, Eastern Arrente		11.	Burarra	400-600
	—Anmatjirra		12.	Ndjebbana	200-
	—Alyawarra		13.	Yindjibarndi	500-600
3.	Western Desert, eastern	3,000+	14.	Nyangumarta	700-800
	—Pitjantjatjara		15.	Jaru	250
	—Pintupi-Luritja		16.	Western Destert, western	1,000+
	—Yankunytjatjara			—Manjiljarra	
4.	Murrinh-Patha	900+		—Yulparija	
5.	Tiwi	1,400		—Martu Wangka	
6.	Dhuwal-Dhuwala dialects (Yolŋu)			—Gugaja	
	—Gupapuyngu	1,700-2,000		—Ngaanyatjara	
	—Djambarrpuyngu		17.	Wik Mungkan	900-1,000
	—Gumatj		18.	Kala Lagaw Ya	3,000-4,000
7.	Gunwinggu	900	19.	Thayore	500
8.	Anindilyakwa	1,000+	20.	Kuku Yalanji	300

Map 7.1 Distribution of strong Aboriginal languages
Source: Schmidt (1990)

If nothing is done about it, almost all Aboriginal languages will be dead by the year 2000. Even the two most likely groups to survive, the Yolngu languages of north-east Arnhem Land and the Western Desert language may not last long beyond that date. [McConvell, 1991: 143]

Once the domains or areas of life in which the language is constructed and used are invaded and restricted, then there is cause for concern. A language might be used only at home or just with the older generation or exclusively for traditional matters. Even the strongest languages, like Pitjantjatjara, are undergoing radical changes. Some domains of vocabulary — for example, names of stars or fine distinctions in the meaning of closely related words — are falling into disuse and are not known by the younger generation. All languages change; new words are invented and some words are lost. That is a natural progression. However, the rate of change in most Australian languages is so rapid and the influence of English so strong that the very integrity of the languages is threatened.

A number of languages in the Pilbara, Kimberley, Northern Territory and northern Queensland have just one or a handful of older speakers remaining. Once those older speakers die, much of those languages will be lost. It is important that as much recording and documentation of Aboriginal and Torres Strait Islander languages as possible is done now, while these speakers remain. Some languages have been lost almost without trace. In other cases a short word list remains; for some only the name remains. Undoubtedly some languages have disappeared without trace. Map 7.2 shows the distribution of severely threatened Aboriginal languages.

In the literature, many Aboriginal languages, including Kaurna, the language of the Adelaide Plains, have been referred to as "dead" or "extinct". For instance, Schmidt (1990: 2) classifies 160 of Australia's 270 languages — that is 59 per cent, as "extinct". But zoological metaphors do not apply well to languages. The language may cease to be spoken "right through", or cease to be spoken as a first language, but memories of a language typically linger on and remain for many years afterwards. For instance, a number of words of Tasmanian languages are still remembered and used within the Koori community there.[1] Invariably the languages are still of considerable significance to the descendants of their speakers. This is certainly the case in Tasmania, where Tasmanian Aborigines have obtained considerable funds under the Aboriginal Languages Initiatives Program to retrieve and reclaim their linguistic heritage.

In some cases, with access to old written records, knowledge in the community can be increased considerably. The Kaurna language of the Adelaide Plains is an interesting case to consider. It is believed that Kaurna ceased to be spoken as a mother tongue back in 1929, or perhaps even earlier, with the death of Ivaritji (Gara, 1990: 66). Nungas in Adelaide are now reclaiming that linguistic heritage and some are beginning to relearn the language. The programs are drawing primarily on early descriptions of the language, especially Teichelmann and Schürmann (1840). For example, Kaurna is being taught to all students at Kaurna Plains School. Greetings such as *Ninna marni*? (Are you good?) and leavetakings such as *Nakkiota*! (Will see [you]!), along with relationship terms such as *ngarpadla* (aunty) and *kauwawa* (uncle), have come back into common usage within that school community.

A number of songs and stories have recently been written in the Kaurna language. Nursery rhymes and European stories have been translated into Kaurna and new terms have recently been developed in Kaurna. For example, *padnipadnitti* (car), *karrikarritti* (aeroplane), *mukamuka karndo* (computer, from brain + lightning), *turraturrarndiappetti* (photocopier) and other terms have been coined by drawing on productive word-forming processes that are described or evident in the early descriptions of the language (see Amery, 1993). The Kaurna language is also being used increasingly to deliver speeches at public meetings, hence one must ask: Is Kaurna really "dead" or "extinct"?

There is growing interest throughout Australia in reviving and reclaiming Aboriginal linguistic heritage. In addition to Kaurna and the languages of Tasmania, revival programs are operating in Nyoongah at Bunbury, south of Perth and in Djabugay, Dyirrbal and other languages in northern Queensland which are no longer spoken in everyday life. A number of languages in New South Wales including Bandjalang, Gumbaynggir, Paakantji, Ngiyampaa, Wangkumara and Gidabul, have also been introduced into schools. In Darwin there is an interest in reclaiming the Larakiya language. In a number of communities and schools across Western Australia and the Northern Territory, where language use has been restricted to the older generations, revitalisation

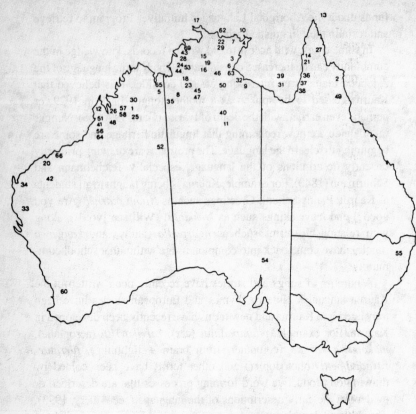

Map 7.2 Distribution of severely threatened Aboriginal languages
Source: Schmidt (1990)

Note to Table 7.1: These speaker numbers are very rough estimates and not final. They are provided to give some indication of the radically low number of speakers for each language. These figures are based on Black and Walsh (1982), Thieberger (1987), McGregor (1989), advice from communities and scholars in each region, and my own observations during the course of this project. Only languages with more than ten fluent speakers are listed. This list is not exhaustive; it is the best estimate possible based on available information at the time of writing this report. All comments and corrections are welcome.

Table 7.1 Severely threatened languages and numbers of speakers

#	Language	Speakers	#	Language	Speakers
1	Walmajarri	1000	36	Koko Bera	50
2	Guugu Yimithirr	400	37	Oykangand	50
3	Nunggubuyu	300-400	38	Yir Yoront	50
4	Dhangu dialects	350	39	Lardil	50
5	Kija	300	40	Mudbura	50
6	Ritharngu	300	41	Yuwarliny	50-
7	Dijinang	200-300	42	Kurrama	50-
8	Gurindji	250	43	Marithiyel	50-
9	Garawa	200+	44	Marri Ngarr	30-50
10	Dharlwangu	200	45	Wageman	50-
11	Warumungu	200	46	Mangarayi	50-
12	Bardi	100-200	47	Wardeman	50-
13	Meriam Mir	100+	48	Nyigina	20-50
14	Wik Nganthana	100-200	49	Dyirbal	40
15	Jawony	100+	50	Alawa	30
16	Ngalkbun	100-200	51	Yawuru	30
17	Iwaidja	180	52	Ngardi	30
18	Ngarinman	170	53	Djamindjung	30
19	Rembarrnga	150	54	Adnyamathanha	20+
20	Ngarluma	100	55	Banjalang	20+
21	Wik Nganjara	100	56	Karajarri	20
22	Gunbalang	100	57	Worrorra	20
23	Ngaliwuru	100	58	Wunambal	20
24	Marri Jabin	100	59	Malngin	20
25	Gooniyandi	100	60	Nyungar	20
26	Ngarinyin	100-	61	Djingili	20
27	Umpila	100-	62	Gungoragone	20
28	Ngankikurungkurr	100-	63	Ngalakan	20
29	Nakara	75-100	64	Mangarla	20-
30	Bunaba	50-100	65	Miriwoong	10-20
31	Kaiadilt	70	66	Ngarla, Nyamal	10
32	Yanyuwa	70-100	67	Madngele	10?
33	Watjarri	50	68	Maramanindji	10?
34	Panyjima	50	69	Batyamal	10?
35	Wanyjirra	50	70	Malak Malak	10?
				Maranungku	??

Source: Schmidt (1990).

programs have been implemented to increase knowledge and use of the language within the younger generations.

Despite the emphasis on the maintenance of viable languages inherent in *Australia's Languages: The Australian Language and Literacy Policy* (1991), the majority of Aboriginal Languages Initiatives Programs identified in that policy are in fact going to support languages other than those deemed to be viable.

The nature of Australian languages

The working assumption among practising linguists is that almost all the languages of Australia are genetically related, sharing a common ancestor (Walsh, 1991: 33). It is not certain, however, that the languages of Tasmania are part of this language family. At the same time, there is nothing to suggest that they are not related.

Within Australian languages, there is a basic division between the languages of the north and north-west of Australia and the languages of the rest of the continent. The languages of the north and north-west of Australia are prefixing (and suffixing) while the languages of the rest of the continent are strictly suffixing. See Map 7.3 for an illustration of the classifications of Australian languages. Schmidt (1919), working with limited data, first proposed this north versus south division. The boundary between these two groups of languages was repositioned by Capell (1956) and revised later by Hale (1964).

The vast majority of Australian languages are thought to belong to the suffixing Pama–Nyungan language family while the prefixing (and suffixing) non-Pama–Nyungan languages are thought to be distributed across twenty to thirty language families. While there is undoubtedly a fairly strict division on typological grounds, the genetic basis of the Pama–Nyungan versus non-Pama–Nyungan dichotomy has been questioned recently. More detailed work is needed to clarify the situation.

There is a remarkable similarity of sound systems of Australian languages in all but a few phonologically deviant languages of the Cape York Peninsula, which have markedly different sound systems. The grammars of Australian languages, too, show marked similarities across the continent, yet there is considerable diversity within the vocabulary of the languages. The phonological similarity plus grammatical similarity combined with a diversity in vocabulary provides a contrast with the way diversity is managed in literate societies.

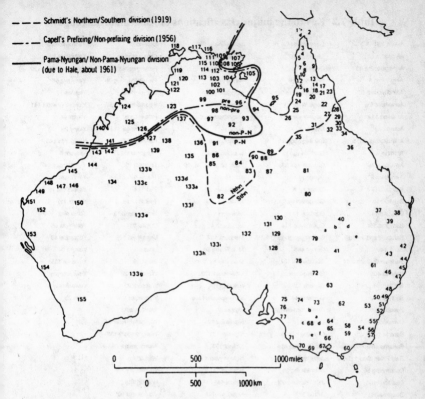

Map 7.3 Major classifications of Australian languages
Source: Dixon (1980)

The matter of vocabulary difference is intriguing. Linguists have pointed to the high rate of vocabulary replacement, contributed to by taboos on the use of names (or words sounding similar) of recently deceased persons and borrowing from other groups as possible causes. The Reverend Bill Edwards records that when he first lived with the Pitjantjatjara, *kapi* was the word for water. It is actually a Yunkunytjatjara word. It was replaced by *mina* and still later by *kumpili*.

The lexical competence of the average speaker of an Aboriginal language is equivalent to that of the average speaker of other languages. The vocabularies of Aboriginal languages allow their speakers to express their mythology, culture, thoughts and feelings. Working vocabularies in excess of 10,000 words are common. Aboriginal

Table 7.2 Key to the major classifications of Australian languages

Alawa 100	Garlyarra 148	Madhi-Madhi 68b	Olgolo 20	Yadhaykenu 3
Alyawarra 84	Girramay 30	Malak-Malak 120	Oykangand 16	Yalarnnga 88
Andegerebina 83	Gog-Nar 24	Malyangapa	Pallanganmiddang 58	Yandruwanhtha 130
Anguthimri 5	Gugada 133i	Mamu 30	Peek Whurrong 70	Yanyuwa 96
Anindilyakwa 105	Gugu-Badhun 32	Mangala 142	Pintupi 133d	Yaralde 77
Anmatjera 85	Gugu-Wara 21	Mangarayi 99	Pitjan(tja)tjara 133f	Yawuru (Yauor) 141
Arabana 132	Gugu-Yalanji 22	Mantjiltjara 133c	Pitta-Pitta 87	Yaygir 44
Aranda 82	Guinay 30	Mara 101	Rembarrnga 113	Yidiny 29
Arandic sbgp 82-6	Gumbaynggir 45	Maranunggu 121	Rithamu 106	Yinggarda 143
Atampaya 3	Gunbalang 115	Margany 40a	Tanganekald 77	Yinwum 6
Awabakai 49	Gundungura 53	Maric sbgp 32, 36, 40, 81	Thargari 152	Yinyjibarndi 147
Awngthim 5	Gunggari 40d	Maung 116	Thawa 57	Yir-Yoront 15
Baagandji 72	Gunggay 29	Mbabaram 27	Tiwi 118	Yitha-Yitha 73
Balyku 150	Gungoragone 112	Mbara 31	Tyeraity 119	Yiwaja 117
Banjalang 42	Gunibidji 111	Mbiyoom 8	Umbuygamu 13	Yolnu sbgp 106-8
Banyjima 150	Gunwinygu 114	Mpalitjanh 4	Umpila 9	Yota-Yota 65
Baraba-Baraba 68d	Gunwinygu sbgp 113-15	Mudbura 137	Ungarinyin 125	Yugambal 43
Bardi 140	Gunya 40b	Muk-Thang 60	Uradhi 3	Yukulta 94
Bariman Gutinhma 14	Gupapuynu 107	Murawari 41	Waga 39	Yulbarija 133b
Bidyara 40c	Gureng-Gureng 37	Murinypata 122	Wagaman 22	Yuwaalarraay,
Biri 36	Gurindji 137	Nakara 110	Wakoora 22	Yuwaaliyaay 61
Biyaygirri 33	Gurrama 147	Ngaanyatjara 133e	Walmatjari 139	Yuyu 75
Bunaba 126	Guugu Yimidhirr 23	Ngajan 30	Wambaya 92	
Bungandij 71	Guwa 81	Ngaliwuru 123	Wangaaybuwan 63	
Burarra 109	Guwamu 40e	Ngamini 131	Wangganguru 132	
Burduna 151	Jab Wurrung 68e	Ngandi 103	Wangkumara 79	
Daly River sbgp 119-21	Jabugay 28	Nganyaywana 46	Wari 30	
Darkinyung 50	Jaitmathang 59	Ngarigo 54	Warlmanpa 136	
Dhalandji 151	Jaja Wurrung 68f	Ngarla 145	Warlpiri 135	
Dharawal 52	Jirrbal 30	Ngarluma 148	Warluwarra 90	
Dharuk 51	Jirru 30	Ngarndji 98	Warndarang 102	
Dhuduroa 59	Kaititj 36	Ngawun 35	Warnman 134	
Dhurga 55	Kala Lagau Langgus 1	Ngayarda sbgp 145-50	Warrgamay 33	
Dhuwala/Dhuwal 107	Kalkatungu 89	Ngayawung 76	Warumungu 91	
Diyari 129	Keramin 74	Nglyambaa 63	Warungu 32	
Djapu 107	Kitja 127	Nhanda 154	Wathawurrung 67	
Djaru 138	Koko-Bera 19	Nhuwala 149	Wemba-Wemba 68a	
Djinan 108	Kolijon 69	North Kimberly sbgp 124-5	Wergaia 68c	
Djingili 97	Kukatj 26	Northern Paman sbgp 3-8	Western Desert 133	
Dyangadi 47	Kuku-Thaypan 18	Ntra'ngith 5	Western Torres Straits Language 1	
Dyirringany 56	Kunggari 80	Nunggubuyu 104	Wik-Me'nh 12	
Eastern Torres Straits Language 2	Kurnu 72	Nyamal 146	Wik-Muminh 11	
Gabi 38	Kuuku-Ya'u 9	Nyanganyatjara 133g	Wik-Munkan 10	
Gadang 48	Kuurn Kopan Noot 70	Nyangatjatjara 133h	Wiradhuri 62	
Gamilaraay 61	Lama-Lama 17	Nyawaygi 44	Worora 124	
Garadyari 143	Lardil 95	Nyigina 141	Wuywurrung 66	
	Linngithigh 7	Nyungal 22	Yabula-Yabula 64	

Note: A single number is used for each language; the location of dialects is shown only for Margany, Wemba-Wemba and Western Desert.

languages belong to different cultures with different values and belief systems to English-speaking cultures. They are rich in ritual vocabulary and in words which express an understanding of spirituality. In some cases, language and vocabulary are taught through ceremony and ceremonial knowledge is a reflection of hierarchical stratification.

Aboriginal vocabularies reflect an intimate knowledge of the physical and social environment. Fine distinctions are made between vocabulary relating to flora, fauna and seasons. Desert groups, for example, have various words for different types of sand and for plants and animals at different stages of development. When referring to plants, reptiles and insects, speakers of Aboriginal languages typically employ specific species names. Unlike plant names in English, such as *blackberry* or *ghost gum*, plant names in Aboriginal languages usually consist of a single word that is totally unrelated to other words in the language.

Aboriginal languages, like other languages, have complex and intricate grammatical structures. A typical Australian language has nine or ten parts of speech including nouns, verbs, pronouns, adverbs and, frequently, adjectives. Some parts of speech such as indefinite articles (words like *a* and *an* in English) are absent, but Aboriginal languages have their own complexities.

Some languages, such as Pitjantjatjara, have a set of independent pronouns, as in English, used alongside pronoun suffixes or bound pronouns that are attached to other parts of speech (for example, verbs). Compare the following Pitjantjatjara sentences:

Ngayulu nyuntunya nyangu. (I saw you.)
Nyangunanta. (I saw you.)
(where the suffix -na = *ngayulu* "I" [subject] and -nta = *nyuntu* "you" [object]).

Australian languages typically employ suffixes or endings, known as a *case system*, instead of prepositions such as *in, to, from, by* and so on. Consider the following words in Yolngu Matha from north-east Arnhem Land:

rangingura	*on* the beach
ranginguru	*from* the beach
rangikurru	*along* the beach
ranglili	*to* the beach
rangipuy	*associated with* or *belonging to* the beach

miyalkthu	*by* the woman (subject: ergative case)
miyalknha	the woman (object: accusative case)
miyalkkungu	*from/by* the woman
miyalkkala	*to/with* the woman

Australian languages are referred to as *ergative* languages by linguists (along with Basque, Hindi and Fijian). Ergativity is a fundamental concept in Aboriginal languages, but is peripheral in English, restricted to constructions such as causatives.

In an ergative language, the subject of a transitive verb (for example, hit, see, hold) is marked differently to the subject of an intransitive verb (for example, sit, stand, sleep). In fact, usually the object of a transitive verb takes the same form as the subject of an intransitive verb. Consider, for example, the Yolngu Matha sentences:

Miyalkthu weti lukana. (The woman ate wallaby.)
Miyalk wandina. (The woman ran.)
Weti wandina. (The wallaby ran.)

Note the suffix *-thu* on *miyalk* (woman) in the first sentence. This indicates that the woman, *miyalk*, is the subject and the one "eating" something. The patient or object is *weti* (wallaby). The suffix *-thu* is defined as the *ergative case suffix*.

English and most other languages use fixed word order to indicate which participant in the sentence is the subject and which is the object. Because Aboriginal languages have case suffixes, this allows considerable flexibility of word order.[2] In fact, any ordering of the constituents in the sentences above is possible.

Aboriginal languages exhibit many structures that make them difficult for English speakers to learn. Typically, Australian languages have pronoun systems that differentiate between singular, dual and plural pronouns. Pronouns, too, take different forms depending on their case, that is, depending on their function within the sentence.

Note the following sentences in Kaurna and their English translations, which illustrate twelve different forms for the second-person pronoun:

Ninna tikkandi.	You (one) are sitting.
Niwa tikkandi.	You (two) are sitting.
Na tikkandi.	You (many) are sitting.
Nindo ngai nakki.	You (one) saw me.

Niwando ngai nakki.	You (two) saw me.
Naando ngai nakki.	You (many) saw me.
Ngatto paru ninnanni yunggi.	I gave (to) you (one) meat.
Ngatto paru niwanni yunggi.	I gave (to) you (two) meat.
Ngatto paru nanni yunggi.	I gave (to) you (many) meat.
Ngu ninko wodli.	That's your house.
Ngu niwadluko wodli.	That's your (two) house.
Ngu naako wodli.	That's your (mob's) house.

In English there are just two second-person pronouns, *you* and *your*, which remain the same whether they are referring to one, two or more people and whether the referent is the subject or object of the sentence. In Kaurna one would have to choose between *ninna* (you: one), *niwa* (you: two), *na* (you: many), *nindo* (you: one as agent), *ninnanni* (to you: one), *niwanni* (to you: two), *nanni* (to you: mob), and between *ninko* (your: one), *niwadluko* (your: two) and *naako* (your: many people's).

Despite the fact that relatively few number terms are employed, a feature shared by many Aboriginal languages, Kaurna has distinctive birth order names for the first, second, third, fourth child, right up to the ninth-born child. These birth order names are also differentiated for gender.

	Female	*Male*
First born	*Kartanya/Kartiato*	*Kartamerru*
Second born	*Waruyu*	*Waritya*
Third born	*Kudnato*	*Kudnuitya*
Fourth born	*Munato*	*Munaitya*
Fifth born	*Midlato*	*Midlaitya*
Sixth born	*Marruato*	*Marrutya*
Seventh born	*Wanguato*	*Wangutya*
Eighth born	*not recorded*	*not recorded*
Ninth born	*Ngadaato*	*Ngadlaitya*

These terms appear to have been frequently used. Birth order names are also used in some other South Australian languages, for example, Nukunu and Adnyamathanha.

Australian languages have many more relationship or kinship terms than English and the kinship systems are organised along somewhat different principles to English. Typically, terms which would most readily translate as *mother* and *father*, for example *ngunytju* (mother) and *mama* (father) in Pitjantjatjara, in fact refer to a number of people. *Mama* (father) refers to father's brothers and others in that "father" relationship to the individual, while *ngunytju* (mother) also refers to one's mother's sisters and others in a "mother" relationship. Some terms are not easy to translate into English, but they are still basic terms within Australian languages.

Many Aboriginal words have no equivalent English meaning. The Pitjantjatjara word *tjukurrpa*, for instance, is often translated as "dreaming". But this does not really capture the essence of the term. *Tjukurrpa* is glossed in Goddard's dictionary as "Dreaming, Law (often, and appropriately, spelt with a capital letter in this usage). Note that there seems to be an emerging Aboriginal preference for this use of the word not to be given an English equivalent at all." (Goddard, 1987: 145).

Place names, in particular, generally cannot be translated from Aboriginal languages into English.

Forms of communication

Prior to the invasion in 1788, Australian languages were not written, though the precursors of writing existed in the symbols used in message sticks, drawings or bark and sand paintings. The writing systems used today were first developed by missionaries and linguists. The Kaurna language of the Adelaide Plains was first written down in the 1830s and first described by Teichelmann and Schurmann (1840). One of the first recorded documents in an Australian language, written by Aboriginal people, was a letter written in Kaurna to Governor Gawler in 1841 by Kaurna children who attended the Native Location School or Piltawodli. This letter appeared just five years after the proclamation of the colony of South Australia. By contrast, the slow spread of European settlement into the more arid areas meant that Pitjantjatjara was not recorded in a written form for another century, until a mission was established at Ernabella in 1937 (Gale, 1992).

In Central Australia, and undoubtedly in other areas as well, sand painting or ground drawings were used to reinforce verbal communication. They were used to illustrate stories told to children, stories related to the group's activities, Dreaming stories and ceremonies. Interestingly, a number of today's coffee table books on Aboriginal art contain illustrations or photos of sand paintings, along with an explanation in English or the language of the artist or both. Hence Aboriginal people are adjusting to new ways of communicating.

In Alice Springs, Aboriginal people have set up their own media services in Central Australian Aboriginal Media Association Radio (CAAMA) and IMPARJA TV. Both CAAMA and IMPARJA produce programs in a number of Central Australian languages.

As well as speaking aloud, Aboriginal people used handsigns or gestures to communicate. This happened when people were hunting and didn't want their prey to hear, when gossiping, if endeavouring to be secretive or when ritual demanded silence be enforced. Australian languages typically have highly conventionalised sign languages, highlighting complexity in this area. Nowadays, sign languages provide a very useful medium for conducting a conversation while travelling in a noisy vehicle.

Secret/sacred languages are limited to certain audiences. In parts of Central Australia, newly initiated boys are secluded from the main group and are required to use a special set of words. In many parts of Australia — for example, Dyirrbal in north-east Queensland — separate vocabularies are used between a woman and her son-in-law. Other special vocabularies consist of words for sacred matters known only to fully initiated men or words revealed at different periods in a man's life as he progresses through rituals. Women also have their own vocabularies for their own cultural activities and rituals.

Trading routes criss-crossed the continent. Trade was facilitated by multilingualism or knowledge of a number of languages. These trading routes facilitated the spread of vocabulary across the continent and terms for new concepts spread from one language to another. It is interesting to consider the terms for *horse* in the languages of Australia. Two terms are widespread. *Yarraman* (horse), originally from around Sydney, spread across eastern Australia and up into north-east Arnhem Land. It seems that the word had been absorbed into some languages even before the first appearance of horses into the region (Dixon, Ramsom and Thomas, 1990: 231). *Nantu* (horse), from *nanto* (kangaroo) in Kaurna, the Adelaide language, spread up through South Australia into the Centre and parts of Western Australia.

Pidgins, creoles and Aboriginal English

In some parts of Australia, new languages, *creoles*, have developed (Mühlhäsler, 1991). Where speakers of different languages have been brought together and need to communicate with each other, a *pidgin* will sometimes emerge. A pidgin language is a simplified code with a reduced vocabulary and a simplified grammar. A pidgin is nobody's first language. It is used for restricted purposes. When a pidgin becomes acquired by children as a first language it rapidly increases in complexity and its vocabulary expands. This new complex language is called a *creole*.

Linguistically, creoles are on a par with any other language. Australian creoles draw words from a number of languages, though the majority originate from English. However, they are not readily understood by English speakers. They have their own grammar and structure. With more than 20,000 speakers, there are now more speakers of Kriol,[3] spoken across the Kimberley, the cattle country of the Northern Territory and into Queensland, than of any other contemporary Australian language. Torres Strait Islanders have developed their own creole, referred to as Broken or Torres Strait Creole.

While the majority of urban Aboriginal people speak English and often have little knowledge of their ancestral languages, they are still typically linguistically distinct in that they may speak a variety of English in their family situations and social networks that is not shared and is often poorly understood by other Australians. Aboriginal English varieties spoken in urban settings are social dialects and are linguistically distinct from standard Australian English (see Malcolm and Kaldor, 1991). They may reflect grammatical structures and features of the sound systems of their ancestral languages which have long ceased to be spoken. They may also incorporate words from those ancestral languages or use English words in different ways or with changed meanings. In some places, Aboriginal English varieties are diverging from Australian English spoken in the same urban centre. The speech of urban Aboriginal people may range from standard English through to varieties of Aboriginal English which on occasion may not be understood by non-Aboriginal Australians. Many urban Aboriginal people are adept at switching between standard English and Aboriginal English varieties, depending on the context and to whom they are talking.

Language policy and language education

Australian society generally is poorly informed about the existence of Australian languages, of their value and uniqueness, and also about the fragile and endangered state of some of them. As these languages are central to Aboriginal identity, it follows that non-Aboriginal Australians are generally ignorant of the expressed needs, aspirations and cultures of Aboriginal people. Many Aboriginal people use their languages to fulfil all their needs. Knowledge about Aboriginal languages and the ways languages are used is vital to the appreciation and understanding of Aboriginal cultures.

Colonisation of Australia caused drastic social changes which have resulted in actual or imminent extinction for many Australian languages. The early missionaries and government officials suppressed the use of Aboriginal languages because they were a major expression of Aboriginal identity. While Aboriginal people continued to speak their own languages, they were also regarded as heathen rubbish, and such use was seen as a threat to imposed authority. The speaking of Aboriginal languages was often viewed by authorities as a sign of failure to conform and assimilate. This was sufficient, in some cases at least, for children to be separated from their parents if they were caught using their own languages.

However, recent government policies (see *Australia's Language: The Australian Language and Literacy Policy,* 1991: 90–96) have supported initiatives which assist the preservation, use and reconstruction of Aboriginal languages. Australian Aboriginal language issues are matters of national significance with respect to Australian heritage and identity. Australian language heritage should be important to all Australians. It is a unique national treasure. It can provide a key to understanding the continent in which Australians live. Australian languages are obviously of even more significance to Aboriginal and Torres Strait Islander people. The continued active use and recording of Aboriginal languages is fundamental to the survival of Aboriginal cultures and identity. Therefore, language maintenance programs for Aboriginal children are necessary for the survival of those Aboriginal languages still being used on a daily basis.

Aboriginal and Torres Strait Islander people live in a range of socio-cultural settings throughout Australia. The term "traditionally oriented" is used to characterise Aboriginal people who follow their own customs and use their own language rather than English in their family situations. Many Aboriginal people in this category are multi-lingual. They may speak more than one Australian language as well as English. In addition, they may use an Australian creole.

The proper provision of government services to traditionally ori-ented Aboriginal communities requires appropriate translating and interpreting services. Professional translating and interpreting services will ensure that non-English speaking Aboriginal people are able to deal with the wider community and are ensured access to information and services which might otherwise not become known to them. These services exist in Alice Springs and are co-ordinated by the Institute for Aboriginal Development.

In the Northern Territory, bilingual education programs were imple-mented in the early 1970s with the primary aim of facilitating the learning of English by establishing early conceptual development at school and literacy skills in the child's first language. In more recent times, language maintenance has been increasingly identified as the reason for implementing bilingual programs. Currently, twenty-one official bilingual programs operate in seventeen languages in Northern Territory schools.

Yipirinya is an independent Aboriginal school in Alice Springs, established so that Aboriginal children learn "both ways" — that is, to read and write in the Aboriginal way and the non-Aboriginal way. The school's curriculum offers a bilingual and bicultural program, with both Aboriginal and non-Aboriginal curriculum components.

Generally, Aboriginal and Torres Strait Islander languages have suffered in the past under both government and non-government education systems. They have seldom been taught as first or second languages in schools or universities. Despite a clearly identifiable need that has been recognised for some time, Aboriginal languages have never been taught at senior secondary level, at least not towards a credential. Thirty-one languages other than English are accredited by senior secondary assessment authorities around Australia, but not one Australian language is included. Some of these languages have several thousand speakers and have been well researched. The House of Representatives Standing Committee on Aboriginal and Torres Strait Islander Affairs, in *A Matter of Survival* (1991: 51), noted that:

The committee finds it intolerable that while most migrant children with a first language other than English have been able to study that language up to matriculation level, most Aboriginal and Torres Strait Islander children cannot study their language at high school.

The Australian Indigenous Languages Framework is a federally funded national curriculum initiative that seeks to address these needs. The project recognises the diversity among Australia's languages and the different historical experiences that each of these languages has undergone. It is intended that the framework be flexible enough to accommodate all Australian languages and linguistic heritage, whether the language be spoken by entire communities and still acquired by children or whether they are no longer spoken. The project aims to teach all Australians about the nature of Australian languages and their importance to both Aboriginal Australians and the wider community. While recognising the loss of linguistic heritage, the main focus will be a celebration of the survival of Aboriginal and Torres Strait Islander languages and their continuing and increasing importance in Australian society.

Furthermore, the study of Australian languages will serve to increase the standing and status of these languages within Australian society, which in turn will impact positively on their long-term survival. Positive attitudes to languages are fundamental to their maintenance and continued use and vitality.

Language centres

Aboriginal language centres are being established now around the country to provide maximum access with limited resources. Language recording, research and publication facilities are made available to a range of language groups within the one centre. Language centres have been particularly active in the Kimberley and Pilbara in Western Australia and in Alice Springs and Tennant Creek in 1993. The most recent to be established was the South Australian Aboriginal Language Centre, also known as Yaitya Warra Wodli, located at the Aboriginal Community College, Port Adelaide. These centres are funded from a variety of sources, including Commonwealth funds.

Work on Australian languages has shifted away from the production of esoteric linguistic descriptions and analyses of languages written primarily for other linguists to the development of more "hands-on" materials for the lay person and school use. The Australian Institute for Aboriginal and Torres Strait Islander Studies (AIATSIS) has co-ordinated an Aboriginal Dictionaries Project, resulting in the production of twenty dictionaries in 1992–93. A further twenty or so dictionaries are in production. Many of these dictionaries concern languages, such as Dharuk from Sydney, Nukunu from Port Augusta, Wiradjuri from the Riverina in New South Wales and Wamba Wamba[4] from north-west Victoria, which are no longer spoken fluently as a first language. Nick Thieberger at AIATSIS is working on a computer software Hypercard resource file on Australian languages which provides information stacks on the distribution, vocabulary, writing systems, pronunciation and other aspects of Aboriginal languages. This will provide an excellent resource for schools and the general community. Macquarie publishers are currently publishing a volume of word-lists in representative languages from around the country, together with a brief description of each associated language and its context. A study guide is also being written to accompany this volume.

Aboriginal language centres, the Australian Institute of Aboriginal and Torres Strait Islander Studies (AIATSIS) in Canberra or universities offering studies in Australian linguistics can provide more detailed information on the languages of Australia. The University of South Australia offers three subjects in Pitjantjatjara language as part of its undergraduate awards within its Aboriginal and Islander Studies program. The Institute for Aboriginal Development in Alice Springs offers courses in a number of central Australian languages and the Centre for Aboriginal and Islander Studies at the Northern Territory University in Darwin offers a short course in Djambarrpuyngu, a Yolngu language from north-east Arnhem Land.

Conclusion

Australian languages are a fundamental part of Australia's national heritage. As such they are of importance to all Australians, but especially to Aboriginal and Torres Strait Islander people. Indigenous Australians are the custodians of this heritage. All the languages of Australia are important. There are, however, many languages which are still spoken, sometimes by just a handful of speakers, which are in need of assistance. It is a matter of national urgency to assist those communities to maintain, revive and reclaim their linguistic heritage should they desire to do so. It is their basic human right to reclaim and maintain that heritage.

Notes

1. Words drawn from Aboriginal languages are often used in preference to *Aborigine* or *Aboriginal*. No universal term is accepted. Different groups have their own in-group terms to refer to themselves — for example, *Koori* in New South Wales, Victoria and Tasmania, *Nunga* in the south of South Australia, *Nyoongah* in the south-west of Western Australia and *Yolgnu* in the north of the Northern Territory. These terms are used when referring to people from those specific areas.
2. By contrast, English employs prepositions such as *in, at, on, by, for, to, through*, etc. where Aboriginal languages typically employ case suffixes or endings attached to the noun in a similar fashion to Latin.
3. Kriol is the name given to a particular creole language spoken in the Northern Territory and Western Australia.
4. Throughout the chapter, some Aboriginal words are spelt more than one way — for example, Wamba Wamba is also written as Wemba-Wemba.

References

Amery, Rob (1993). "Encoding new concepts in old languages". [To appear in *Australian Aboriginal Studies*.]

Blake, Barry J. (1991). *Australian Aboriginal Languages: A General Introduction*. 2nd edn. St Lucia: University of Queensland Press.

Capell, A. (1956). *A New Approach to Australian Linguistics*. Sydney: Oceania Linguistic Monographs.

Department of Employment, Education and Training (DEET) (1991). *Australia's Language: The Australian Language and Literacy Policy*. Canberra: AGPS.

Dixon, R.M.W. (1980). *The Languages of Australia*. Cambridge: Cambridge University Press.

—— Thomas, W.S. and Thomas, Mandy (1990). *Australian Aboriginal Words in English: Their Origin and Meaning*. Melbourne: Oxford University Press.

Edwards, W.H. (1988). *An Introduction to Aboriginal Societies*. Wentworth Falls: Social Science Press.

Gale, Mary-Anne (1992). *Dhangum Djorra'wuy DhSwu: The Development of Writing in Aboriginal Languages in S.A. and the N.T. Since Colonisation*. Masters of Education thesis. Darwin: Northern Territory University.

Gara, Tom (1990). "The life of Ivaritji ('Princess Amelia') of the Adelaide Tribe". In *Aboriginal Adelaide*. Special issue of the *Journal of the Anthropological Society of South Australia*, vol. 28, no. 1, pp. 64-104.

Goddard, Cliff (1987). *A Basic Pitjantjatjara/Yankunytjatjara to English Dictionary*. Alice Springs: Institute for Aboriginal Development.

Hale, Ken (1964). "Classification of the Northern Paman Languages, Cape York Peninsula, Australia: a research report". *Oceanic Linguistics*, vol. 3, nos 248-65.

House of Representatives Standing Committee on Aboriginal and Torres Strait Islander Affairs (1992). *Language and Culture — a Matter of Survival. Report of the Inquiry into Aboriginal and Torres Strait Islander Language Maintenance*. Canberra: AGPS.

McConvell, Patrick (1991). "Understanding language shift: a step towards language maintenance". In *Language in Australia*, edited by S. Romaine. Cambridge: Cambridge University Press.

Malcolm, Ian G. and Kaldor, Susan (1991). "Aboriginal English — an overview". In *Language in Australia*, edited by S. Romaine. Cambridge: Cambridge University Press.

Mühlhäusler, Peter (1991). "Overview of the pidgin and creole languages of Australia". In *Language in Australia*, edited by S. Romaine. Cambridge: Cambridge University Press.

Schmidt, Annette (1990). *The Loss of Australia's Aboriginal Language Heritage*. Canberra: Aboriginal Studies Press.

Schmidt, W. (1919). *Die Gliederung der Australischen Sprachen*. Vienna.

Teichelmann, C.G. and Schürmann, C.W. (1840). *Outlines of a Grammar, Vocabulary and Phraseology of the Aboriginal Language of South Australia*. Facsimile edition 1982. Largs Bay: Tjintu Books.

Walsh, Michael (1991). "Overview of indigenous languages of Australia". In *Language in Australia,* edited by S. Romaine. Cambridge: Cambridge University Press.

Yallop, Colin and Walsh, Michael (1993). *Language and Culture in Aboriginal Australia*. Canberra: Aboriginal Studies Press.

Chapter 8

Living Wisdom: Aborigines and the Environment

Olga Gostin and Alwin Chong

Introduction

This chapter explores the place of technology and science in Aboriginal Australia and investigates how this relates to Aboriginal attitudes towards the environment. These aspects of Aboriginal culture have perhaps been the least understood or most misinterpreted by Europeans, whose own attitudes to science and technology were cast in a completely different mould.

The Aboriginal world view is essentially inclusive or holistic. Humans and all aspects of human endeavour, as well as nature and all natural phenomena, including animals and plants in all their diversity, are seen as equal manifestations of a timeless spiritual or cosmic order whose origins, meaning and integrity are not challenged. Thus the Kaurna people of the Adelaide Plains of South Australia have a markedly different perception of the role and place of science and technology and their very perception of the environment is different to that of non-Aborigines.

For example, the Mount Lofty Ranges represent the body of the ancestral hero Urabilla. It forms the boundary between Kaurna and Peramangk territory. Based on an expression of their personal belief system, the Kaurna, therefore, see the Mount Lofty Ranges differently from non-Aboriginal people for whom the ranges are a geological feature that has no necessary personal connection to anybody at all.

The European world view tends to separate the spiritual, natural and human domains whose characteristics and attributes are ever open to challenge, debate and reinterpretation. In this lies another important distinction between the two cultural traditions as expressed in attitudes towards knowledge. In the Aboriginal world view, knowledge is an extension of the cosmic order and comprises the accumulated wisdom of the group since time immemorial, handed down from generation to generation by word of mouth. This does not mean that the body of knowledge is changeless or finite, but rather that changes and additions become incorporated into the collective wisdom of the group. The individual acquires this knowledge progressively and cumulatively during a lifetime punctuated by periods of intense learning now described in many parts of Australia as "going through The Law". Knowledge is acquired both by imitation in day-to-day contact with peers and older persons, and by bestowal by specialist older persons. The latter is often undertaken in a highly charged ritual setting which is both secret and separate from those who are not undergoing the same experience. It does not invite debate or challenge. The individual progresses through these stages of specialised learning and graduates as a different person with new knowledge, new privileges and new responsibilities. This change in status is universally accepted by the group whose acceptance enforces the person's new role and responsibilities, derived directly from having tapped into the ancient wisdom of the group. At present the diversity of Aboriginal Australia is such that not all Aboriginal people necessarily access the same sources of knowledge. Even so, the role of older persons and kin groups in passing on knowledge remains very important.

The European quest for knowledge, by contrast, is markedly different in character. It is essentially an individual search driven by specialist interests backed by open access to the accumulated knowledge of past generations stored in libraries. The cosmic order has itself been secularised and the quest is to establish verifiable facts and theories in an atmosphere of detached critical analysis and intellectual debate.

This impersonal academic tradition is a far cry from the highly ritualised bestowal of knowledge upon a neophyte by the custodians of ancient wisdom. The end product of the two traditions results in a very different reading of the environment and a different perception of what, in the West, is identified as technology and science and, in Aboriginal culture, is celebrated as ancient wisdom and traditional skills. This is not to say that Aboriginal people did not or cannot think about the environment in a scientific or rational way. They can and do.

Technology and science

In the past, and to some extent even today, Westerners have tended to pass judgment on Aboriginal cultures and peoples by regarding their level of technological sophistication and achievements in material culture as the gauge of so-called cultural advancement. In the words of George Taplin, missionary among the Ngarrindjeri of South Australia:

> Man, in order to get his living, must have an implement ... In this very necessity lies all the capacity for unlimited advances in human condition. The improvement of the human race has its origin in this necessity for the use of an implement. The "zero of humanity" will be the tribe which has fewest and rudest tools, the most imperfect weapons, and which obtains its subsistence most from the spontaneous productions of the country where it lives. [Taplin, 1979: 9]

Such an equation, based on only one aspect of culture, the technological or material, completely misses the spiritual, ethical and social dimensions of living as expressions of the quality of life.

Advanced technology and scientific thinking are not the exclusive prerogative of the West, even though science has evolved there, as a specific methodology characterised by highly specialised disciplines operating in a reductionist, analytical and experimental framework. For some other cultures, scientific thinking is incorporated into a total body of knowledge, the collective wisdom of the elders, as it were. Scientific principles do inform these traditional forms of knowledge, as well as many practices of indigenous cultures. The distinguishing factor is that Aboriginal cultures make no firm demarcation between so-called scientific thinking, social values and beliefs, technology and other aspects of culture. Indigenous cultures have evolved a detailed and profound knowledge of nature and humankind seen as an inseparable whole, expressed in ritual and song cycles, oral traditions, ceremonies and practices which do not necessarily conform to conventional scientific norms, yet embody a wealth of often precise and detailed verifiable knowledge. Sometimes these spheres of knowledge overlap in an intriguing way.

Thus, looking at the night sky, the Western Desert people will focus on the dark patches in the Milky Way and discern the outline of an emu with the head approximately in the area of the Southern Cross. At different times of the year, the night sky emu will be fully extended as though running, or compactly "sitting". This corresponds in real life to the time when emus may be hunted or when they are nesting and should not be disturbed. Similar associations apply to seasonal cycles, the life cycle of animals and the fruiting of plants, though it must be noted that not all groups have access to the same knowledge about the Sky Beings.

In the harsh Central Australian desert environment, two species of bloated frogs were reservoirs which yielded safe water when they were excavated from their hiding places in hard-baked mud. The small green and yellow frogs would burrow a foot or so below the surface during droughts when their waterholes were baked dry. Bloated with the water they stored, the frogs would "shut down" for months through a dry spell until the rains filled up the waterholes again. However, they could be tricked by stamping firmly on the ground above.

> The noise, perhaps sounding like the thunder which precedes rain, some-
> times provoked hidden frogs into croaking, thus revealing their presence.
> Unearthed by the probes of a digging stick, they were snatched up and
> squeezed like a lemon, so that their water ran into a waiting bowl or mouth.
> [Blainey, 1978: 180]

The indigenous Australians have also had a long association with technology and their understanding of the environment and natural processes has stood the test of time. Changes in world view and attitudes to the environment no doubt can and did occur, but always in the context of a hunter-gatherer lifestyle. For Aboriginal people, technology is an extension of everyday living, an extension of the self. In such a society there is no redundancy, no mass production and no impersonal manufacturing.

Aboriginal culture is popularly described as Stone Age in the sense that stone tools were the basic implements which, in turn, helped to fashion wooden tools as well as bone and shell implements. Archae-ologists vary in their categorisation of the stone tool sequence, though most would agree that the oldest tools tend to be larger, and of the so-called core tool and scraper tradition, while a more distinctive small tool assemblage made up of geometric points appeared about 6,000 years ago (Flood, 1989; Mulvaney, 1975). These tools were carefully selected, shaped and fashioned into spearhead-like shapes. Other tools, such as adzeheads, were hafted or attached to wooden handles with spinifex resin, wax, animal sinew and/or string made from bark or human hair. An interesting feature of Aboriginal technology is that modern media were incorporated into the traditional tool kit very soon after first contact and sometimes even ahead of actually meeting the first Europeans (Reynolds, 1981: 7). Thus beautifully worked glass tools can be found, as well as implements using steel. Later still, hub caps, bicycle spokes and beer cans were fashioned into functional tools such as digging implements and scoops.

Some non-Aboriginal people today make blanket generalisations about Aboriginal technology without understanding the degree of specialisation of individual tools or the extent of regional diversity across the continent. For example, the boomerang and the didgeridoo are promoted as ubiquitous Aboriginal symbols. In fact, the distribution of these artefacts was localised and their use determined by gender and/or limited to certain members of a community. The boomerang was not found in all parts of Australia and varied greatly in size and mode of use. Some were returning, most were non-returning. Likewise, the didgeridoo originated in the north of the continent as a strictly male artefact.

Altogether some 120 distinct artefacts have been recorded on the mainland, ranging from the beautiful and intricate basketry of the Ngarrindjeri of the Coorong of South Australia to the multifunctional, highly specialised *woomera*, or spear thrower, of the Western Desert people. The eastern seaboard people used complex fishing equipment including bone hooks, while the Murray–Darling dwellers fished from their bark canoes with the aid of fire at night to attract the fish. In the Torres Strait, the outrigger canoe, possibly an innovation adapted from Macassan traders, gives stability to hunt sea turtles and the dugong and facilitates safe movement in the open sea. Other artefacts include digging sticks, carrying dishes (*coolamon*), which double up as water dishes and/or scoops, clubs, spears and a great variety of boomerangs, both returning and non-returning. The characteristic feature of these artefacts is that they were portable, generally multi-functional and an expression of the identity of their owner/maker. Some tools, because of their size (e.g. grinding stones) or because of their ritual uses, were not transported but kept in special places.

The Tasmanian enigma

In European countries, technology has assumed an impersonal dimension characterised by anonymous mass production and is no longer necessarily related to simplicity, function or even usefulness. In a general way, technological know-how, as expressed through the proliferation of material goods, has become the criterion for gauging so-called cultural development. Starting from this Western point of view, Rhys Jones raises a contentious issue in his film, *The Last Tasmanians*, when he identifies a tool kit of only twenty-two artefacts and argues that this so-called decline in technological skill is an indication that the Aboriginal Tasmanians were in a process of cultural degeneration when compared with the richer cultures of the mainland.

It could, however, be argued that the Tasmanians had refined their management of resources and satisfaction of needs to the point where they needed only minimal technology. Even so, it remains a mystery why Tasmanians appear to have abandoned the making of bone tools and the eating of scaly fish some 3,000 years ago (Allen, 1979; Jones, 1977). Whatever the reason, it in no way detracts from the remarkable achievements of the Tasmanians whose hand stencils in Kutikina Cave, dated at some 20,000 years ago, testify to their presence at the peak of the last glacial period. At that time, the Tasmanians represented the southernmost point of human occupation on earth.

Adapting to environment

Aboriginal Australians have indeed proved successful in adapting to their environments — which range from the tropical island habitat of the Torres Strait to the desert of the Centre; from the rainforests of the tropical north to the temperate rainforests of Tasmania; from the riverine basin of the Murray Darling to the lacustrine environment of Lake Eyre.

The successful adaptation and survival of Australian hunting and gathering communities in this vast continent was firmly founded on a detailed understanding of nature and natural phenomena. This knowledge was integrated into socioeconomic structures which facilitated successful adaptation to a variety of environments. This approach was very different from the attitude towards the environment which evolved over centuries in Europe. It was characterised by the notion that humans are dominant over nature and that "progress" lies in being able to evade, if not control, the vagaries of climate, environmental adversity and other natural phenomena.

Adaptation in the Pleistocene[1]

Versatility and adaptability are indeed the most striking feature of Aboriginal cultures, not only in historical times but extending to the very earliest periods of Aboriginal settlement of Australia. Geological evidence suggests that for the last 100,000 years, during the so-called late Pleistocene period, Australia experienced several glacial peaks about 100,000, 60,000, 40,000 and 18,000 years ago. During these times, sea levels fell by up to 140 metres, creating the greater Australian land mass known as the Sahul, which included Papua New Guinea and Tasmania in a continuous land mass one-seventh larger than present-day Australia.

During the inter-glacial periods, when the polar ice caps melted due to global warming, the ocean levels rose again, flooding areas which had hitherto sustained human occupation. Aboriginal people not only coped but thrived in these highly changeable periods, colonising the continent and the extended coastal areas during the ice ages and retreating inland or to the new coastal margins as the sea levels rose.

This would have had implications for economic systems as people moved into new ecological areas. No doubt there would have been political and demographic implications too, as the flooded coastal people encroached upon the inhabited hinterland. The ritual and spiritual adaptation which ensued is open to speculation. The constant factor was the need to adapt to each successive period of change. The latest flooding of Bass Strait, about 10,000 years ago, isolated the Tasmanians, who went on to develop their culture in a unique way.

Torres Strait Islands

The Torres Strait was flooded about 8,000 years ago and the people of the Sahul plains between Papua New Guinea and the Australian mainland found themselves retreating to the higher points in their territory — now the islands of the Torres Strait. Here the new maritime society developed a uniquely vibrant culture blending features of its Melanesian neighbours to the north and cultural attributes of the Aboriginal people to the south (Arthur, 1992).

The Strait covers a total area of over 40,000 km², made up mostly of open ocean. Some 100 islands and islets dot this vast continental shelf habitat, which has been described as one of the most ecologically complex areas in the world (Nietschmann, as quoted by Mulrennan, 1992). Four separate island groups can be distinguished, as shown on Map 8.1.

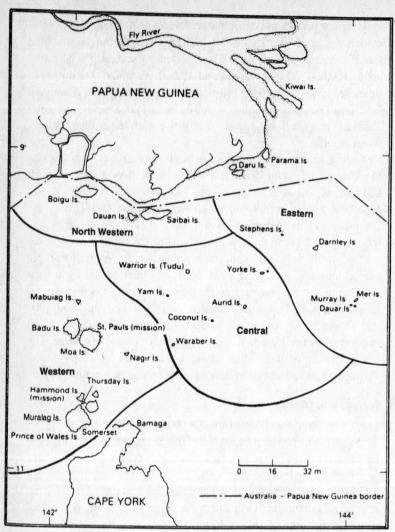

Map 8.1 Map of Torres Strait Islands
Source: Beckett (1987)

The Torres Strait comprises four separate island groups:

- A western group of high islands of acid volcanic and granitic rocks characterised by a mixed economy of fishing and gardening. The main islands here include Badu, Moa and Mabuiag. Thursday Island, the administrative centre for the Torres Strait, forms part of the Prince of Wales group of islands which falls within the geographic boundaries of the western group.

- A central group of low coral cays surrounded by coral reefs whose inhabitants depend almost totally on fishing as there is very little soil that can be cultivated. These include Coconut, Warraber (Sue), Yorke and Yam Islands.

- An eastern group of high islands with fertile volcanic soils derived from the eroded remnants of volcanic cones. These include Mer (home of the famous Mabo land claim), Erub (Darnley) and Stephens Island. The islanders here enjoy a mixed economy based on fishing, pig husbandry and gardening.

- The north-western islands of Boigu, Saibai and Dauan lie close the Papuan mainland and consist of low lying mangrove swamps and peats. The people on these islands survive by trading with their neighbours. [Mulrennan, 1992: 7]

The inhabitants of these four island groups show subtle cultural adaptation to the limitations of resources provided by their different island habitats.

Today some 6,000 Islanders reside on sixteen inhabited islands in the Strait and two communities (Seisia and Bamaga) on the tip of Cape York. Another 15,300 Islanders live on the Australian mainland where they maintain links with their home islands, particularly at times of communal ritual importance such as mourning feasts which culminate in the unveiling of tombstones (Beckett, 1987).

Megafauna[2]

Just as the Torres Strait Islands, with their distinctive culture, emerged as a result of the dramatic rise in sea levels at the end of the last ice age, other parts of the continent also experienced vast environmental changes as a result of associated climatic shifts. For example, the Lake Eyre Basin was once part of a large inland water system which sustained humans and unique Pleistocene animals known as *mega-*

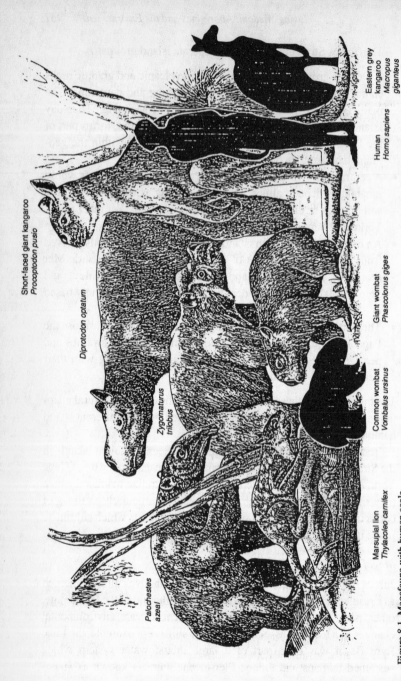

Short-faced giant kangaroo
Procoptodon pusio

Diprotodon optatum

Zygomaturus trilobus

Marsupial lion
Thylacoleo carnifex

Palochestes azeal

Human
Homo sapiens

Common wombat
Vombalus ursinus

Giant wombat
Phascolonus gigas

Eastern grey kangaroo
Macropus giganteus

Figure 8.1 Megafauna with human scale
Source: Smith (1986)

fauna: creatures such as Diprotodon, Procoptodon and Zaglossus, corresponding to giant wombats, kangaroos and echidnas (Quirk and Archer, 1983; Vickers-Rich, 1991). These large animals, which were also found in other parts of Australia and which were unique to this continent, became extinct in Central Australia about 35,000 to 40,000 years ago, yet lingered around the coastal margin until as recently as 14,000 years ago (see Figure 8.1).

The circumstances of their extinction are still debated. Some scientists argue that megafauna were victims of changes in climate which led to marked changes in habitat and hence to the demise of the large herbivores. Others have taken the view that Aboriginal hunting practices were responsible, while others still have sought an explanation in a combination of climatic factors, habitat changes and human impact (Horton, 1980). Be it as it may, the megafauna disappeared but Aboriginal people survived the vagaries of climate and habitat change with characteristic versatility.

Lake Mungo

Two examples highlight the contrasting adaptation of Aboriginal people to the challenge of climatic and environmental changes. In both incidents, technological skills and detailed knowledge of the environment ensured survival and the development of a prosperous lifestyle. The first example refers to Lake Mungo in western New South Wales. It is one of a series of lakes making up the Willandra Lakes system. Over the last 50,000 years, Lake Mungo has undergone periodic rises and falls in water level, corresponding to changes of climate over the continent. They culminated in the lake totally drying out about 15,000 years ago. When the Willandra Lakes were full they provided a resource-rich environment which saw the flowering of a civilisation featuring ceremonial burial practices rating among the oldest recorded on earth (Bowler, 1990; Flood, 1989).

It was here that Mungo Lady was buried after being cremated about 26,000 years ago. Some 500 metres from this site an even older burial shows a fully extended recumbent adult male whose body had been anointed with ochre. Dated at 36,000 years, Mungo Man conclusively shows that Aboriginal people were engaged in metaphysical thinking and elaborate burial practices far earlier than conventional thinking had suggested.

More importantly, the uniform size of fish remains (as noted by the otoliths or ear bones) found in 30,000-year-old hearths not far from the burial sites suggests that the Mungo people engaged in gillnet fishing. This implies that a fairly sophisticated technology of weaving and making string was in place at that time. When the lake finally dried up 15,000 years ago, the local Aboriginal people adapted from a lacustrine resource-rich economy to one focused on the grass plains, involving a mixed economy based on hunting game and harvesting native grasses and local produce. Today, the Mutthi Mutthi, Barkindji and Ngyiampaa groups form a living link with this ancestral place and are directly involved in passing on knowledge to the younger generation. The vital importance of Lake Mungo in world prehistory was recognised in 1981 when it was placed on the World Heritage List (Gostin, 1993).

Lake Condah

A second example of successful technological adaptation by Aboriginal people occurs at Lake Condah in western Victoria. Here the Kerrup-Jmara people turned the eruption of Mt Eccles about 6,000 years ago to their advantage by arranging volcanic basalt boulders into an elaborate system of weirs, channels and stone walls which effectively regulated the flow of the local Darlot River. This complex of structures described by archaeologists as a marvellous piece of prehistoric hydro-engineering ensured the harvesting of a steady supply of fish and migratory eels (Coutts, Frank and Hughes, 1978). This enabled the local populace to live semi-permanently in the area as shown by the foundations of some 200 stone houses. Complex stone structures used as a means of channelling and trapping fish have also been found at Brewarrina on the upper Darling River and even on coastal estuaries in northern New South Wales (Dargin, 1976).

Firestick farming[3]

Aboriginal people have shown versatility in the face of major climate and environmental changes. In recent times, some environmentalists have promoted Aboriginal people as model conservationists. But it must be remembered that the original Australians had an impact on the whole continent for tens of thousands of years and to some extent it would be true to say that the whole of Australia is an Aboriginal artefact. The reference here, of course, is to *firestick farming*, which

Aboriginal people have practised from the earliest times. This involved systematic burning of the countryside in a chequered or mosaic pattern which had the multiple effect of flushing out game, rejuvenating plant growth and attracting animals once new regrowth started. Such burning was founded on precise knowledge of seasonal and local weather patterns as well as on botanical knowledge of what plants were pyrophyllic (fire loving) and what plants were not fire tolerant.

Burning was controlled and "safety zones" were left around areas vegetated by plants which disliked regular burning. On the other hand, burning helped stimulate the simultaneous fruiting of *macrozamia* plants of the cycad family to the extent that ceremonies could be planned months ahead in expectation of a bountiful supply of food from this plant. The use of *macrozamia* as a food raises the question of how and why it became a food staple given that in its natural state the fruit is highly toxic and has to be treated by elaborate soaking and leeching procedures before it can be safely eaten. In fact, archaeological evidence suggests that macrozamia became part of the Australian diet only as recently as 5,000 years ago.

It is possible that the long-term effect of firestick farming changed the plant succession in the continent from Casuarina dominance to Eucalyptus and other fire-loving plants as early as 100,000 years ago. This remains a contentious issue and awaits confirmation if and when human occupation is proved at this early time (Blainey, 1978; Singh et al., 1981; Smith, 1986).

In any case, Aboriginal people, while managing their resources, were actively engaged in modifying the landscape. Systematic burning on a regular basis resulted in low-intensity fires which gave rise to an open landscape favouring the proliferation of herbivores like kangaroos. Ironically, the original Australians thereby set the scene for the pastoral invasion of the British settlers.

From the earliest days of contact, the British commented on the "burning continent" and the firestick practices of the Aboriginal people. As the European frontier extended inland and Aboriginal land management practices were forcefully repressed, the plant succession hitherto managed by firestick burning was radically modified (Smith, 1992b). Clearings gave way to a tangle of undergrowth. When burning occurred, whether by design or by accident, this gave rise to devastating high-intensity fires which destroyed both the undergrowth and the tall tree canopy. The scene was thus set for plant destruction and soil erosion on an unparallelled scale.

Aboriginal practices revisited

Careless farming practices, deforestation, over-fertilising, the practice of monoculture and over-stocking have resulted in land degradation and soil erosion across the continent, indicating major environmental mismanagement. It is only in comparatively recent times that non-Aboriginal people have turned to the management practices of the original Australians as a method of possible alternative land use. Thus regular, low-intensity burning has been reintroduced at Kakadu National Park (Birckhead et al., 1992; Lewis, 1989). The joint management of parks is increasingly being regarded as the ideal means of combining indigenous knowledge and land care practices with the management skills and technical know-how of non-Aboriginals.

Permaculture is also finding acceptance and respectability as a more sustainable form of land use (Mollison and Holmgren, 1984). In effect, this mirrors the Aboriginal practice of harvesting a variety of crops in a sustainable way in the natural environment. One of the benefits of this new-found respect for Aboriginal botanical knowledge and land management skills is a rediscovery of Aboriginal pharmaceutical and medicinal practices (Low, 1990; 1991). Many of these are firmly based on verifiable scientific facts and have generated a flurry of activity to retrieve and safeguard this knowledge, lest it be lost to humankind.

The same point is made in the ABC-TV series *Bushtucker Man*, which explores the rich diversity of the Australian environment and, most importantly, reveals the depth of knowledge and understanding of the natural environment of the original Australians. However, many Aboriginal people believe that the series would have been more appropriate with Aboriginal persons identified who provided the focal and unifying point. As it stands, the series is regarded as a form of cultural appropriation. While they are proud of the belated recognition given to the richness of their cultures, Aboriginal people nevertheless resent the way aspects of their ancient knowledge and wisdom were recorded and interpreted in the past and are handled today. More recently, leading Aboriginal academics like Marcia Langton have been most outspoken against cultural appropriation and commercialisation, seen as the latest expression of colonial dispossession.

Conclusion

Against the current anxiety over anticipated land claims by Aboriginal people, it could be argued that land in Aboriginal custody is land in safekeeping pending a reorientation and reassessment of attitudes to land use and land management which have proved less successful in the past two centuries. It should be clear from our exploration of Aboriginal scientific knowledge, technology and attitudes to the environment that a more enlightened way ahead lies in the marrying of the two systems of knowledge. The collective wisdom of both cultures could then ensure a more holistic approach to everyday life. In an ideal setting, science, technology and the environment would no longer be discrete units, but vital connections between human beings and the natural environment in which they live.

Notes

1. Pleistocene is the Geological period characterised by ice ages covering the last two million years, but excluding the last ten thousand years known as the Holocene.
2. Megafauna are large animals, which in Australia were distinctive and became extinct during the late Pleistocene period.
3. Firestick farming is a term coined by Rhys Jones (1969) referring to systematic and deliberate seasonal burning practised by Aboriginal people as a form of land management.
4. Permaculture is a system of crop production based on a variety of perennial plants which are compatible and self-sustaining.

References

Allen, H (1979). "Left in out in the cold: why the Tasmanians stopped eating fish". *The Artefact*, vol. 4, pp. 1-10.

Arthur, W. (1992). "Culture and economy in border regions: the Torres Strait case". *Australian Aboriginal Studies*, vol. 2, pp. 15-33.

Beckett, J. (1987). *Torres Strait Islanders: Custom and Colonialism*. Melbourne: Cambridge University Press.

Birckhead, J., De Lacy, T. and Smith, L. (1992). *Aboriginal Involvement in Parks and Protected Areas*. Canberra: Aboriginal Studies Press.

Blainey, G. (1978). *Triumph of the Nomads: A History of Ancient Australia*. Melbourne: Sun Books.

Bowler, J. (1990). "Human occupation and environmental change: the ancient records of the Willandra Lakes". In *The Mallee Lands: A Conservation Perspective*. Proceedings of the National Mallee Conference, Adelaide,

1989, April, edited by J.C. Noble, J. Joss and G.K. Jones. Melbourne: CSIRO.

Coutts, P., Frank R. & Hughes, P. (1978). "Aboriginal engineers of the Western District, Victoria". *Records of the Victorian Archaeological Survey,* vol. 7.

Dargin, P. (1976). *Aboriginal Fisheries of the Darling-Barwon Rivers.* Brewarrina: Brewarrina Historical Society.

Flood, J. (1989). *Archaeology of the Dreamtime.* Sydney: Collins.

Gostin, O. (1993). *Accessing the Dreaming: Heritage, Conservation and Tourism at Mungo National Park.* Adelaide: Aboriginal Research Publications.

Horton, D. (1980). "A review of the extinction question: man, climate and megafauna". *Archaeology and Physical Anthropology in Oceania,* vol. 15, pp. 86-97.

Jones, R. (1969). "Firestick farming". *Australian Natural History,* September, pp. 224-28.

—— (1977). "The Tasmanian paradox". In *Stone Tools as Cultural Markers: Change, Evolution and Complexity,* edited by R. Wright. Canberra: Australian Institute of Aboriginal Studies.

Lewis, H. (1989). "Ecological and technological knowledge of fire: Aborigines versus park rangers in Northern Australia". *American Anthropologist,* vol. 91, pp. 940-61.

Low, T. (1990). *Bush Medicine: A Pharmacopoeia of Natural Remedies.* North Ryde: Angus & Robertson.

—— (1991). *Bush Tucker: Australia's Wild Food Harvest.* North Ryde: Angus & Robertson.

Mollison, B. and Holmgren, D. (1987). *Permaculture One: Practical Design for Human Settlements.* Tyalgum: Tagari

Mulrennan, M. (1992). *Coastal Management: Challenges and Changes in the Torres Strait Islands* (Discussion paper number 5). Darwin: North Australian Research Unit.

Mulvaney, D. (1975). *The Prehistory of Australia.* Ringwood: Penguin.

Quirk, S. and Archer, M. (1983). *Prehistoric Animals of Australia.* Sydney: Australian Museum.

Reynolds, H. (1981). *The Other Side of the Frontier.* Townsville: James Cook University.

Singh, G., Kershaw, A.P. and Clark, R. (1981). "Quaternary vegetation and fire history in Australia". In *Fire and the Australian Biota,* edited by A.M. Gill, R.H. Groves and I.R. Noble. Canberra: Australian Academy of Science.

Smith, J. (1986). "Biogeography of Australian flora and fauna". In *A Natural Legacy: Ecology in Australia,* edited by H. Recher, D. Lunney and I. Dunn. Sydney: Pergamon Press.

—— (1992a). "The burning bush". In *The Unique Continent: An Introductory Reader in Australian Environmental Studies,* edited by J. Smith. St Lucia: University of Queensland Press.

——— (1992b). "The ecology and history of bushfires in Eastern Australia". In *The Unique Continent: An Introductory Reader in Australian Environmental Studies*, edited by J Smith. St Lucia: University of Queensland Press.

Taplin, G. (1879). *Manners, Customs and Languages of the South Australian Aborigines*. Adelaide: Government Printer.

Vickers-Rich, P., Monaghan, J.M., Baird, R.F. and Rich, T.H. (eds) (1991). *Vertebrate Palaeontology of Australia*. Lilydale: Pioneer Design Studio in co-operation with the Monash University Publications Committee, Melbourne.

Chapter 9

Education: The Search for Relevance

Howard Groome

Introduction

Schools and schooling have been key elements in the relationships between Aboriginal and non-Aboriginal Australians. Schools may be seen as arenas in which the negative encounters between the two parties are regularly replayed in the experiences of individual Aboriginal children. They have been places where the power of non-Aboriginal authority has been reinforced.

In their first months at school, and often in each subsequent meeting with a new teacher, many Aboriginal children have to confront another world. This is a world in which their own values are denied, their language and communication strategies are challenged and their identity and self-confidence are threatened (Malin, 1989). They recognise that, to survive, new rules have to be learnt. They have to learn to handle the shame of being invisible as an individual person and yet highly visible racially. Some learn survival strategies and succeed. But too many others learn only to expect failure. This inevitably affects their academic achievement. In the sorting and grading process of school, many Aboriginal children find themselves continually losing ground until — often prematurely — they leave, with inadequate social, academic or economic skills (Binnion, 1975; Duncan, 1987).

It is possible to identify the elements which contribute to this situation; it is far harder to achieve an improvement. Behind it lies the colonising attitude described by Mulvaney (1989) as a mixture of contempt, fear, total lack of understanding, and guilt. The product of this is a suffocation of conscience which has made the history of Aboriginal education, as much as that of the nation, one of indifference.

In this brief survey of the field, the three major phases in the history of Aboriginal education are considered, followed by a discussion of the current issues. First, however, it is necessary to consider the form of education practised in Australia prior to colonisation.

Education and socialisation in Aboriginal Australia

In Aboriginal Australia, the whole continent was a school. Everyone was a teacher. All community members, even young children, had some educational role (Hamilton, 1981).

The foundation of the curriculum was The Dreaming. From this source, through The Law which it generated, sprang knowledge and skills. There have been several detailed examinations of the nature of the learning emphasised in traditional Aboriginal societies (Harris, 1984; Coombs, Brandl and Snowden, 1983; Nganyinka, 1991).

The Law emphasised harmony in relationships. It was reflected by a concentration on developing skills of co-operative living in the young. At the same time, personal autonomy and independence were valued. The individual was required to develop to the full those personal attributes which would enhance the life of the group (Coombs et al., 1983).

The ways in which these values were transmitted were essentially practical. Learning was through observation and imitation, with an emphasis on learning by doing (Harris, 1984). The learning was achieved through the telling of stories, the singing of songs, the modelling of skills, the instilling of increasing levels of responsibility (Broome, 1982).

As children in a group grew older, the learning became more sophisticated, until in their teenage years the boys (and to a lesser degree the girls) were engaged in highly demanding residential "universities". In these settings they were beginning the lifelong learning of advanced survival skills, coupled with the complex spiritual knowledge and values of their people (Coombs et al., 1983).

The Anglo-Europeans, with very few exceptions, were as blind to the existence of this complex and finely tuned system as they were to most aspects of Aboriginal life (Rowley, 1972).

Early government schools 1830s and 1840s

Schools for Aborigines were among the first to open in Australia. During the 1830s and 1840s there were small schools operating in or near all of the small coastal settlements which are now the major cities of Australia. The majority of these were government schools in that, while the teachers were usually Christian ministers, the schools operated with the strong support of the local British governors (Rowley, 1972).

The establishment of these schools reflected the spirit of the colonisers. While individual motives varied from centre to centre, the basic drive was a strong evangelical belief in the need to "civilise and Christianise" the children of a people who were regarded as living in total degradation. The values and lifestyles of hunters and gatherers were incomprehensible and threatening to Europeans who believed that they themselves were the benefactors of the most advanced civilisation yet known (Broome, 1982).

These schools were modelled on overseas practices, thus introducing a pattern which was to recur frequently in Aboriginal education. Two influences were evident: strategies which had proved successful in colonising the Pacific Islands, and those developed in Britain itself. The British model was the school system designed to transform the redundant peasantry into a disciplined workforce appropriate to the needs of the new factories.

The Aboriginal communities whose children were recruited into these institutions were not aware of the significance of these imported strategies. However, they were soon to recognise the schools as yet another attack on their lifestyle and freedom. Traumatised by the shock of invasion, with their numbers declining under the multiple impacts of introduced diseases, sub-standard diets and random murders, Aborigines failed to see why they should surrender their children to be inducted into alien ways (Broome, 1982). They saw that those children who had gained significant literacy and numeracy skills in the successful early months of these schools failed to gain a place in the highly stratified colonial societies. They were learning a lesson that was to be an ongoing experience with education: despite all the promises, schooling was not able to deliver to Aboriginals a place in Australian society. By itself schooling was no guarantee against endemic racism.

There were other themes evident in these early schools which have emerged frequently with respect to the education of Aboriginal people in subsequent decades.

The basic motivation behind schooling was assimilation. There was very little understanding, and even less appreciation, of Aboriginal culture, and no place for it in schools. The two exceptions, the bilingual schools in Western and South Australia, were forced after only a few years to drop education in the mother tongue in the face of public opposition (Broome, 1982).

There was no consultation with Aboriginal parents. Relationships were limited to bribes of blankets and food to persuade reluctant parents to send their children to school.

The colonists themselves were not blind to these tensions and contradictions. They plied the newspapers with spirited debates about Aboriginal issues, especially on the topic of education. Some of them, such as James Bonwick, understood the Aboriginal position:

> We teach [the Aboriginal lads] to read, and their fathers want to instruct them in woodcraft. We show them how to handle the pen, and they want to guide their arm with the spear. We give them light upon other countries, and they are losing time in learning the haunts of birds, the retreat of the wombat, and ways of the emu. We can train them in the elements of astronomy, but cannot give them the practical arts of the forest — the means of their life, and the source of high animal enjoyment. We cultivate their mental faculties, but dwarf their physical capabilities. The old warrior finds the schoolboy less fleet in the chase, less cunning on the trail, and less merry in the leafy glades as they despise the training we give the lads. [Bonwick, 1862: 127]

This first phase of schooling for Aboriginal children ended within a relatively short time. The high death rates and low birth rates among Aboriginal groups living close to the major population centres meant that there were few children to attend the schools. It was generally seen by both their supporters and opponents that the schools were a failure (Rowley, 1972).

With their closure, the direct involvement of governments in the education of Aboriginal children ceased in most areas of Australia until the early decades of the following century. For the next hundred years the main responsibility for the education of Aboriginal people was to pass to churches and welfare groups who operated the missions and reserves which were established throughout rural and remote Australia.

Aboriginal schooling 1850 to 1960

Some of the missions and reserves were a safe haven for a dispossessed people. Their founders were frequently talented visionaries with a strong sense of social responsibility. They conceived of these missions as agriculturally based re-education centres which aimed to teach the "arts of industry" (Rowley, 1972).

The more successful were self-supporting and provided Western-style training and employment for many Aboriginal men and women. They provided a place of social readjustment and some economic security for many of the thousands of people driven off their lands by white pastoralists. Broome (1982) claims that without them many groups would have faced certain death.

It is impossible to generalise about missions and reserves. Each one tended to reflect the capabilities and interests of the individual white managers. There was a wide range of administrations, ranging from the benevolent to the despotic. They shared, however, one major agenda — to break the remaining traces of Aboriginal culture and replace it with an Anglo-European work and faith ethic. The way in which this was pursued varied according to local emphasis. Charles Rowley (1972) has called this process "civilisation by tuition".

There was purposeful planning behind these missions and reserves. They were conceived as model villages in which even the ordered and compact town plan would assist in the training and disciplining of the Aboriginal residents (Attwood, 1989).

The school was the major feature of most of the communities. Many were boarding schools, "safe places" where the children could be educated away from the "harmful influences" of the older people. The typical timetable contained a great deal of Christian activity and practical domestic training for both boys and girls. Lessons of health and hygiene were strongly emphasised (Broome, 1982). The 1860s diary of Reverend George Taplin at Pt McLeay demonstrates the typical outlook of the missionary/teachers of the middle years of last century:

> The first step was to have them all well washed with warm soap and water, have their hair cut and put on clean clothes. Their parents were very averse to the hair-cutting process for the bigger boys. It is the custom of the natives to let a youth's hair grow from the time he is ten years old until he is sixteen or seventeen — that is until he is made a young man, or *narumbe* ... But I insisted that my pupils must have their hair cut, and after some scolding from their mothers I carried the point.
>
> The schoolboys are glorying in the fact that they have done several things in defiance of native customs, and have received no harm. They have eaten wallaby, and yet have not turned grey. They have eaten *tyere* (fish), and

have no sore legs. They have cooked *ngaikunde* (fish) with *palye*, and yet there are plenty more. [Mattingley and Hampton, 1988: 101]

There was, of course, a great deal of distress among the parents about such situations.

The Aboriginal who tried to maintain his Law fought the missionary for the minds of his children. The missions attempted to split the generations and wreck the traditional pattern of socialisation in order to save the soul of the child. [Rowley, 1972: 102].

There were considerable variations among the mission and reserve schools over time and place. However, the majority appear to have been totally ineffective, erratic in both their hours of opening and in the quality of instruction (Reynolds, 1989). In this period, when trained teachers were not readily available in the general community, the persons employed as teachers on Aboriginal missions were frequently untrained and incompetent. Education departments in some states had deliberate policies which ensured that literacy and numeracy skills among Aboriginal children were kept lower than those in mainstream schools (Broome, 1982). Very few students gained skills of independent living and self-management. The presence of one concerned and gifted teacher was significant enough to ensure that he or she passed into folk memory (Mattingley and Hampton, 1988).

The children of those Aboriginal families who managed to avoid being drafted on to missions met with mixed fortunes. Some attended local state schools. Many others were barred in some states from attending government schools if local white parents objected. Others lived on remote station camps where schooling was unavailable (Reynolds, 1989).

The alienation of Aboriginal children

Throughout Australia in the early years of this century governments began to realise that while the component of the Aboriginal population comprised of people of full Aboriginal descent was decreasing, the population as a whole was increasing. The assimilation of these "mixed-race" children and young people into the Australian community was seen as an urgent need. All states introduced *protection legislation* which claimed to "protect" Aboriginal people from the worst effects of white society. In reality, such legislation supported a thoroughgoing program of assimilation through institutionalisation.

The various state acts gave the Protectors of Aborigines total power over Aboriginal people, and the authority to remove their children.

> The 1911 Act in South Australia dealt with such matters as who was an Aboriginal to be controlled: who might remove or confine Aborigines; who might visit them and the penalties for "enticing" them away. The Chief Protector was the legal guardian of every Aboriginal or half-caste child, overruling parental authority, until twenty-one years of age; and could take over the property of an Aboriginal or half-caste. [Rowley, 1972: 221]

The Acts reinforced the already common practice of forcibly removing Aboriginal children, especially those with lighter skin colouring, from their mothers. Under this legislation, many hundreds of Aboriginal children all around Australia were forcibly taken from their parents and committed to an institution for care, control and training. This practice continued in some states until the 1970s.

Very few of these children gained anything positive from this experience. The great majority lost all self-confidence and their Aboriginal identity. Many of them experienced emotional trauma which fostered alcoholism and destructive behaviours (Radford et al., 1990). Only a few gained acceptance in the white world and the vacuum of their lost homes and families was rarely filled (Reid, 1982; Mattingley and Hampton, 1988).

In this period, too, theorists in the newly emerging human and social sciences became interested in Aboriginal children. Psychologists carried out extensive investigations into Aboriginal children. Their findings, that Aboriginal children were intellectually inferior to non-Aboriginal children, served to confirm official and popular views of Aboriginal people and were used to legitimise assimilationist policy directions (McConnochie, 1981).

The work of the psychologists was to have long-term effects on the education of Aboriginal children. Educational administrators used these findings to support their policies of providing lower levels of support for Aboriginal children and limiting them to lower levels of achievement. Many classroom teachers have been influenced by these findings towards either "writing off" Aboriginal students or to not making the same demands on them as they have on non-Aboriginal students.

Thus, while the time places and action had changed, the themes had not. The basic motive remained to "improve" and "civilise" children who, because of their membership of an "inferior" group, were regarded as being unacceptably below the standards (norms) of a civilised (democratic) society (Broome, 1982).

The new wave in Aboriginal education: 1960s on

During the 1970s and 1980s the distinctive field of expertise now known as Aboriginal education began to emerge. This was due to several factors:

- With the passing of the 1967 referendum, the welfare mentality of the states began to be challenged.
- The control of Aboriginal missions began to pass from churches and welfare agencies to communities themselves. Responsibility for the schools was taken by Education Departments and this usually, but not always, led to improvements in the quality of teaching.
- As employment opportunities reduced in rural Australia, increased numbers of Aboriginal families moved into major cities (Broome, 1982).
- Compared with the rest of Australia, the Aboriginal birth rate has been high over recent decades, creating a population with a large juvenile sector.
- In the 1960s there were significant worldwide changes in the understandings of the educational needs of children from minority and indigenous groups.

The influence of these theories was felt in many aspects of Aboriginal education, most noticeably in the various programs funded by the Van Leer Foundation in the 1960s and 1970s (Teasdale and Whitelaw, 1981).

The influential cultural deficit and deprivation theories arrived in Australia from the United States and Britain in the early years of the 1960s. These theories focused on the social and cultural settings of under-achieving children. The failure of minority-group children to achieve was explained by the disadvantaged or deprived nature of their homes and communities. These theorists claimed that these homes lacked stimulating learning and language, and so these children were unable to benefit from schooling to the same degree as children whose homes were enriched (Nurcombe, 1976).

The programs developed by these theorists aimed to create the development experiences which these children were believed to have missed due to their "deficient" home backgrounds. To achieve their goals these programs generally proposed far-reaching intervention into the lives of the children and their families.

A positive factor of this period was the graduation of the first cohorts of Aboriginal teachers from Teachers' Colleges.

The current situation: Issues and needs

It appears that educators have learnt few lessons from a century and a half of experience with Aboriginal children and schools. Throughout the period, there has not been significant improvement in the educational experiences and outcomes of these students. The words of the 1985 Senate Select Committee on Aboriginal education are still appropriate:

> [Education] has failed to cater for the needs and aspirations of Aboriginal people, the majority of Aboriginal parents do not have confidence in the education provided for their children. [Senate Select Committee, 1985: 120]

When measured on four key indices, the inadequacy of the education provided for Aboriginal students becomes apparent: in general they tend to have lower achievement levels and higher levels of absenteeism. In one area of Adelaide during 1988, 40 per cent of Aboriginal students attended for less than four days a week. Aborigines record lower school retention rates and lower numbers of matriculants than non-Aboriginal groups (Hughes, 1988). The national percentage of Aboriginal students staying at school in 1986 was 18 per cent compared with the national average of 60 per cent.

Aboriginal students today can be described as being at high risk in schools for a variety of complex reasons.

Aboriginal parents and schools

The interactions between generations of Aboriginal people and educators have been generally negative.

Many Aboriginal parents view schools in the light of their own experiences and communal perceptions. Because of their experiences on missions, reserves and in fostering institutions, many older people have no tradition of needing or respecting European education. The close association between education and the management of the institutions made schooling an unpleasant controlling and limiting experience rather than an empowering one. School became just another aspect of white domination, something to be avoided. This long history of negative experiences fostered a persistent mistrust of schooling among many families (Pierson, 1977).

Teachers and Aboriginal parents

There is evidence that teachers as a group are ignorant of many aspects of modern Aboriginal life (Tannock and Punch, 1975). The Select Committee (1985) found that many teachers did not understand the attitudes and motives of Aboriginal students and were unresponsive to their needs. In their training, teachers have not received guidance on how to work with Aboriginal students.

Researchers have found that two-thirds of Aboriginal parents had never met the teachers of their children. As a result, many of them, especially fathers, lacked knowledge about school matters. They were not aware of the subjects their child was studying and how they were progressing. They did not understand how a child's progress was measured and reported, or the significance of regular attendance and homework (Watts, 1976; Eckermann, 1984).

Racism in schools

Many Aboriginal parents are concerned about the impact of racism on the lives of their children (Tannock and Punch, 1975). They see it as causing pressures and strains which can sidetrack their children away from participation in school life and into a marginalised position where they may adopt a disruptive role.

The common experience of parents is that schools tend to condone racism. Despite recent legislation, racism is only rarely treated in the same way as issues such as smoking and violations of the uniform codes (Groome, 1988).

Many Aboriginal parents become preoccupied with assisting their children to cope with racism in all its various forms, and in preventing them from becoming marginalised through it.

In addition to the reality of verbalised racism, there is a hidden or institutionalised racism which operates through the refusal of teachers and schools to recognise the distinctive cultural needs of Aboriginal children in their organisation, teaching and management policies.

Failure to recognise the needs of Aboriginal children

The range of cultural differences among contemporary Aboriginal people is being increasingly documented, as are the ways in which these affect the schooling experiences of Aboriginal children (Malin, 1990).

Recent research has highlighted the major differences between the values and behaviours which are emphasised in many Aboriginal homes and those emphasised in the majority of Australian classrooms. Among many Aboriginal families there are patterns of socialisation which reflect, in varying degrees of intensity, the values and forms of socialisation practised in Aboriginal communities prior to white arrival.

Malin (1990) has shown how many Aboriginal families socialise their children into values and behaviours of autonomy and affiliation; these frequently conflict with the middle-class white expectations of many junior primary classrooms. Schools frequently fail to recognise the significant differences in language (Eades, 1985) and in communication and learning styles among Aboriginal children (Christie, 1985).

The struggle for identity

All of the factors described above mean that there may be very real difficulties for Aboriginal children as they seek to establish their own identity and role in life against the background of the very differing worlds of home and school. Maureen Watson, an Aboriginal cultural communicator, believes that Aboriginal children are alienated, isolated, misunderstood and neglected by the school system (Watson, 1982: 7).

Many Aboriginal students in upper primary and lower secondary years have a negative awareness of both their racial identity and their comparatively lower level of performance thrust upon them. Some face the dilemma that if they improve their academic level they may face rejection by their Aboriginal peer group.

School, which is not necessary for Aboriginal social contacts, may appear irrelevant, restrictive and authoritarian to many young Aboriginal teenagers who are leading independent adult lives. For them, dropping out may seem the most sensible option when school becomes totally destructive of self-esteem and when job prospects appear to be very remote (Binnion, 1975).

The reality of poverty

The Aboriginal community has been identified in several reports as having the highest proportion of its members living in poverty. Poverty adds considerably to the difficulties of Aboriginal children seeking to cope with schooling. Many Aboriginal families have structural problems in trying to support their student children in matters such as regular attendance, homework and the wearing of school uniform.

In 1991 the unemployment rate for Aboriginal people in South Australia was 28.1 per cent compared with 11.7 per cent for the total population (Census, 1991). These figures are similar to those in other states. Unemployment affects Aboriginal children in several ways. Boys, especially, have few models of success and regular employment to encourage them. They realise that few Aboriginal students have achieved good jobs. They may become convinced that school is a waste of time and that it is not relevant to their lives. These perceptions increase their lack of confidence and inferiority and lead to a further reduction in effort. This situation is aggravated by racial prejudice in the school. Many students develop a hostility to society which is expressed by an increasing reluctance to participate in school. They may develop anti-social behaviour and persistent non-attendance which will serve to aggravate the conflict with school staff and tend to reduce their chances of receiving support (Binnion, 1975).

Family dislocations, which frequently accompany unemployment, can also make regular schooling difficult. In 1991, 34.5 per cent of Aboriginal families in South Australia with dependant children were single-parent families (Census, 1991).

As a direct result of poverty many Aboriginal children suffer from acute health problems which affect their ability to learn and their attendance at school. Vision and hearing difficulties occur very commonly and Aboriginal children are very susceptible to a broad range of infectious diseases (Choo, 1990). A recent survey of Aboriginal children in central Sydney revealed that 81 per cent had major ear problems with 23 per cent having hearing loss which would impair learning ability.

For these and other reasons, Aboriginal children are frequently irregular attenders at school. They also tend to have a high level of mobility between schools which further disrupts their learning.

The way ahead in Aboriginal education

Aboriginal students can still be described as being "at risk" in schools and educational institutions around Australia. This risk is generated when educators continue to ignore the distinctive values and needs of Aboriginal students, and as they refuse to involve Aboriginal parents in the planning and delivery of education to their children.

There are, however, some positive signs. There is an increasing number of schools which are achieving success in reversing the negative patterns and providing an education which is genuinely responsive to the needs of Aboriginal students. These schools are characterised by staff committed to meeting the social, emotional and educational needs of Aboriginal students. It usually begins with the principal and it is strengthened by a high level of support from Aboriginal families and educational networks.

Aboriginal involvement in schools

Despite the failure of the education provided for their children, and despite their own negative experiences, the majority of Aboriginal parents still value education as being essential for their children to achieve a better future. Many have a concept of what is a good education and are idealistic about schools.

Many are concerned that their children develop in "both ways". This involves developing a strong sense of Aboriginal identity at the same time as developing strong academic skills (Watts, 1976). They are concerned also to ensure that teachers are culturally responsive, and that they ensure that the values and language styles of Aboriginal children are reflected and endorsed in their classrooms (Hughes, 1988).

Aboriginal parents have struggled over the last twenty years to gain effective control over the education of their children, so that it better meets their needs. In 1975 the Aboriginal Consultative Group to the

Schools Commission presented a report which indicated that Aborigines wanted involvement in, and control of, their own education.

At the national level, the National Aboriginal Education Committee (NAEC) was a major agenda-setting body, establishing policy and practice and continually presenting Aboriginal viewpoints on education from 1977 to 1988. One of the major achievements of the NAEC was to launch the successful program for the training of 1,000 Aboriginal teachers by 1990.

At the present time there is no national group reflecting Aboriginal education needs. Aboriginal Consultative Committees in each state advise their respective education ministers on all aspects of Aboriginal education. Their work covers a wide field, as significant numbers of Aboriginal students are now enrolled in TAFE Colleges and universities as well as the majority of state primary and secondary schools. In many states the leadership of Aboriginal education planning is ostensibly in the hands of Aboriginal educators, but programs still have to function within the constraints of the system.

In 1989 the Commonwealth launched the National Aboriginal and Torres Strait Islander Education Policy. This very comprehensive policy, designed to bring about substantial improvements in Aboriginal education, was negotiated with governments in each state and territory. There was not the same level of consultation with Aboriginal education interest groups. Several Aboriginal groups have rejected the policy as not being representative of their concerns.

There have, however, been some successful outcomes from the policy. The most notable has been the formation of local action groups and parents' committees in schools with significant Aboriginal enrolments. Among the initiatives developed by these committees are after-hours homework centres, organised and supervised by parents.

Since the mid-1970s there have been increasing numbers of Aboriginal people employed in schools as teachers, aides and advisers. They have played a vital liaison role between their communities and the schools. The involvement of Aboriginal parents in the planning and teaching of Aboriginal Studies by some schools is another important advance.

In some areas, Aboriginal parents have taken the initiative to gain complete control of the education of their children. Yipirinya school at Alice Springs was begun because local parents despaired of their children gaining an effective education in the existing government and church schools in the town. Other Aboriginal communities, notably in Western Australia, have also started their own independent schools in recent times. At present there are approximately a dozen independent Aboriginal schools in the country.

There are variations on this theme. The Pitjantjatjara people are in the process of gaining management over education in their Central Desert homelands. The schools will continue to be funded and staffed by the state governments.

There are several government schools, such as Yirrkala in the Northern Territory, which have a majority of Aboriginal staff, including principals. They are beginning to reflect community concerns more closely in their curriculum and teaching strategies.

The challenge that faces all these groups is to develop schools which will better educate Aboriginal students. Just how this will be achieved is a matter of some debate.

One approach, practised by the Yirrkala school, is that there must be an integration of Aboriginal and Anglo knowledge and values into the one curriculum. They believe that it is possible to have "both ways" working together. They have already achieved this in the difficult area of mathematics curriculum.

An alternative view, represented currently in the Pitjantjatjara schools, maintains that integration is not feasible and that the two domains of Anglo and Aboriginal learning must be kept separate in all aspects of the children's experience.

Some of the most significant developments in Aboriginal education in recent years have come in the post-secondary area. There are now a range of institutions, many of which are Aboriginal controlled, which seek to meet the educational needs of mature-age Aboriginal students, providing specialised instruction ranging from para-professional training to short-term preparatory courses for university entry. Among these are Tranby College in Sydney and the Aboriginal Community College in Adelaide.

Batchelor College in the Northern Territory is an independent Aboriginal TAFE institution which offers teacher training and a range of other specialised courses such as media, health and management.

Many universities are now offering specific training opportunities in education, health, law and other professional areas. The University of South Australia, Edith Cowan University (Mt Lawley) and Monash have the longest history of dedicated Aboriginal courses.

There are increased numbers of Aboriginal children going on to matriculation. In 1992 there were 5,105 Aboriginal students enrolled in universities. The ultimate measure of success will be if the quality of education for all Aboriginal students is seen to improve.

References

Attwood, B. (1989). *The Making of the Aborigines*. Sydney: Allen & Unwin.

Binnion, J. (1975). *Secondary Education for Aborigines*. Adelaide: Education Department.

Bonwick, J. (1862). *Rides Out and About, Rambles of an Australian School Inspector*. London: Religious Tract Society.

Broome, R. (1982). *Aboriginal Australians*. Sydney: George Allen & Unwin.

Choo, C. (1990). *Aboriginal Child Poverty*. Melbourne: Brotherhood of St Laurence.

Christie, M. (1985). *Aboriginal Perspectives on Experience and Learning: The Role of Language in Aboriginal Education*. Geelong: Deakin University Press.

Coombs, H., Brandl, M. and Snowden, W. (1983). *A Certain Heritage*. Canberra: CRES, Australian National University.

Duncan, P. (1987). "A teacher's life". In *Fighters and Singers*, edited by I. White et al., Sydney: Allen & Unwin.

Eades, D. (1985). "You gotta know how to talk: information seeking in SE Queensland Aboriginal society". In *Cross Cultural Encounters: Communication and Miscommunication*, edited by J. Pride. Melbourne: River Seine.

Eckermann, A., Watts, B. and Dixon, P. (1984). *From Here to There*. Canberra: Department of Aboriginal Affairs.

Groome, H. (1988). *Relationships Between Aboriginal Parents and Schools*. Adelaide: University of South Australia.

Hamilton, A. (1981). *Nature and Nurture*. Canberra: Australian Institute of Aboriginal Studies.

Harris, S. (1984). *Culture and Learning; Tradition and Education in Northeast Arnhem Land*. Canberra: Australian Institute of Aboriginal Studies.

Hughes, P. (1981). *Report of the Aboriginal Education Policy Task Force*. Canberra: Department of Employment, Education and Training.

Ilyatjari, Nganyintja (1991). "Traditional Aboriginal learning: how I learned as a Pitjantjatjara child", *The Aboriginal Child at School*, vol. 19, no. 1, February/March.

Malin, M. (1990). "The visibility and invisibility of the Aboriginal child in an urban classroom". *Australian Journal of Education*, vol. 34, no. 3.

Mattingley, C. and Hampton, K. (1988). *Survival in Our Own Land, Aboriginal Experiences in South Australia Since 1836*. Adelaide: Wakefield Press.

McConnochie, K. (1981). "White tests, black children: Aborigines, psychologists and education". In *Aborigines and Schooling*, edited by Menary. Underdale, SA (UniSA): Texts in Humanities.

Mulvaney, D. (1989). *Encounters in Place*. St Lucia: University of Queensland Press.

Nurcombe, B. (1976). *Children of the Dispossessed*. Hawaii: East-West Centre, University of Hawaii.

Pierson, J. (1977). "Voluntary organisations and Australian urban adaptions in Adelaide". *Oceania*, vol. XLVIII, no. 1, September.

Radford, A. et al. (1990). *Taking Control* (Monograph number 7 of the Department of Primary Health Care, Flinders University, Adelaide). Adelaide: Flinders University.

Read, J. (1982). *The Stolen Generations: The Removal of Aboriginal Children in New South Wales, 1883 to 1969* (Occasional paper number 1). Sydney: NSW Ministry of Aboriginal Affairs.

Reynolds, H. (1989). *Dispossession, Black Australians and White Invaders*. Sydney: Allen & Unwin.

Rowley, C. (1972). *The Destruction of Aboriginal Society*. Ringwood: Penguin.

House of Representatives Select Committee (1985). *Aboriginal Education*. Canberra: AGPS.

Tannock, P. and Punch, K. (1975). *A Report on the Equal Status of Aboriginal Children in Western Australia*. Perth: University of Western Australia.

Teasdale, G. and Whitelaw, A. (1981). *The Early Childhood Education of Aboriginal Australians*. Melbourne: ACER.

Watson, M. (1982). *Black Reflections*. Adelaide: Wattle Park Teachers' Centre.

Watts, B. (1981). *Aboriginal Futures*. Brisbane: Schonell Education Research Centre.

Chapter 10

Health: A Holistic Approach

Jenny Burden

Introduction

In 1986 the Better Health Commission stated that good health is dependent upon:

> a variety of material and non material factors: adequate shelter, suitable nutrition, companionship, income and a healthy environment. [Saggers and Gray 1991a: 82].

To this can be added the many prerequisites for good psychosocial adjustment. These include a firm sense of individual identity and group belonging; a sense of security, purpose, personal involvement, satisfaction and achievement; the knowledge and skills to allow an individual to function effectively in society; the freedom to make choices of benefit to self and others; as well as a sense of control over important aspects of one's life. These conditions were, according to Boyden (1987), amply provided for in hunter-gatherer societies, such as those that occupied pre-colonial Australia.

However, in Australia, as the lives and lifestyles of Aboriginal people were radically altered by encroaching Europeans, very few — if any — of the conditions necessary for the maintenance of physical and psychological health survived intact. Not surprisingly, Aboriginal health began to deteriorate, until today the health status of Aboriginals throughout Australia is a cause for grave concern.

Aboriginal health today

> Aborigines have the worst health status of any identifiable group in Australia: they carry a burden of poor health and mortality far in excess of that expected from the proportion they comprise of the total Australian population. [National Aboriginal Health Strategy Working Party, 1989: 7]

Throughout Australia, for almost all disease categories, rates for Aborigines are worse than for other Australians: death rates are up to four times higher and life expectancy is up to twenty-one years less (Thomson, 1991: 37). In some areas of Australia — for instance, in the arid desert country around Kalgoorlie in Western Australia — the general health of Aboriginal people has been estimated to be ten times worse than that of other Australians (Western Australian Health Department, 1992).

In many instances, the health status of Aboriginal people in rural and remote areas of Australia is comparable to that of many Third World countries. However, while the people of the Third World countries are, in the main, the victims of the so called "diseases of poverty" (acute infectious diseases, malnutrition, parasitic diseases), the irony of the Aboriginal population is that they suffer not only the "diseases of poverty" but also the "diseases of affluence": the degenerative "lifestyle" diseases characteristic of developed countries. These include heart disease, lung disease, hypertension, cancer and diabetes. Aboriginal people throughout Australia carry a double burden of disease.

Over the last twenty-five years, spiralling death rates from these lifestyle diseases among young to middle-aged Aboriginal adults have offset the improvement that has occurred in infant mortality and child health in the same period. A recent Western Australian report shows that diseases of the circulatory system are now the leading cause of death, a trend that is not confined to Western Australia but has also been noted in other states and territories. One very disturbing aspect of this increase in diseases of the circulatory system is that among young to middle-aged Aboriginal adults, deaths from this cause occur at ten to twenty times the expected rates for other Australians (Western Australian Health Department, 1992: 61).

While it is the lifestyle diseases which, in the main, affect disproportionate numbers of the adult Aboriginal population, it is the acute infectious diseases that inflict major illness and suffering on Aboriginal infants and young children. Among this group, preventable diseases, such as gastroenteritis and acute respiratory disease, are serious cause for concern, as is the high rate of ear disease which leaves a significant proportion of Aborigines with a marked hearing deficit.

Many possible explanations have been advanced by researchers in the field to account for the plight of Aboriginal people in relation to health status. Factors such as the physical and psychological effect of dispossession, poverty, high levels of unemployment, inadequate housing, unsatisfactory sanitation and hygiene, alcohol abuse, malnutrition and faulty diet, as well as lack of appropriate medical services, have all been implicated as causative or contributory factors.

While it is generally acknowledged that there are many causes for the high morbidity and mortality rates within the Aboriginal population, researchers differ in the relative importance they attach to each of these causes (Saggers and Gray, 1991a: 17). The argument presented in this chapter seeks to draw attention to the fact that, as these factors rarely (if ever) occur in isolation, it is their cumulative and interactive effects that have to be considered.

Aboriginal health prior to colonisation

In order to understand the complex nature of Aboriginal health problems today, it is essential that an historical perspective be taken and that the contemporary pattern of ill health should be analysed within the context of the lifestyle changes that have occurred for Aboriginal people throughout Australia since 1788.

While there is scant information recorded regarding the health of Aboriginal people with little or no alien contact, all the indices are that their health prior to European invasion was good. Reports from early European explorers and settlers often stated that, when first encountered, Aboriginal people appeared to be in good health and free from disease.

This view of pre-contact health status is supported by contemporary evidence (Lee and De Vore, 1968) which suggests that traditional hunter-gatherer societies throughout the world provided for their members' lifestyles which, prior to European contact, "were ... enviable in terms of health, nutrition and leisure" (Saggers and Gray 1991a: 19). Within such societies:

> the existence of an effective psychological support network, a certain amount of creative behaviour and situations which promote a sense of personal involvement ... are (also believed to have been) conducive to human health and well being. [Boyden, 1987: 40]

There is no evidence to suggest that the hunter-gatherer societies within Australia, prior to 1788, in any way departed from these generalisations.

For pre-contact Aboriginal people, daily life was lived within small, close-knit groups of kin whose size varied according to the availability of water and other essential resources. Generally, these small kin-based groups followed a seasonal pattern of movement within a known and defined territory, to which they had deep spiritual ties. Periodically they would congregate in larger numbers for ceremonial purposes or when a seasonal abundance of some food source drew them to a particular site.

Kinship was the organising principle around which social life revolved and prescribed each person's relationships and responsibilities to others within the local group and the larger language group of which it was a part. These social responsibilities and obligations were inculcated from childhood and "the individual was much aware of his or her responsibilities to the community" (Boyden, 1987: 73).

From a psychological perspective, the social links between the people within the larger language group were of significance, for they not only ensured that people lived their lives within a known and "expectable" social environment, but also "allowed for greater social harmony at times of congregation and for interdependence between groups during periods of scarcity" (Morice, 1978: 25). In addition,

> the ease with which individuals could be accepted into other groups, by virtue of the ... (prescribed) ... relationships, enabled the resolution of conflict and tension by fission to occur [Morice, 1978: 75].

When serious tensions or conflicts arose within a group, it was possible for members to leave their local group temporarily and join a neighbouring group. As Morice (1978) and others have pointed out, this mitigated against the deleterious effect of prolonged stress which is so often a concomitant of unresolved interpersonal conflict and tension.

For Aboriginal children:

> psychological development was attuned to both the physical and social environment. The infant Aborigine was reared in an atmosphere which stressed physical contact and immediate gratification. Throughout childhood years permissiveness was the rule, so that when adolescence was entered, the average Aborigine could have been expected to have developed a sense of basic trust, autonomy, initiative and an absence of inferiority. The stage of adolescence was marked by a series of ... rites of passage, through which the young person was prepared for, and accepted into, the spiritual and secular life of the tribe. [Morice, 1978: 25]

This formalised process of identity formation provided the basis for the development of a strong sense of individual identity and group belonging (Morice, 1978).

In relation to physical well-being, the hunter-gatherer lifestyle dictated frequent exercise which minimised the risk of obesity and associated health problems. In addition, the environment provided a wide range of naturally occurring plants and a great diversity of animal life which allowed for a well-balanced, nutritious diet of protein and plant foods, high in fibre and low in salt, sugar and fat.

The actual composition of the pre-contact diet was, of course, dictated by regional and seasonal variations in the availability of food. In coastal and riverine areas, fish and shell fish provided a dietary addition not available in the inland areas of Australia, and larger, more permanent settlements were possible. Within the most arid regions of Australia, such as Ooldea on the Transcontinental line and the Western Desert region of (Western Australia), the range and variety of food was more limited than in more fertile regions and the population was, of necessity, more widely dispersed across the country. However, even in these harsh and arid environments there were still many different varieties of plant and animal food available to provide a nutritionally adequate diet.

In 1941, the anthropologists Ronald and Catherine Berndt (1988) recorded some indigenous foods which could be easily obtained in the spinifex area immediately around the Ooldea Soak and Mission Station. The list included eighteen varieties of mammals and marsupials, nineteen birds, eleven reptiles, eight insects, six water roots, seventeen varieties of seeds, three vegetables, ten fruits and berries, four other plants and fungi, as well as a variety of eggs. Berndt and Berndt (1988) considered this a very conservative list, with many varieties of plants and animals not recorded.

Similarly, in the Western Desert region, Gould (1980) recorded

a minimum number of 37 staple plant species and 48 animal species ... (and) ... reported that even in times of extreme drought, the people were assured of a regular, if sometimes monotonous, diet. (Saggers & Gray, 1991a: 28, 41)

As is typical of hunting and gathering communities which follow a more or less nomadic lifestyle, most Aboriginal groups were spread sparsely over the continent. This mitigated against the spread of disease. Many contagious and infectious diseases cannot take hold in a population as sparsely spread and relatively isolated with defined group territory, as was the case with pre-contact Aboriginal society. Hygiene was not a problem.

Diseases indigenous to Aboriginal people appear to have been few. Dental disease was relatively rare and, according to Abbie (1976: 75–77), smallpox, influenza, measles, whooping cough, tuberculosis, leprosy and syphilis were unknown. The common cold, yaws and some skin diseases were probably endemic. Trachoma may also have been present.

This pre-contact situation is in sharp contrast to the situation which developed after the arrival of the First Fleet.

Aboriginal health after colonisation

From the beginning of European occupation, Aboriginal people have been subjected to pressures which have had disastrous consequences with respect to their health and also led to a decimation of the population. Many groups became extinct. The economic historian and demographer, Noel Butlin, in 1983 estimated a 1788 pre-contact population of over a million people, which had been reduced to 150,000 by 1850.

This drastic population decrease resulted, in large part, from the devastating effect of introduced diseases to which the Aboriginal population had no immunity and which, in epidemic proportions, began their sweep when smallpox ravaged the Aboriginal population around Sydney Cove in 1789.

> Watkin Tench gave the first account of a smallpox outbreak in 1788. He recorded that boat parties exploring the foreshores found the bodies of "Indians" (meaning the Aboriginals) in many of the coves and inlets of the harbour. Pustules, like those caused by smallpox, were spread thickly on their bodies. Tench could not understand how a disease, to which the natives seemed strangers, could have been introduced and spread so quickly. [He] ... did not realise that the disease had been introduced by the settlers themselves. Many of them were carriers and although they did not develop the disease themselves, they had spread it among the Aboriginals. [McEwan, 1979: 66]

Disease spread ahead of European settlement, so that Sturt, on his riverine journeyings in 1828, commented on the piles of bones seen and the evidence of pox-marked faces as testament to the fearful toll taken on Aboriginal communities (Butlin, 1983). The evidence of venereal diseases was not so easy to recognise, but its scourge was already wreaking silent havoc. Other infectious diseases, such as measles, tuberculosis and influenza, also ravaged the Aboriginal population.

Violence was another potent factor responsible for population reduction but, as Reynolds (1982) has pointed out, its importance has been seriously underplayed in official accounts of the history of settlement.

Punitive expeditions of Europeans formed genocidal bands, moving along the ever-widening frontier in bloody retribution for perceived villainies and imagined wrongs. Aboriginal resistance in defence of land, lifestyle and society was seen by authorities and settlers alike as deviant hostility, to be put down with the strongest possible force. Systematic killings took place, sometimes under military leadership, with self-righteous justification the answer to any qualms of conscience from more humane members of the wider public. *Settler justice* ruled the frontier.

The death toll resulting from this conflict has been estimated by Reynolds (1982) to have been at least 20,000 with massacres continuing well into this century. The *Bulletin*, in 1880, reported on the situation in Queensland:

> The blacks have been murdered by thousands ... there is ... wholesale massacre of human beings; a relentless violation of women. [I have] seen the brains of an infant dashed out against a tree after the mother had been murdered. This is not a fiction but the statement of one who, not three years ago, saw in Queensland scrub the sunburned corpses of men and women and children who had been murdered by officers of "justice" and left for the crows. [*Bulletin*, 1880, cited in Pollard, 1988: 24]

The rapid population decline which resulted from disease and violence had a dramatic effect on the ability of Aboriginal groups to maintain themselves as social entities. With the death by violence of many adult males and the loss of countless numbers of people through disease, Aboriginal societies were shattered. These factors, in conjunction with the forced dispossession from homelands, dealt a fatal blow to Aboriginal life as it had been prior to 1788.

Dispossessed from their land, the dispirited and disoriented remnants of broken tribes were forced into unfamiliar and often alien territory. Many were relocated on missions and reserves. Some lived as fringe dwellers on the outskirts of European towns, newly sprung up on traditional land, or worked on sheep and cattle stations in order to remain close to their own land. Most Aboriginal people lived in squalid conditions, far removed from their traditional lifestyle.

On the Eastern seaboard and in other areas of European occupation, the once-vibrant hunter-gatherer societies were reduced to little more than collections of sick, impoverished and undernourished mendicants, forced to eke out an existence on the fringes of European settlement, cut off from their country, their sacred sites and their religion. The essence of their life had been taken from them.

For those forced to live on missions and reserves, likened by many to prisons or reformatories (Stanner, 1979; Nathan and Japanangka, 1983), the experience was one of almost total loss of freedom. They were virtual prisoners, totally at the mercy of whichever local or official government policy happened to be in place at the time.

In many instances, as well as experiencing the confusion, grief and trauma resulting from loss of country and kin, Aborigines were forced to live together, under mission or reserve control, with people from totally different language groups. They thus lost not only their land and their freedom, but had to endure the stress of discord and violence frequently generated in such situations. The recent unrest at Aurukun in far North Queensland is a classic example of this.

In all areas of their lives, Aboriginal people lost the right to self-determination and became a subjugated people. Not even their family life was safe, as children of mixed ancestry were forcibly removed from their mothers and reared in isolation from their kin. The majority of these children were placed in institutions, with the intent of training them to become domestic servants or farm workers in the non-Aboriginal community. Many never saw their parents again. Others did so, but only after years of heartbreaking searching. This policy, which was relentlessly pursued until twenty-five years ago, left a significant proportion of young Aboriginal people with a severe emotional handicap and a debilitating identity crisis.

The psychological trauma which accompanied the disruption of Aboriginal family, social and cultural life was frequently accompanied by a deep sense of despair. This led to feelings of hopelessness, powerlessness and helplessness — of life empty of meaning and purpose — and resulted in widespread apathy among the Aboriginal population. All too often, escape into alcoholic oblivion became a panacea for the psychological pain experienced by vast numbers of Aboriginal people. It remains so for many to this day.

Physical as well as psychological well-being suffered. Cut off from natural food sources, Aboriginal people were forced to exist on meagre and nutritionally inadequate rations of tea, flour and sugar, with the occasional addition of meat.

In some instances, the people living on missions or reserves in the Northern Territory were subjected to the ultimate indignity of having their daily food provided for them through communal kitchens, with the menus dictated by the white authority. This mass feeding arrangement was bitterly resented, for it removed from the parent generation one of their primary and few remaining responsibilities: the provision and preparation of food for themselves and their children.

Those living on cattle stations fared no better. The adult able-bodied men were expected to work as stockmen and the women as domestic servants, but were not necessarily paid until the 1960s. Many commentators have drawn attention to the plight of *station blacks* in the earlier part of this century. Markus says of the situation in the 1920s and 1930s that many Aboriginal people were "left to starve or to live their lives undernourished" (Markus, 1990: 63).

Most of the station owners were not concerned with the condition of "their" camp blacks, or even with those who had previously been employed, but were now too old or sick to work:

> generally the only food they received ... [was] the offal of the beasts on killing day. [Markus 1990: 63]

For these people there was nothing to be gained by moving to government ration depots, as the Aboriginal people living at such depots were also undernourished and emaciated.

In the 1930s, Dr Charles Duguid found a similar situation on cattle stations around Alice Springs.

> The old men and women I saw were scraggy specimens existing on government rations. Not more than 5 lbs of flour, 1 lb of sugar and 1/4 lb of tea per week.

He described this as "a ludicrous diet for people who, in tribal days, lived largely on raw natural foods" (Duguid, 1972: 101), and reported that the ration for the Aboriginal working men was grossly inadequate, with insufficient calories for the work they had to do. The women and children were even worse off and many older people simply starved to death.

In 1945, Ronald and Catherine Berndt (1987: 72) found no improvement in the Northern Territory. At Wave Hill, one of the Vestey stations, they reported that each working man and woman was given, three times daily,

> a slice of dry bread, one piece of usually cooked meat (sometimes in the form of a bone), and a dipper of tea.

From time to time a beast was killed but the Aborigines received only bones and offal. The situation at Birrundudu outstation was even worse and Aboriginal people "faced circumstances of near starvation" (Berndt and Berndt, 1987: 217). Despite serious health problems among the resident Aboriginal population at Birrundudu, medical treatment was only available if it was requested, and usually such requests were refused.

In 1974 Frank Stevens published a similar account of living conditions on cattle stations in the Northern Territory.

> while the masters at some stations sat down to dine in virtual baronial splendour, being waited upon by up to as many six highly trained domestics, occasionally decked out in monogrammed aprons and caps, the husbands and children of the maids sat in the dust picking at the offal from their disgusting pottage, and eventually crawling into "dog kennel-like" structures to sleep. [Stevens, 1974: 108]

Other factors, besides diet, also took their toll under the new conditions in which Aboriginal people were forced to live. One of these was housing. From the beginning of European settlement and the forced removal of Aboriginal people from their homelands, housing has been a sadly neglected area. In 1976 the Senate Select Committee on Aborigines and Torres Strait Islanders (SSCATSI) reported that:

> visits to local communities undertaken during four years of inquiry impressed on the committee time and again the fact that housing conditions for Aboriginal families are appalling ... [with] an estimated minimum of 4,455 Aboriginal families throughout Australia ... living in humpies, shacks, abandoned car bodies, and other makeshift shelter and ... thus in dire need of adequate accommodation ... (with) an even larger number of families living in substandard and overcrowded accommodation. [SSCATSI, 1976: 169]

In such situations, with high-density sedentary populations living in unsatisfactory accommodation, sanitation and hygiene became a major problem. A population which was once protected against infectious and other diseases (particularly illnesses associated with contaminated water supply and unsatisfactory disposal of waste) by its low density and semi-nomadic lifestyle became susceptible to such diseases in the settlement environment.

> The change from small, semi-nomadic communities into large aggregates of people ... led to a rapid increase of ... communicable diseases. [Saggers & Gray, 1991b: 385]

From this summary of historical events it can be seen that the enforced change from a hunter-gatherer way of life to an impoverished sedentary existence had disastrous consequences for both the physical and psychological health and well-being of Aboriginal people.

In particular, the dramatic change in diet and nutrition and the effects this had on health cannot be stressed too strongly. As Saggers and Gray (1991a: 39) point out, the:

> link between poor nutrition and ill health is now well known ... Normal growth and development and resistance to disease depend on adequate nutrition, but many Aborigines have been deprived of healthy food and their children have grown up ... where food is scarce and not particularly nutritious.

With inadequate nutrition and living under appallingly unhygienic and overcrowded conditions, the deterioration in health was inevitable. Under such conditions, Aboriginal people became susceptible to all manner of illness to which they had not previously been vulnerable.

Medical services

Despite the serious deterioration in health which occurred from 1788 onwards, very little real attempt was made to provide comprehensive medical services to the Aboriginal population. Up until the 1960s, the special provisions for Aboriginal health were primarily directed at protecting the white Australian population from the ravages of infectious disease sweeping through the Aboriginal population (Saggers and Gray, 1991b), with responsibility for such "health care" in the hands of the police or government officials.

Nathan and Japanangka (1983) report that the enforced treatment programs, hospital admissions and house searches and the use of violence by the police "protectors" in carrying out their caretaker role have left a deep impression on Aboriginal people. As late as the 1980s, many recalled how

> the police used to force people into hospital ... for ... checkups ... If people left the hospital, they'd get the police onto it. They'd be under police guard all the time. [Nathan and Japanangka, 1983: 29]

The situation improved only marginally when, more recently, government doctors took over the role of "protector". In this role, doctors had

> enormous power over their wards ... and many Aboriginal people ... experienced feelings of intimidation and humiliation in a health care setting. [Mobbs, 1991: 315]

In the light of these highly adverse experiences, it is little wonder that many Aboriginal people have, over the years, shown a marked reluctance to make use of the health services that were available in rural areas. In bigger towns and cities, where mainstream health services were, in theory, available to everyone, a similar reluctance was the norm. In these situations, the health services were unacceptable because of the impersonal nature of the clinic or hospital setting and the presence of an exclusively non-Aboriginal nursing and medical staff, who were perceived by Aboriginal people to be either indifferent to their plight or demonstrably racist in their attitudes. This under-utilisation of available health services often exacerbated health problems, as all too often minor ailments which were left untreated developed into serious illnesses.

In the late 1960s and early 1970s, recognition was finally given to the fact that Aboriginal health needs warranted special attention, when it was found that Aboriginal mortality and morbidity rates were significantly higher than for non-Aborigines. Not only was Aboriginal health status found to be significantly worse than that of non-Aborigines, it was also realised that Aboriginal health showed "little or no improvement over that of the last century" (Reid and Lupton, 1991: 23).

The specific health strategies introduced in the late 1960s and early 1970s (targeted in particular at maternal and infant health problems) were, however, based on the culturally alien and inappropriate Western biomedical model of health care. As Nathan and Japanangka (1983) have pointed out, the authorities at the time did not question the appropriateness of mainstream services in relation to Aboriginal health care and acted upon the assumption that Western medicine had all the knowledge and technical skills necessary to rectify Aboriginal health problems. All that was needed, it was believed, was an injection of funds to provide a proper system of health care, with "highly qualified practitioners, clinical settings and medical equipment and systematic research" (Nathan and Japanangka, 1983: 2). In the event, however, apart from achieving an initial dramatic decline in infant mortality rates, these special provisions failed to have an impact on Aboriginal health and "provided little more than 'bandaid' curative services" (NAHSWP, 1989: 59).

One of the major deficiencies with the biomedical model of health care is that it is primarily interested in the recognition of treatment of disease and defines health negatively, as an absence of infirmity or disease. It has been criticised, generally, for its mechanistic, curative approach and for focusing too narrowly on biological malfunction as a cause of illness while paying too little attention to the psychological, social and environmental factors which affect health in any population, not just the Aboriginal population (Powles, 1979; Sobel, 1979; Taylor, 1986).

Aboriginal conceptions of health are radically different from this biomedical perspective. Health, to Aboriginal people, is a much broader concept and relates not simply to "the physical well-being of the individual ... but [encompasses] the social, emotional, and cultural well-being of the whole community ... a whole-of-life view" [NAHSWP, 1989: X]. Such a perspective places health and well-being within a wider context that relates to:

> all aspects of their life including control over their physical environment ... dignity ... community self esteem ... and justice. It is not merely a matter of the provision of doctors, hospitals, medicines or the absence of disease and incapacity. [NAHSWP, 1989: ix]

Western medicine has not only failed to come to grips with the conceptual gulf which exists between its own philosophy and Aboriginal traditional beliefs with respect to health matters, but has also failed to address the complex web of factors which affect Aboriginal health status.

Psychosocial factors and health

Among the many factors responsible for the high rate of morbidity and mortality in the Aboriginal population today, the psychosocial factors already discussed are of particular importance. These include the trauma and social dislocation associated with loss of land, the powerlessness associated with loss of autonomy, the dependency which has accompanied institutionalisation and the inertia and "general anomie that ... [has] so widely characterised Aboriginal life during their association with us" (Stanner, 1979: 235). The importance of such psychological stress factors in the aetiology of disease is now widely acknowledged (Gatchel et al., 1989; Boyden, 1987; Taylor, 1986).

In addition to these psychological factors, the depressed socioeconomic status of most Aboriginal people is also a major factor in relation to poor health status. As Franklin and White (1991: 31) point out, in the 1990s the majority of Aborigines "living in an otherwise affluent Australia are still trapped in a vicious cycle of poverty and powerlessness from which they feel they can never hope to escape".

This level of poverty has important implications for health, as it frequently acts as a barrier to achieving adequate nutritional status. It is not only the case that many Aboriginal children are failing to thrive but, as Harrison (1991) has shown, unsatisfactory nutritional status leaves many Aboriginal young at increased risk of infectious and other illnesses through lowered resistance. It is also believed that childhood malnutrition can predispose to obesity in adulthood.

For Aboriginal adults, nutritional status is also an important factor in relation to health. A diet high in refined carbohydrates (sugar, flour and canned drinks), with an absence of fresh fruit and vegetables and high in fat and salt, is believed to be a contributing factor in relation to obesity, hypertension, diabetes and cardiovascular disease, all of which are major causes of illness and death among adult Aborigines.

Environmental living conditions and health

Similarly, environmental living conditions continue to play a significant role in Aboriginal ill-health. A majority of Aboriginal people throughout Australia continue to live under conditions that are wholly unsatisfactory, with inadequate water and electricity supplies, poor sanitation and sewerage and overcrowded and inappropriate housing.

This situation persists today despite the fact that in 1979 the House of Representatives Standing Committee on Aboriginal Affairs gave high priority to the environmental health conditions, especially a safe water supply. Without basic facilities which other Australians take for granted — adequate housing, without facilities for bathing, washing clothes, blankets and eating utensils — it is virtually impossible for any sedentary population to remain healthy. Aboriginal people are no exception.

For remote communities, the situation is particularly bad, especially in relation to water supplies and related ablution and sanitation facilities. In some instances the problem lies not simply with the adequacy of good quality water supplies, but rather with the availability of any water at all, regardless of quality. In situations such as these, washing and bathing facilities cannot be a reality and hygiene remains a problem (Saggers and Gray, 1991a).

In communities where a water supply and other essential services have been provided, it is often the case that the residents are little better off than those without such facilities. Too often the facilities provided are simply not appropriate. All too frequently, the residents in these remote communities do not understand the operating principles of the technologically sophisticated water reticulation and sewerage systems that have been provided and, once broken, these facilities remain out of action until outside technical assistance can be brought in to replace or repair them (NAHSWP, 1989). In the meantime, the blocked and often overflowing flush toilet, the broken or crushed plastic or polythene water or drain pipe and the dripping tap which creates pools of stagnant and fouled water constitute a serious health hazard.

Such environmental contamination and lack of facilities for personal hygiene have important implications in the aetiology of many of the infectious diseases which afflict Aborigines. Gastrointestinal diseases, for instance, occur with a much higher frequency among Aboriginal people than among non-Aboriginal people.

The overwhelming reason for the seriousness of these gastrointestinal diseases in Aborigines is the inferior standards of housing, hygiene and nutrition which they experience since most of these diseases are infections which are spread in overcrowded, unhygienic and contaminated conditions. [NAHSWP, 1989: Appendix 1]

The significance of environmental living conditions in relation to illness has been confirmed by a recent study of ten Aboriginal communities in the Northern Territory (Munoz et al., 1992). This study provides evidence that, in relation to health status, the important variables are housing, water supplies, sanitation, electric power and levels of literacy and hygiene. Those communities with poorly developed and maintained physical facilities had the highest hospital admission rates.

Other factors related to health status include unemployment and alcohol abuse. In the 1990s the level of employment among Aborigines remains low and a high percentage of the Aboriginal population continues to subsist on welfare payments. With a lack of meaningful activity to occupy their time, many adult Aboriginal people today continue to seek solace in alcohol or other substance abuse. Money which would otherwise be spent on food and other essentials for a family is all too often spent on alcohol. And so the poverty–illness cycle perpetuates itself.

But perhaps of even more concern is the role that alcohol plays in adult morbidity and mortality in the Aboriginal community. During the period 1974–88, for instance, nearly half of the town camp deaths in Alice Springs "were due to alcohol-related disease, accidents and murder" (Langton, 1990: 304).[1]

If significant improvement is to occur in the health status of Aboriginal people, it is essential that these underlying causes of Aboriginal ill-health be addressed and that a preventative, holistic — rather than a curative — approach be adopted. It is also imperative that medical authorities take cognisance of the Aboriginal perspective with respect to health and well-being and accept that in:

> contrast to the more focussed clinical and disease oriented approach of non-Aboriginal health professionals, Aboriginal people's collective concerns are to regain their land, to ensure that their children have tucker and to be able to undertake social obligations including ceremonial duties. Health business includes all of these as well as access to reasonable housing, freedom to have their babies "on the land" and having good water to drink.
> [SA Health Commission, 1993: 3]

As early as 1978, Hollows (1978) expressed the view that Aboriginal health problems would only be resolved when Aboriginal people regained control over their lives and their land. Waterford (1982), in similar vein, argued that the whole complex of ill-health could only be changed by Aborigines themselves and this would occur only when Aboriginal people were given control over the many factors which, from their perspective, determine health — the whole living environment.

Regaining control: Community-controlled health services

In the last thirty years the granting of land rights and the return of some Aboriginal groups to traditional homelands has gone part of the way towards meeting these objectives. At the same time, Aboriginal-initiated political action — starting with the Yirrkala bark petition in 1963, the Gurindji Walk-off from Wave Hill in the mid-1960s and the Tent Embassy in Canberra in 1972 — has brought about a situation where, today, Aboriginal people have a greater degree of control over their lives and destiny than at any time since 1788.

Aboriginal-controlled health services are an example of such political action. In 1971 the first Aboriginal community-controlled health service was established at Redfern. Other communities followed and in the ensuing years set up their own health services — in Fitzroy in 1973, Perth in 1974 and in Alice Springs, where the Central Australian Aboriginal Congress was established in 1974. As these community-controlled health services developed, attitudes began to change among Aboriginal people.

The Aboriginal-controlled health services are based on a broad, holistic concept of health which takes into account the wider social, economic and political issues affecting Aboriginal life and lifestyles. Throughout Australia, Aboriginal controlled health services — such as the Central Australian Aboriginal Congress — in addition to providing medical care, have sought to address the political, social, economic and environmental factors that underlie so much Aboriginal illness. Their aim is to improve the quality of life at both the individual and community level. Saggers and Gray (1991b) believe that the community development functions of these health services are probably as important as those of health care delivery.

By the end of the 1980s there were more than sixty Aboriginal-controlled health services in existence, with an additional ninety-one centres awaiting funding to establish their own health services. In 1990–91, following the recommendation of the National Aboriginal Health Strategy Working Party, the commonwealth government allocated $6.74 million to fund sixty-seven additional health projects. Some new health services were included among these projects.

The real strength of these alternative and culturally appropriate health services lies in the fact that they are community owned and community controlled — they are run *by* the local community *for* the community. The philosophy of community control on which Aboriginal health services are based is of singular importance. Aboriginal people believe that in order for improvement in health status to occur, "they must be able to control their own destiny and ... [assume] responsibility for their own decision making" (NAHSWP, 1989: XIII).

Community control gives Aboriginal people the opportunity to exercise such rights. Furthermore, it not only allows the local community to have control over the issues that directly affect their lives, but

> the mere fact that community control shuns dependence on non-Aboriginal systems is of benefit ... [for] it promotes responsibility and allows communities to be active participants. [NAHSWP, 1989: XVI]

Such active community participation is as vital an element today as it was in pre-contact Aboriginal society, where responsibility for health and well-being was shared by the community. Today, it allows Aboriginal communities to be involved not only in defining the health-related problems facing the communities and identifying their own solutions, but also in shaping the services to meet the specific health needs of their particular community.

These community-controlled health services, in conjunction with other Aboriginal-controlled organisations, such as land councils, community councils, legal services and housing associations, have demonstrated to Aborigines that, although they remain the poorest and most disadvantaged segment of the Australian population, "they are not completely powerless and can organise to improve the conditions under which they are forced to live" (Saggers and Gray, 1991b: 403). This has had the vital effect of raising Aboriginal self-esteem and of restoring to many a sense of control over important aspects of their lives.

One of the outstanding features of Aboriginal Health Services has been their acceptability to the Aboriginal population. This acceptability is due not only to the fact that these services are "owned" by the community they service, but also to the fact that most Aboriginal Health Services are staffed largely by Aboriginal people who are perceived as being more approachable. They not only know how to listen and talk to their Aboriginal patients but, because Aboriginal staff members are usually drawn from the local community, they are likely to have an understanding of the types of problems their patients are facing. While the doctors and some of the trained nursing staff working in Aboriginal Health Services are non-Aboriginal, they are nevertheless accepted because they are perceived as having an empathy with Aboriginal people and a genuine interest in their well-being.

Some of the larger health services, such as the Central Australian Aboriginal Congress, now provide a wide range of programs, including dental services as well as rehabilitation, welfare and public health programs. One recent innovative service has been the establishment of the Congress Alukura, a culturally appropriate birthing centre for Aboriginal women in Alice Springs.

Preventative health programs are a strong feature of Aboriginal Health Services, with specific programs directed at lifestyle factors including diet, exercise, smoking and alcohol use in an attempt to reduce the risk factors associated with obesity, diabetes, strokes, hypertension, heart disease, acute respiratory disease, sexually transmitted diseases and alcoholism. This particular aspect of Aboriginal Health Services is of crucial importance, as obesity and diabetes are major causes of illness in the adult Aboriginal population, as are diseases of the circulatory system.

Alcohol abuse is another area for grave concern, and many attempts have been made by Aboriginal people over the years to combat the problem. An increasing number of communities throughout Australia have taken matters into their own hands and now ban the use of alcohol within their boundaries. Drying out and rehabilitation centres are another means used to address the problem, but many programs have been hamstrung in the past by a lack of support from funding bodies (Langton, 1990).

One innovative Aboriginal approach which has recently been developed in Alice Springs through the actions of Congress and other

Aboriginal organisations is the Central Australian Aboriginal Alcohol Prevention Unit (CAAAPU). CAAAPU's aim is to raise community awareness with respect to the dangers of alcohol and to develop culturally appropriate Aboriginal-controlled rehabilitation and treatment centres.

Other Aboriginal health services have sought to address the range of problems arising from unhealthy living environments in an attempt to reduce the high rates of morbidity among Aboriginal infants and young children from illnesses such as gastroenteritis and pneumonia.

In the late 1980s, the Nganampa Health Council conducted a wide-ranging survey of public and environmentally based health issues in the Pitjantjatjara homelands in the north-west of South Australia. This project, the UPK (Uwankara Palyanku Kanyintaku), provides an excellent model for developing an approach to environmental and public health in remote Aboriginal communities. It not only provides guidelines with respect to healthy living practices and the health hardware necessary to achieve them but also highlights the need for Aboriginal communities to be given the opportunity to acquire the knowledge and skills to maintain healthy environments (Saggers and Gray, 1991a: 94).

The work being done by Aboriginal Health Services throughout Australia is of the utmost importance and has brought about a situation where more Aboriginal people now have access to culturally appropriate and acceptable health care services than at any time since white occupation began. However, many Aboriginal communities (especially in remote areas) are still without adequate and appropriate health care. Additional funding must be provided to allow Aboriginal communities throughout Australia to establish their own health services.

The National Aboriginal Health Strategy Working Party (1989), in recommending that all Aboriginal primary health care services be transferred to Aboriginal community control, recognises the critical importance of community participation and control and asserts the right of Aboriginal people to determine their own destiny in this and other aspects of their lives.

Improvements in health will not occur unless Aboriginal people throughout Australia are given the right and the responsibility to identify their own problems and to determine their own solutions. All governments — local, state/territory and commonwealth — must make this their priority.

Note

1. Alcohol was not a feature of traditional Aboriginal society. The introduction of alcohol to Aboriginal communities in Central Australia is a recent phenomenon and "there has not developed in the quarter of a century that it has been available, the kinds of inhibitions and social rules for consumption and drinking behaviour" (Langton, 1990: 302) that are characteristic of Western societies.

References

Abbie, A.A. (1976). *The Original Australians*. Sydney: Rigby.

—— (1941). *Survey of the Half-caste Problem in South Australia*. Proceedings of the Royal Geographical Society of Australasia, SA, vol. XLII.

Berndt, R.M. and C.H. (1988). *The World of the First Australians*. Canberra: Australian Studies Press.

Boyden, S. (1987). *Western Civilisation in Biological Perspective*. Oxford: Clarendon Press.

Branson, D., Kinnear, A. and Sumner, P. (eds) (1993). *South Australian Health Statistics Chartbook*. Supplement 4, "Aboriginal Health". Adelaide: South Australian Health Commission, Public and Environmental Health Service.

Butlin, N. (1983). *Our Original Aggression: Aboriginal Population in South Eastern Australia 1789–1856*. Sydney: Allen & Unwin.

Duguid, C. (1972). *Doctor and the Aborigines*. Adelaide: Rigby.

Franklin, M.A. and White, I. (1991). "The history of politics of Aboriginal health". In *The Health of Aboriginal Australians*, edited by J. Reid and P. Trompf. Sydney: Harcourt Brace Jovanovich.

Gatchel, R.J., Baum, A. and Krantz, D.S. (1989). *An Introduction to Health Psychology*. New York: Random House.

Gould, R.A. (1980). *Living Archaeology*. Cambridge: CUP.

Harrison, L. (1991). "Food, nutrition and growth in Aboriginal communities". In *The Health of Aboriginal Australians*, edited by J. Reid and P. Trompf. Sydney: Harcourt Brace Jovanovich.

Hollows, F.C. (1978). *Australian Aboriginal Eye Health — and What Must Be Done*. Submission to the House of Representatives Standing Committee on Aboriginal Affairs — Health problems of Aboriginals. *Hansard*: 3602-11.

Langton, M. (1990). "Too much sorry business." *The National Report of the Royal Commission into Deaths in Custody,* vol. 5, Appendix D [1].

Lee, R. and De Vore, I., (eds) (1968). *Man the Hunter*. Chicago: Aldine.

McEwan, M. (1979). *Great Australian Explorers: The Courageous Exploits of the Men who Challenged the New Land*. Sydney: Bay Books.

Markus, A. (1990). *Governing Savages*. Sydney: Allen & Unwin.

Mobbs, R. (1991). "In sickness and health: a socio-cultural context of Aboriginal well-being, illness and healing". In *The Health of Aboriginal*

Australians, edited by J. Reid and P. Trompf. Sydney: Harcourt Brace Jovanovich.

Morice, R. (1978). "Central Australian Aborigines, changes in lifestyle and the effect on health". *New Doctor*, no. 8, April.

Munoz, E., Powers, J.R. and Matthews, J.D. (1990). "Hospitalisation patterns in children from 10 Aboriginal communities in the Northern Territory". *Medical Journal of Australia*, vol. 156, no. 8.

Nathan, P. and Japanangka, D.L. (1983). *Health Business*. Melbourne: Heinemann Educational Australia.

National Aboriginal Health Strategy Working Party (1989). *A National Aboriginal Health Strategy.* Canberra: AGPS.

Pollard, D. (1988). *Give and Take: The Losing Partnership in Aboriginal Poverty*. Sydney: Hale and Iremonger.

Powles, J. (1979). "On the limitation of modern medicine". In *Ways of Healing*, edited by D.S. Sobel. New York: Harcourt Brace Jovanovich.

Reid, E.J. and Lupton, D. (1991). "Introduction". In *The Health of Aboriginal Australians*, edited by J. Reid and P. Trompf. Sydney: Harcourt Brace Jovanovich.

Reynolds, H. (1982). *The Other Side of the Frontier*. Ringwood: Penguin.

Saggers, S. and Gray, D. (1991a). *Aboriginal Health and Society*. Sydney: Allen & Unwin.

—— (1991b). "Policy and practice in Aboriginal health". In *The Health of Aboriginal Australians*, edited by J. Reid and P. Trompf. Sydney: Harcourt Brace Jovanovich.

Senate Select Committee on Aboriginal and Torres Strait Islanders (1976). *The Environmental Conditions of Aboriginal and Torres Strait Islanders and the Preservation of the Sacred Sites*. Canberra: AGPS.

Sobel, D.S. (1979), "Introduction". In *Ways of Healing*, edited by D.S. Sobel. New York: Harcourt Brace Jovanovich.

Stanner, W.E.H. (1979). *White Man Got No Dreaming*. Canberra: ANU Press.

Stevens, F. (1974). *Aborigines in the Northern Territory Cattle Industry.* Canberra: ANU Press.

Taylor, S.E. (1986). *Health Psychology*. New York: Random House.

Thomson, N. (1990). "A review of Aboriginal health issues." In *The Health of Aboriginal Australians*, edited by J. Reid and P. Trompf. Sydney: Harcourt Brace Jovanovich.

Western Australian Health Department (1992). *Mortality in Western Australia 1983–1989.*

Chapter 11

Economics: Independence or Welfare

Colin Bourke

Background

Most people think of the economy as being involved with money, finance, banking, the stock exchange and business. Primary industry, mining and manufacturing are also considered to be integral to any discussion of the economy. Economies do not have to be so involved. Some societies developed economies which were much more easily understood, even though they had other complexities such as kinship obligations as their base.

The word "economy" is derived from two Greek words: *oikos* is a house or household, while *nomos* is rule, law or custom. When combined as *oikonomos*, they indicate the management of a house or household. An *oikonomos*, then, is the person involved — the manager. So, originally, economics meant the management of the resources of a household. It therefore involved the gathering, production, distribution, sharing and consuming of goods, products and services for the well-being of the household's members.

Today, economics has evolved into an academic discipline which is crucial to industry, finance and government. The modern concept of economics can be traced back to Adam Smith, who in 1776 published *An Enquiry into the Nature and Causes of the Wealth of Nations*. In this classic work, Smith was as interested in the political as he was in the economic aspects of society.

Economics is not a separate entity. It involves large, complex social and community realities, including personal relationships and expectations. It covers the processes of production, distribution, exchange and consumption and involves land, labour and capital.

Prior to 1788, Aboriginal people in Australia had a different economic system from that of the people who were to colonise Australia. Aborigines owned no valuable treasures that appealed to Europeans. Their economic life was based on sharing and co-operation. There were no individuals who possessed great wealth or land in European terms.

In most cases the people moved around their ancestral lands as hunters and gatherers, so many possessions would have been a hindrance. Their movements around their country were not haphazard, but had a purpose. They were part of Aboriginal mastery over the resources of the land.

Due to environmental conditions and cultural practices, there was great diversity in the economic activities of Aboriginal people. The contrast in the economic life between the Pintubi of the Simpson Desert and the Kerrup-Jmara of the Lake Condah region in Victoria would have been sharper than the contrast between China and Australia today.

The various Aboriginal groups utilised the edible plants of their lands, worked their mines, developed the use of drugs and medicines, developed new manufacturing techniques and a large range of resources which ranged from raw materials for cosmetics and paints to hidden supplies of water.

As Professor Geoffrey Blainey (1975: v–vi) has written:

> In one sense Aborigines resembled today's nations of Europe rather than Asia for the growth of their population was slow and their material standard of living was relatively high. Indeed, if an Aborigine in the 17th Century had been captured as a curiosity and taken in a Dutch ship to Europe, and if he had travelled all the way from Scotland to the Caucasus and had seen how the average European struggled to make a living, he might have said to himself that he had seen the third world and all its poverty and hardship.

Fire and smoke

The Aboriginal economy has been described as a fire economy. Fire was central to their way of life, affecting nearly every activity (Blainey, 1975: 71). When Captain Cook sailed north up the Pacific Coast of Australia, he and his crew saw fires burning in the bush on most days. When the British arrived in 1788, they noticed Aborigines carrying lighted sticks. When they eventually ventured inland, they were surprised to find large tracts of blackened country.

Although firesticks were carried, fire could be made with wood by friction generated through twirling or sawing. In some areas, percussion was used by striking iron pyrite with flint to give sparks.

Fire was important in traditional life. It affected most activities and was central to Aboriginal technology. Fire cooked meat, vegetables and damper. In some regions it cremated the dead. In others it was used to make body scars to adorn the living. Smoke was an insect repellent, while flames were used to hunt animals. Along the Murray River, hot ashes were used as a poultice.

Fire kept away evil spirits at night, while a large bush thrown on to a fire lit up the surrounding countryside for a considerable distance at night unless the moon was full. Fire was the only light on moonless nights. In Arnhem Land, burning a pandanus palm provided a beacon for canoes at sea. Around Botany Bay, the early settlers noted the Eora people with small fires on clay hearths in their canoes while fishing at night.

Fire was used to straighten spears, shape wood, burn down trees for firewood, or to flush out animals. Most Aboriginal people had few clothes, so fire was important for personal warmth. It was common practice to sleep between small fires at night and to carry a firestick during the day for warmth. An experienced person could enjoy the warmth of a firestick for hours.

Fire was also used for communication. Smoke signals could identify the location of groups and co-ordinate hunting and gathering activities. Early Europeans such as Jardine noted that in Queensland there was communication between the islanders and the natives of the mainland and that the rapid manner of carrying news from tribe to tribe for great distances was astonishing. He was informed of the visit of the HMS *Salamander* two days before the ship arrived.

For Aboriginal people, uncontrolled fire was no real problem. Their possessions were such that they could be carried. They had no special structures, animals or fences to save. They did not have to fight fire; they merely used it. Their observation skills and knowledge of the countryside meant that they were seldom surprised by fires.

Through their use of fire, Aborigines undoubtedly changed the vegetation of Australia. Repeated burning over countless thousands of years resulted in the survival and flourishing of plants, animals, birds and insects which adapted best to the situation. Many Australian species of plant are relatively fire-resistant and some need extreme temperatures for germination. Continuous burning turned forests into grasslands and increased the carrying capacity of edible grass-eating animals. Nearly all the larger native animals were grass-eaters.

Food and trade

Prior to 1788, agriculture was not practised on the Australian mainland, although Aborigines on Cape York Peninsula knew it was practised in the Torres Strait. Instead, the women went out each day to gather edible roots, fruits and seeds. Some of these were eaten raw, but some had to be treated and cooked in a fire. Women also collected small animals. If they lived near the sea they gathered shell fish. Men usually hunted for the larger animals or fished, but women were also major providers of food — perhaps 50 per cent of the daily diet. Aborigines have been criticised for not making gardens and domesticating animals. As the Berndts (1988:108) noted,

> before European settlers came to Australia there were no ... animals which could be domesticated.

Later anthropologists such as Peter Sutton have suggested the lack of domestication and agriculture was cultural rather than ecological.

Although they were not a gardening people, the Aborigines were intimately concerned with the growth cycles of the plants they depended on for food. Their economy was a subsistence one, but it was not a matter of thoughtless, hand to mouth existence, or needless waste of natural resources.

It is now clear that traditional Aboriginal people enjoyed a balanced diet of meat, fruit and vegetables. Most early historical records indicated that indigenous Australians were mainly meat eaters. However, Blainey (1975) noted that in a normal year Aborigines in many parts of the country ate a variety of plant foods that no present greengrocer or fruiterer in an Australian city would hope to display. He noted that on Cape York, seventy-three different fruits and forty-six different roots were eaten, while nineteen kinds of seeds and nuts and eleven varieties of greens and shoots were consumed. In Arnhem Land, at least thirty-five different fruits and thirty-four types of vegetables were available to Aborigines, while on Wilson's Promontory in Victoria, about 120 edible plants existed. In 1979–80, Altman (1984) reported 170 species of flora and fauna being consumed.

As well as plant food, meats, fish, shellfish and eggs of various types were popular. Aboriginal people also knew how to prepare their food, which types to cook and which could be eaten raw. Some foods were poisonous unless properly prepared. For example, some tubers and the cycad palm nut require a preparation involving many processes over several days.

The groups were generally self-sufficient in food and, as there were transportation and preservation problems, food was not usually an important trade commodity before 1788. However, William Buckley, an escaped convict, reported that groups around Geelong traded fish for other goods (Morgan, 1967: 38).

A system of trade by barter or exchange connected the people of Australia from one end of the continent to the other. Some tribes had plenty of raw materials, such as paint pigments or special stones for tool making, and they would swap these for weapons, ornaments or even corroborees or rituals. Trading took place on the boundaries of the groups concerned, often at ceremonies and other gatherings. The method of exchange varied. If groups were hostile, a silent exchange took place. One group placed its products at a selected spot and then withdrew to provide an opportunity for the other group to place goods there. If both parties were satisfied, after separately examining the goods, the exchange was made. If not, other goods were included until a satisfactory conclusion was reached. Goods frequently traded or exchanged included pigments, hairbelts, pearl shell, boomerangs, weapons, stone axes and knives, dilly bags and adhesive gums.

Trade between Aboriginal groups was not carried out for profit as it is in Australia today. In Arnhem Land, a ceremonial exchange cycle was recorded by Professor Donald Thomson (1949). Goods passed continually from person to person along trade routes. In this way, goods could end up hundreds of kilometres from their original location. The goods usually moved in one direction, thus ensuring they were never returned to the donors.

According to Thomson, the Mildjingi clan of the Lower Glyde River in Eastern Arnhem Land were involved with a range of goods:

- From the east, iron-headed spears and a particular type of heavy stone used to crack cycad nuts.
- From the north, calico cloth, tobacco, blankets, glass, steel tomahawks and knives, belts and smoking pipes. All these goods and the iron spear heads were introduced into Arnhem Land by Macassans from Indonesia long before the Europeans arrived.
- From the north-east, hooked spears and heavy clubs.
- From the south east, boomerangs, chain mesh dilly bags and possum fur aprons.
- From the south-west, boomerangs (on another trade route), hooked spears and ceremonial human hair belts.

Trade routes criss-crossed Australia, many following the original paths of The Dreaming Ancestors who had first travelled the country. Along these routes, the totemic ancestors linked different people as brothers and sisters across group boundaries. The routes were often clearly marked tracks which followed rivers, valleys and skirted mountain ranges and coastal shores.

Various items have been followed along a chain of connecting exchanges. Red ochre from the quarry at Parachilna in the Flinders Ranges (SA) was traded throughout South Australia, the Lake Eyre Basin, western New South Wales and south-eastern Queensland. Pearl shell ornaments from the Kimberley coast were traded all over Western Australia and western Arnhem Land, south and Central Australia and western Queensland. Bailer shells from Cape York were exchanged all over Queensland and Western New South Wales, Central Australia and the Northern Territory. Pitjuri (native tobacco), grown in south-western Queensland and central Australia, was traded as far as Western Australia.

Outside influences

Aborigines from Broome to Cape York exchanged goods with Indonesians (Macassans) for some 500 years before the European invasion. The Indonesians travelled south using the prevailing winds, stayed for the dry season, bartering for trepang (dried sea-cucumber), pearl shell, tortoise shell and other items. Aborigines helped them and were paid with metal implements, food and clothing. Trepang had a reputation as an aphrodisiac and was traded right through to China.

Aboriginal family histories record that some family members even travelled to Indonesia. This contact with the Macassans introduced new words, ideas, techniques and concepts into Australia. One of these was the dugout canoe.

Until 1788, Aborigines had been able to choose what they wanted from other cultures. They didn't adopt agriculture apparently, because it wouldn't fit into their maintenance of sacred sites and attendance at ceremonies as they moved around their lands.

Ideas appear to have spread fairly slowly, because hunting and gathering peoples really cannot afford to experiment boldly. A mistake can mean disaster. However, while it spread slowly, change did occur. Aboriginal cultures were constantly changing. Ceremonies were exchanged, customs changed and new goods were introduced. But this was done slowly. Iron tools and macassan pipes had been in Arnhem Land for some 400 years before Cook, yet they hadn't reached south-eastern Australia by the 1830s.

Aboriginal economic life changed forever once the Europeans arrived. While it took nearly 100 years for the colonising encroachment of Aboriginal land to spread from Sydney to the Kimberley, European diseases had disastrous effects on many Aborigines long before they knew a white man. Smallpox, the common cold, measles and venereal disease were the frontline troops of European occupation. They wiped out countless indigenous people who had immune systems that were inadequate to counter European diseases.

Aborigines resisted the European invasion and generally did not get involved in the European economic system even though they did take on some aspects of European life, such as material goods and tools. The European concepts of ownership of private property and animals, buying, selling, profit, wealth and distribution of goods were based on different values and concepts to those underlying Aboriginal economic life. The rejection of each other's concepts and values was mutual because basically they were incompatible, with the exception of the pastoral industry. Aboriginal skills were not valued by the colonisers since these did not seem to have an economic value in European terms.

Aboriginal groups physically resisted the colonisers and hindered the spread of Europeans. Generally, there were initial hostilities with varying levels of intensity, then the Aborigines were ejected from their lands and force was used to keep them from white society.

Aboriginal employment

In the early years of the colony, some Aborigines were used as house servants by the wealthy, but the incompatibility of the differing value systems meant Aborigines saw few advantages in the European system of work. Aboriginal people were pushed to the fringes of settlements and generally remained fringe dwellers around Australia until the 1950s. Many found employment in the pastoral industry — the men as stockmen, the women in domestic work.

Non-acceptance by white society resulted in Aborigines not gaining the requisite education and skills to be useful employees. In 1986, 31 per cent of Aboriginal males over fifty-five years reported they had received no schooling (Australian Bureau of Statistics, 1991). During the nineteenth century and the first half of the twentieth century, Aborigines were generally offered seasonal work: picking fruit, cutting cane, casual employment in the rural areas and labouring jobs elsewhere. Children of mixed ancestry, who were forcibly removed from their families by government policy, were only trained to be domestics or semi-skilled farm workers.

Aborigines employed on stations across the north of Australia were not paid wages in most cases. Rations of dubious quality were given to them and their families. When the federal government legislated for equal wages in 1965, many station owners sacked their stockmen and evicted them from their land. But it was Aboriginal stockmen who had made the Australian cattle industry viable in the north of Australia.

Aborigines had assisted European occupation of the country. First, much of what Major Mitchell described as Australia Felix, vast grasslands, appears to have been the result of Aboriginal firestick farming. These grasslands were highly desired by the European squatters for their flocks of sheep.

Aborigines were used by many of the more successful European "explorers" to find their way over Aboriginal lands. One of the better known partnerships was Edward Eyre and Wylie. In many cases, the name or value of the Aborigine was never mentioned in the journal of the explorer.

Socioeconomic factors

In 1788, the Aboriginal population was spread across Australia. In the nineteenth century and early twentieth century, the majority of Aborigines lived in rural areas. But the introduction of equal wages for Aborigines and increased mechanisation in the agricultural and pastoral industries quickly reduced Aboriginal employment in rural areas. Their role in the economy as cheap and convenient labour, always readily available and not unionised, came to an end in the 1960s. The importance of Aboriginal people in the rural economy declined rapidly and the Aboriginal movement to the cities began to accelerate.

Since the 1960s, Aborigines have endeavoured to improve their economic situation. They have struggled to have their rights to land recognised and have agitated for better education, health, employment and social justice.

Economic and social statistics are well-documented in Australia, but it is difficult to isolate those which are Aboriginal. Aborigines still live in all parts of Australia and engage in a wide range of economic activities, as do other Australians.

At the risk of over-simplification, there is some justification in considering the Aboriginal economic situation according to the following groupings:

- outstations, homelands and other small groups;
- Aboriginal towns;
- small non-Aboriginal towns;
- cities and large towns.

Outstations, homelands and other small groups make an interesting category. The movement grew rapidly in the 1970s and 1980s. It has received encouragement and assistance from the government. This has benefited the communities both socially and economically.

The homelands movement provides its member Aborigines with a refuge from the mainstream social and economic system. People can live in a way more in keeping with their cultural traditions and often on land with which they are culturally and emotionally associated.

Where the subsistence base is good, a judicious mixture of hunting and gathering using traditional skills and introduced technology such as guns, motor boats and motor vehicles allows a high level of subsistence. This is often augmented by cash income from the sale of arts and crafts and, in more recent years, by pensions, family allowance, Job-Start allowance, NewStart and unemployment benefits or Community Development Employment Projects where communities agree to work for their unemployment money.

There are limitations and disadvantages to homelands life. Usually the remote location of the homeland adds to costs and restricts the choice of supplies from the market economy. This results in high prices and irregular supplies. The high prices are offset somewhat by lower housing rental costs in most of these areas.

Towns and settlements on Aboriginal lands differ considerably from the homelands in economic and social structure, although most homelands have close ties with and are serviced by Aboriginal towns such as Ernabella, Yuendumu and Maningrida. The towns have a larger population as well as social and economic amenities not normally found at the homelands.

While the economic base of these towns is limited, there may be a certain amount of paid employment at schools, retail stores, council and other government institutions and perhaps a cattle station. Job opportunities are usually restricted, but such centres generally have reticulated water, some permanent housing and a health centre.

Most towns and settlements depend on the central government, whether through social welfare payments, wage employment generated by public investment or government schemes where unemployment benefits are paid in full and the community and people work for their share.

In most states there are small non-Aboriginal towns with a significant Aboriginal population. They differ in several respects from Aboriginal towns. The chief economic difference is that some Aborigines in these situations are more fully integrated into the larger Australian economy as productive units. Aboriginal employment in such towns is more likely to be integrated into the economy as a whole than is the case in Aboriginal towns. This happens simply because most non-Aboriginal towns are sited to exploit some economic resource or opportunity. They have a substantial economic role in the total economy and do not exist solely to provide services to the residents, as most Aboriginal towns do.

Although most Aboriginal employment is in unskilled areas, Aborigines have to compete for jobs against other ethnic groups, whereas in Aboriginal towns they generally have the unskilled field to themselves.

Amenities in the country towns are generally good. Many Aborigines migrate into these townships from fringe camps and reserves, where the level of amenities and of housing, in particular, is often poor. Those who do secure steady employment in these towns, who qualify for assistance with housing and who successfully adapt to town life do well. Those who do not are ultimately worse off than those in Aboriginal towns.

In cities and large towns, the Aboriginal population is usually less differentiated from that of the rest of the population than in the other cases. Aboriginal people generally have more dependants, fewer marketable skills, less relevant work experience and less education than the majority of the population, and are thus generally poorer, with a higher unemployment rate.

The economic roles of Aborigines in the cities are basically similar in type to those of the majority of city dwellers — that is, they are either persons in paid employment, pensioners, unemployed or dependants. It is the proportion within each of these categories that differs from the majority. They are rarely employers, managers or highly paid professionals.

Aborigines in the economy today

Most economic discussions relating to Aborigines concentrate on Aborigines as consumers, employees or welfare recipients. The role of Aborigines as entrepreneurs in the private sector has generally been overlooked. Aboriginal individuals and organisations make important contributions in arts and crafts, the cattle industry and tourism.

As consumers, Aborigines are an important component of the Australian economy, especially in those parts of Australia, such as the Northern Territory, where Aborigines are a significant proportion of the total population. Many towns depend on Aboriginal people for their existence. The 1991–92 Aboriginal and Torres Strait Islander Program totalled $1,161 million (*Social Justice for Indigenous Australians*, 1992–93: 31). When added to earned incomes, social security payments, mining royalties and miscellaneous incomes, this results in a total of well over $1,600 million of goods and services flowing into the Aboriginal sector of the economy (Altman and Smith, 1993). Refer to Figure 11.1 for more detail.

Little research has been done on the levels of Aboriginal savings. It is generally believed that savings are extremely low, and therefore all income is spent almost immediately in the private sector in which there are few Aboriginal entrepreneurs. The Aboriginal sector of the economy does not benefit from a multiplier effect which would be achieved when Aborigines buy goods and services from one another.

Over the last two decades, the federal government has provided additional funds for Aboriginal employment programs. Despite this, the unemployment rate is nearly three times that of other Australians. Aborigines have been employed by government bodies and government-funded Aboriginal organisations, but few have been employed in the private sector.

1991/92
$ million

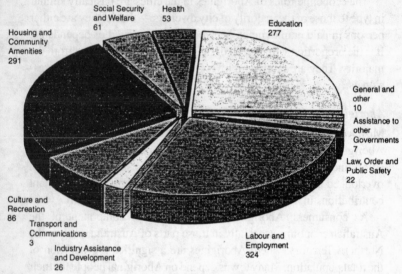

Total $1,161 million

Figure 11.1 Commonwealth outlays by function, Aboriginal and Torres Strait Islander Programs 1991/92 ($ million)
Source: Social Justice for Indigenous Australians, 1992–93.

Technological advances in the private sector, especially the pastoral and agricultural industries, have lessened the demand for unskilled labour, the location of much of the potential Aboriginal workforce. Low levels of education and skills mean there are few opportunities for Aborigines in the private sector.

Aboriginal people and the mining industry have had a difficult relationship. Mining has grown rapidly but unevenly over the past decade, and it has had a large effect on the Australian economy. It has directly affected some Aboriginal communities.

Mining constitutes about 20 per cent of Australian exports. It is big business. Many new towns, rail links and port facilities have been constructed near Aboriginal communities. With the exception of the Northern Territory, where some royalties are paid to the land owners, there has been little benefit to Aboriginal people. In the rest of Australia, royalties are paid into state coffers. Very few Aborigines are employed by mining companies. Less than 5 per cent of their total workforce is Aboriginal, even though many mines are in areas where, before mining, the majority of the population was Aboriginal.

Many companies generally employ Aborigines in unskilled positions. Staff positions are seldom filled by Aborigines. Aboriginal employment is usually concentrated in ancillary services, where continuous production or process operations are not affected. Mining companies still offer limited training opportunities.

In 1973, Peter Rogers wrote:

> Australia has not done itself justice in the handling of the modern industry versus Aborigines conflict ... the lack of preparation ... is a disgrace to government, private organisations and unions alike.

Some twenty years later, the situation appears to be little improved.

The Aboriginal economic structure has changed since colonisation. The pre-contact situation of Aborigines has been summarised in the following equation (Fisk, 1985):

$Y = S$

Where Y is the total goods and services available to the Aboriginal sector and S is the self-subsistence production for consumption within the group

While today it is:

$Y = S + W + R + G_1 + G_2$

Where W is the income (mainly wages and salaries) earned by the sale of goods and services to the non-Aboriginal economy (private and public sector).

Where R is property income derived as rents and royalties from the non-Aboriginal economy.

G_1 is money, goods or services which accrue to individuals as transfers from the Australian economy such as age pensions, unemployment benefits and family allowances.

G_2 are transfers from the Australian economy which do not accrue to individuals, but comprise services to Aboriginal groups. Examples include grants to community organisations.

While the terms W, R, G_1 and G_2 are undoubtedly positive quantitatively and tend to increase Y, the term S has been reduced to a very small amount overall. In many Aboriginal communities it is no longer a factor.

Policy

New policies in Aboriginal employment and economic development were announced by the government in the 1986-87 Budget. The Aboriginal Employment Development Policy (AEDP) was the government's response to the Miller report on Aboriginal employment and training programs.

The Prime Minister referred to a policy shift away from the welfare dependency approach of the past towards measures to enhance Aboriginal economic independence. A feature of the new policy was to be the development of strategies for improved Aboriginal access to the private sector and the creation of jobs in Aboriginal enterprises.

The government anticipated that some two-thirds of the employment growth required to achieve employment equality for Aborigines could be met through increased opportunities in the private sector. The private sector was seen as consisting of Aboriginal-owned businesses and Aboriginal service organisations, as well as employment with non-Aboriginal employers. The target set was an extra 1,100 jobs per year for the remainder of this century. It could be argued that Aboriginal service organisations should not have been classified in the private sector while the bulk of their funds came from governments.

In the past, government assistance to promote Aboriginal wage and salaried employment in the private sector has focused almost exclusively on wage subsidies under the Training for Aboriginals Program (TAP).

The Aboriginal Employment Action (AEA) program was introduced in 1985 to develop group intake strategies for the recruitment of Aboriginals to the private sector. Activities funded include:

- Aboriginal Employment Executives who have been employed by participating organisations on a contract basis for fixed terms to co-ordinate the development of Aboriginal employment and training strategies within each organisation;
- other costs of preparation and initial implementation of employment development strategies;
- the design and delivery costs of cross-cultural training for non-Aboriginal staff and of work information seminars with Aboriginal community groups.

The government is continuing to provide wage subsidy assistance to private-sector employers for the training and recruitment of unemployed Aboriginal job-seekers. Four major approaches have been adopted:

- negotiating group training and recruitment packages wherever possible;
- ensuring that training placements are only made when the prospects for recruitment after the training period are high, which requires employers to enter into recruitment as well as training agreements;
- making all placements on a negotiated fee basis, whether for individual or group training; and
- linking the numbers of placements made to the target already identified as that required to achieve equity in Aboriginal employment in the private sector.

Because of an estimated 30 per cent training attrition rate and an expected employment turnover of at least 2,750, negotiated fee placements in private-sector wage and salaried employment would be required to achieve a net growth of at least 750 in the stock of jobs held by Aborigines each year.

Small business

The government's aim is to achieve equality in the self-employment of Aboriginal people in Aboriginal-owned businesses by the year 2000. To achieve equity with non-Aborigines in small-business self-employment, the proportion of Aborigines in small business would need to increase by about 350 each year.

The government's major program in this area has been the Small Business Funding Scheme. This scheme involved either loans assistance to prospective Aboriginal entrepreneurs at concessional interest rates, or joint loans packages partly funded by government at concessional interest rates and partly funded by commercial financial institutions at market interest rates, depending on individual circumstances.

An Aboriginal Enterprise Incentive Scheme (AEIS) was also established by the government to assist unemployed people to establish businesses. This alternative approach to job creation for Aborigines required only small amounts of capital to establish sole trading businesses for self-employment.

An Enterprise Employment Assistance program commenced in 1986. It provided assistance for labour costs in Aboriginal community enterprises and involved the payment of employment subsidies to Aboriginal community enterprises equivalent to the overall unemployment benefit payments that eligible Aboriginal participants would otherwise have received. This program was later extended to all Aboriginal businesses where the employment or self-employment of an eligible Aboriginal person was involved.

The assumption of the government's strategy is that around 80 per cent of those assisted by the private-sector element of the Enterprise Employment Assistance program will be assisted into permanent jobs. This assumption clashes with the government's own view that 66 per cent of the workforce in the private sector turns over every three years. Today some 30 per cent are still unemployed and Aborigines have not achieved equality in Australian society.

Aborigines are a diverse group living in different situations throughout Australia. Consequently, any single policy will have difficulty meeting the needs of all Aborigines.

The government's Aboriginal Employment Development Policy (AEDP), which has at last recognised that Aborigines must move into the private sector as employees and entrepreneurs, is aimed at creating an economic base which will generate jobs. However, according to Tesfaghiorghis and Altman (1991), there is no concrete evidence to date that this strategy which incorporates a focus on enterprise development is having any success. John Taylor (1993) reports that the CDEP scheme has increased from 6,000 participants in 1986–87 to more than 22,000 in 1993.

Aboriginal and Torres Strait Islander Commission

The Commission has set itself three tasks to achieve in socioeconomic development (ATSIC Report, 1990–91):

- to enable Aboriginal and Torres Strait Islander communities or groups to undertake community development activities (including community enterprises) designed and valued by the community or group and which involve the employment of community members;
- to provide training to the staff and executive Aboriginal and Torres Strait Islander community councils, organisations and community

enterprises to enable them to perform their existing duties more efficiently and to achieve more effective self-management;
- to promote the number of self-employment opportunities through Aboriginal and Torres Strait Islander enterprises.

ATSIC is one of several agencies involved in developing the Aboriginal Employment Development Policy (AEDP). It forms the basis of the Commission's approach to the economic development of Aboriginal and Torres Strait Islander people. In 1990–91, AEDP strategies related to community development employment projects ($194 million), business and enterprise development ($21 million) and training and planning ($9 million).

ATSIC realises that the AEDP depends on other programs which involve skill acquisition, employment and economic development opportunities. An AEDP Task Force has provided a forum for discussion and has had a co-ordinating, overseeing and monitoring role to increase the effectiveness of the program.

The Community Development Employment Projects (CDEP) scheme employed some 22,000 indigenous Australians in 1993. It offers an opportunity to replace unemployment with work on a variety of community projects and enterprises. It is commonly known as the "work for the dole" scheme. The Royal Commission into Aboriginal Deaths in Custody Report indicated that the scheme was a source of dramatic change in many communities. It highlighted social benefits and an improvement in race relations in some country towns. Critics of the scheme have questioned its effect on individual human rights, the concealing of unemployment numbers and the large number of non-Aboriginal administrators involved. A further fundamental criticism of CDEP has been its inability to achieve income equality between indigenous and non-indigenous Australians. Jon Altman, in a personal communication, states that income is a more significant measure of economic equality than employment. He also points out that income equality is a major plank of the AEDP.

The funding of enterprises and businesses is seen as essential if indigenous Australians are to participate in the full range of Australian economic activity. This part of the AEDP has had difficulty with the staff resources available, arrears control and the development of adequate management information systems. One inbuilt difficulty is that ATSIC officers are public servants with backgrounds, abilities and knowledge which may not be suitable for dealing with private enterprise.

AEDP also offered an enterprise incentive scheme, management advice and training for people desirous of establishing small businesses. Training was also available for staff and directors of Aboriginal organisations to increase effectiveness and achieve a higher degree of self-management. For a statistical analysis of the AEDP based on the 1986 and 1991 Census data, see Taylor (1993).

Community development planning has enabled communities to plan for an integrated framework of development and co-ordination of government services provision. These community plans are developed into regional plans, but are centrally managed by ATSIC. At this stage, there appears to be some difficulty in co-ordinating community and regional needs into a national program.

Conclusion

Since 1788, Aboriginal people have ceased to be fully employed, self-sufficient individuals with high self-esteem. Today they are the poorest identifiable sector of the Australian community. Various government programs have been in place for many years, but progress is difficult to achieve.

Some 30 per cent are officially recognised as being unemployed and Aborigines are still not achieving equality in an increasingly technologically sophisticated Australia. Aboriginal society consists of many diverse groups. Consequently, centralised policies do have difficulty meeting the needs of all Aborigines.

The Aboriginal Employment Development Policy Statement is a very optimistic document which, in some areas, has not come to grips with the private sector. A positive feature of the policy is that the government has at last recognised that Aboriginal people must move into the private sector as employees and entrepreneurs.

Government-funded Aboriginal organisations are not in the private sector and should not be considered as such. The policy includes a gross over-simplification of what it takes to succeed in small business (over 35 per cent of all small businesses in Australia fail in the first year, this increases to over 50 per cent by the second year). This over-simplification is understandable because the policy was written by public servants with little background in business and a vested interest in maintaining Aboriginal people as a client group.

Despite this criticism, there is a recognition of the importance of Aboriginal economic development and that Aboriginal people have to become involved in the private sector of the Australian economy to move out of the welfare sector.

The Miller Committee (1985) found that Aboriginal people had low economic status. The Committee's recommendations resulted in the AEDP focusing on two broad policy goals:

- ensuring Aboriginal economic equality, using employment, income and education indicators, by the year 2000; and
- achieving a corresponding reduction in Aboriginal welfare dependency to the same level as other Australians.

Initial analysis of data indicates that the AEDP will have great difficulty achieving its goals. The CDEP scheme, because it is based on unemployment benefits, works against income equality, a goal of AEDP. The more Aborigines who go under CDEP, the more who will receive below-average wages.

Measuring the success of AEDP will probably require dependence on census data, because statistical data on Aboriginal people are very limited. The comparison between 1991 and 1996 census data is of immense policy interest when examined on an Australia-wide basis. Any correlation between government expenditure on economic programs and improvement in social indices at a regional or community level is of great importance to the bureaucratic policy-makers, but it is ultimately crucial to an improvement in Aboriginal economic well-being. The economic development of Aboriginal people is vital to all Australians. Welfare dependence must be reduced and Aboriginal independence advanced through programs based on Aboriginal growth through self-determination.

References

Aboriginal & Torres Strait Islander Commission (1990-91). *Annual report*.

Altman, Jon C. and Nieuwenhuysen, John (1979). *The Economic Status of Australian Aborigines*. New York: Cambridge University Press.

Altman, Jon and Smith D.E. (1993), *CAEPR Discussion Paper*, no. 47. Canberra: Centre for Applied Economic Policy Research, Australian National University.

Berndt, Ronald M. and Berndt, Catherine H. (1988). *The World of the First Australians: Aboriginal Traditional Life, Past and Present*. Canberra: Aboriginal Studies Press.

Blainey, Geoffrey (1982). *Triumph of the Nomads: A History of Ancient Australia*. Melbourne: Macmillan.

Daylight, Phyllis and Johnstone, Mary (1986). *Women's Business: Report of the Aboriginal Women's Task Force*. Canberra: Australian Government Publishing Service.

Edwards, W. H. (1987). *Traditional Aboriginal Society: A Reader*. South Melbourne: Macmillan.

—— (1990). *An Introduction to Aboriginal Societies*. Wentworth Falls: Social Science Press.

Fisk, E. K. (1985). *The Aboriginal Economy in Town and Country*. Sydney: Allen & Unwin.

Committee of Review of Aboriginal Employment and Training Programs (1985). *Aboriginal Employment and Training Programs: Report of the Committee of Review*. Canberra: Australian Government Publishing Service.

Morgan, John (1852, republished 1967). *The Life and Adventures of William Buckley*. Melbourne: Heinemann.

Roger, Peter (1973). *The Industrialists and the Aborigines: A Study of Aboriginal Employment in the Australian Mining Industry*. Sydney: Angus & Robertson.

Rowse, Tim (1992). *Remote Possibilities: The Aboriginal Domain and the Administrative Imagination*. Darwin: Australian National University.

Social Justice for Indigenous Australians (1992–93). Budget-related paper no. 7. Circulated by the Honourable Robert Tickner, Minister for Aboriginal & Torres Strait Islander Affairs and Minister assisting the Prime Minister for Aboriginal Reconciliation. Canberra: Australian Government Publishing Service.

Taylor, John (1993). *The Relative Economic Status of Indigenous Australians 1986–1991*. Canberra: Centre for Applied Economic Policy Research, Australian National University.

Tesfaghiorghis, H. and Altman, J. (1991). *Aboriginal Socio-economic Status: Are There Any Evident Changes?* Canberra: Centre for Applied Economic Policy Research, Australian National University.

Thomson, D. F. (1949). *Economic Structure and the Ceremonial Exchange Cycle in Arnhem Land*. Melbourne: Macmillan.

Chapter 12

Art: Interpreting Reality

Franchesca Albert and Christopher Anderson

Introduction

The art of Aboriginal Australia is one of the oldest, richest and most complex forms of creative expression in human history. In the earlier days of European occupation, it was mistakenly believed that Aboriginal people had no art, only basic craft and ritual-related decoration. Europeans found it incomprehensible that a people living in such a harsh environment and possessing such minimal material culture could have had more than a rudimentary notion of art. When the spectacular rock paintings in north-western Australia, now known as Wandjina figures, were first described by Sir George Grey in 1837, it was assumed that they must have been done by alien visitors to Australia (Jones, 1988). Today Aboriginal art is recognised around the world as an exciting, major contribution to world art and an expression of deepest humanity and unity with nature.

In spite of this, there remain erroneous beliefs — for example, that bark paintings are the only real Aboriginal art form or that bark painting was done over the whole of Australia; that works made for sale today are somehow not genuine; or that modern written works, dance and music by Aboriginal artists are not "traditional" and hence not genuinely Aboriginal.

Aboriginal art is as much alive today as it was 40,000 years ago. As in that ancient past, the art is not easily separable from everyday life. It is a lively and positive art which describes and engages the world in a variety of guises: song, word, performance and paint, among others.

The art of Aboriginal Australians today takes on many forms. Despite significant change and diversity, the art retains an underlying unity of inspiration — the land and human relationships that are associated with it. It has solid links with the past, but is firmly rooted as political, social and creative action in the present.

What is Aboriginal art?

Aboriginal art is the oldest continuous art tradition in the world. Recent scientific dating of engraved concentric circles on rocks in the Flinders

Ranges of South Australia revealed them to be over 35,000 years old (Dorn and Nobbs, 1992: 56–60).

While the meaning of the art and its symbolism have undoubtedly changed in this time, the form of the art — common to much of Aboriginal art today — has remained strikingly similar for thousands of years. This art, as an expression of Aboriginal people's relationship to the land and to each other, was being generated at a time when art and its association with a spiritual world were apparently unknown to the inhabitants of northern Europe.

The Aboriginal art of today has profound links with that of the past. The last several hundred years up to and including the present have seen a great variety of Aboriginal art forms around the country (see Berndt et al., 1982; Caruana, 1993; Isaacs, 1980; 1984; Sutton, 1988).

Across the continent, there are regional differences in artistic forms varying broadly in relation to the environment, with major differences between arid, tropical and temperate zones. In the visual arts and crafts, including ritual and everyday design, there are:

- concentric circles, dotting, tracks and meandering lines and use of more abstract imagery (Central Australia and much of the arid portions of Australia);
- the ubiquitous rock art of the Top End (of the Northern Territory), with heavy figurative emphasis, use of x-ray figures and cross-hatching in-fill;
- the use of heavy and broad white and red bands, a tradition of wood carving and beeswax sculpture in some areas (north Queensland);
- geometric, square incising, figures and forms incised on pearl shell (Kimberley);
- elaborate weaving and basketry tradition, finely incised wooden implements and weapons (Murray–Darling system).

The art of the Top End, the tropical region east of Darwin in northern Australia, is probably the best known. Here, people expressed themselves in body painting for ceremony, in rock painting and through decoration of everyday objects. In addition, at least in western and north-eastern Arnhem Land and on Groote Eylandt, people painted on sheets of bark. Sometimes bark sheets were used as parts of shelters and were occasionally painted (Edwards and Guerin, 1969). The sheets were taken from suitable trees, stripped, flattened and dried. Natural ochres were then applied with stick brushes. Dreaming stories were painted as a means of teaching novices and to "prove" the veracity of the stories' content.

Bark paintings, though, were confined to a limited area of the tropical north and generally were not found elsewhere in Australia. In other parts of the continent, Aboriginal people used other media for creative and spiritual expression.

In Central Australia, for instance, there were no trees suitable as bark "canvases". In addition, as Aboriginal people there say, "It is not part of our culture". In the arid and desert regions, people painted with a great variety of ochres, on their bodies, on rock surfaces, on their weapons, ceremonial objects and on everyday domestic implements. Using plant substances, ochres and sand, they also created elaborate ground sculptures for ceremony. Sometimes these covered hectares of ground and took many people months of preparation. Often they were secret and restricted only to initiated men. However, in some areas of Central Australia, women created ground paintings for public ceremonies (Anderson, 1993).

From the Lake Eyre region come *toas*, small, sculpted objects of wood, gypsum and ochre, often acting as bases for hair, plant material or feathers. Each one represents a Dreaming place and part of a related story, linking a particular group with the land and its Dreaming heritage. Although debate exists about their origin and function (Jones and Sutton, 1986), the toas are clearly an art form with real and long-standing roots in Lake Eyre Aboriginal culture.

Large-scale rock engravings and carvings were also produced in south-eastern Australia by Aboriginal people — for example, in the Sydney area even fifty years after first European settlement. Large-scale wooden sculpture and fine-line incising were another major tradition in the south-eastern parts of the continent. The largest and most spectacular examples are the carved trees of New South Wales and inland Victoria.

In other parts of the country, such as west Cape York Peninsula in far north Queensland, sculpted animals and other beings in wood and beeswax depicted ancestral figures which were part of complex myth cycles and used in ceremonies.

The epic myth stories of Aboriginal Australia must also be seen as narrative, song and performance events equivalent to the best of

European theatre, dance and literature. The unity of these forms in ceremony has tended to mask their artistic qualities for non-Aboriginal people.

Contrary to the common stereotypes, Aboriginal art took a multitude of forms and was manifest in different media right around the country. In terms of intent and inspiration, however, it shared a great deal.

In traditional Aboriginal society the distinctions between art and non-art, art and craft were meaningless. There was design inherent in both nature and in the manufacture and decoration of all human products. The designs were all "left" by the Ancestors; humans merely brought the religious force to visible form in different contexts.

All forms of art were not equal, however. There was a hierarchy of power, degrees of sacredness. In a sense, all art was sacred. But some was so sacred that it was kept secret from certain groups — the young, the untutored, men in some cases and women in others. This separation of different art for different situations and audiences still applies today in many Aboriginal societies.

Art was integral to traditional Aboriginal society. It was part of everyday life. Each person was expected to be able to depict in terms of the relevant art form their own place in the universe. Art was thus an integral part of religious life. Aboriginal people executed their ancestral stories in the various media: body painting during ritual, ceremonial ground designs and rock paintings or engravings, song, stories and performance.

Art gave people a means of describing their relationship to the land and to each other. It thus provided the bridge between nature and culture. It became a means for the affirmation of identity, an expression of individual creativity and feeling and a way of communicating with people, both living and dead. Through song, dance and painting, people enacted and recreated their histories and affirmed their inalienable place in the landscape. Men and women each had their own artistic domains and particular means of fulfilling their social obligations to each other and to their Ancestors, to The Dreaming.

People shared rights in The Dreaming — that is, a man and his brother or sister would share the right to produce particular motifs and designs. They inherited these from one of their parents and they had the right, indeed the obligation, to produce their Dreaming designs in all possible media. Hence today, as before, some Aboriginal art is produced by individuals and other art by groups of people who share similar rights. Artistic production is thus not only a function of individual creativity; it is also a social activity related to the web of kinship on which the society is based.

This is not to say, however, that "art" did not exist in Aboriginal society, that there were not people with special artistic skills and a desire to describe the world around them through art. However, this was always done through the filter of culture, and people were limited by the media presented to them in their environment.

It is probable that the great variety of art existed at least at the time of first colonial settlement and probably before. Many of the forms still exist today, as integral parts of both everyday and religious life. In many cases, Aboriginal people now make a living in cash terms from their art.

Generating art, in any form, in pre-European days was seen as necessary to ongoing life. The art of Aboriginal Australia was not static, however. It changed as fashion, trade and contact with other groups brought new ideas and innovations to local art. The existence of change and of art as a reflection of particular circumstance, as part of a flexible and adaptive way of life, can be seen as far back as the first days of contact with non-Aborigines.

Opportunity and adaptation

Many people believe that Aboriginal people once did "traditional" art and that now people do art that is somehow corrupted, either by the use of non-traditional materials or because it is being done due to "outside" influences.

Contrary to this view, the art of Aboriginal Australia has always been dynamic and changing to reflect people's circumstances. Aboriginal people have seized opportunities to either express themselves artistically in new ways or to achieve their own ends via art in new situations. This adaptability was probably always the case. It may be that one of the forms now thought of as very "traditional" — for example, rock painting — was once an innovation. In the post-contact era, one of the main factors influencing art was that Aboriginal people saw the political importance of teaching outsiders about their land and world view. The view of the static, unchanging "traditional" is contradicted by a new and different look at the art history of Australia.

Bark paintings are often seen as the definitive Aboriginal art. However, in a sense, bark paintings are not "real". As we have seen, they were confined to one small part of Australia — Arnhem Land — and even here, painting on bark to produce portable art was probably not done prior to the early twentieth century. Bark was used for shelter and it often happened to be decorated. As mentioned above, sheets of bark were also used for didactic purposes during ceremony. However, it was really only the demand created by missionaries, buffalo hunters and other key local Europeans, stimulated in turn by outsiders such as Professor Baldwin Spencer, N.B. Tindale and C.P. Mountford, that created bark painting as an art form. This, however, does not make bark painting less authentic. Rather, it reflects, in content, northern Australian Aboriginal culture; in aim, the economic and political realities of Arnhem Land in the early twentieth century.

In a similar way, the rock paintings of north Queensland contain many examples in which Aboriginal artists depicted the new objects, people and events around them, following the arrival of Europeans (see Walsh, 1988). In the Laura region of Cape York Peninsula, for example, Aboriginal people were attempting to affect and alter with their art the events and forces which appeared in their country in terms of their own culture. The depiction in rock art of Europeans and Chinese on the Palmer River goldfields, for instance, was often part of the sorcery attempts by Aboriginal people to deal with these intruders. The native troopers and other police were also depicted, sometimes with horses and guns. Other north Australian examples include Macassan ships from Indonesia.

Elsewhere, Aboriginal artists made rapid use of new media and materials which seemed to appear out of nowhere. Just after the turn of the century, in the Gulf country of the Northern Territory, unknown Borroloola artists painted their Dreaming stories on to the boards of food packing crates which may have been washed up on the beach. We know little about these works, but it is apparent that artists were using the chance appearance of new materials to continue or elaborate an existing tradition.

In the Kimberley, Aboriginal artists of Karadjeri and Nyangamada descent began from the early 1960s onwards to carve stone heads. This innovation came as a result of a dream-visitation experienced by a Karadjeri/Nyangamada man. In this visitation, a Dreaming being, Walkarurra, taught the man a new ceremonial sequence and insisted that human figures be carved. In similar fashion, the famous Nyangamada tin masks in the South Australian Museum are examples of introduced materials being used for "normal" Aboriginal religious practices (Kean et al., 1990).

In Central Australia, there are a number of significant examples of artistic opportunism which demonstrate the pre-existing Aboriginal tradition of art as education and political act, operating in a situation of radical change.

The first of these examples is crayon drawings. Aboriginal people from the desert regions of central Australia, many of whom had never seen Europeans, jumped at the chance to use introduced materials and media to portray their world view. With the arrival of South Australian Museum expeditions to Cockatoo Creek, Mt Liebig, the Warburton Ranges, the Mann Ranges and other parts of Central Australia in the 1920s and 1930s, Aboriginal men drew unprompted maps of their country, their Dreaming stories and the elements of their environment in the same way they did with "traditional" body, rock and ground paintings.

The technique, developed by the anthropologist Norman Tindale, consisted of giving Aboriginal people (usually men) crayons in colours normally available to them (red, yellow, white and black). They were then also given paper sheets, usually 50cm x 30cm. No suggestions were made as to what people should draw, only that they put "marks" on the paper.

In general, the iconography is the same as for that in other art forms of Aboriginal Central Australia: concentric circles represent mythic sites in the landscape (usually waterholes or campsites), with straight lines connecting the circles representing travelling paths. "U" shapes represent people sitting and domestic implements and weapons such as spears and boomerangs are often shown near them. The tracks of animals such as kangaroos, dingoes and birds are also common.

The fact that they were using crayons and brown paper and were drawing the paintings for Europeans is irrelevant. The artists were trying to teach the newcomers about their land, in the same way that they taught young Aboriginal people. The artists were also making statements about their affiliation to the land and their rights to it. These drawings are a unique and significant record, not only of the art of Central Australian Aborigines, but of a momentous encounter between two very different cultures.

The water-colours of Central Australia, the so-called Namatjira school, provide another example of Aboriginal artistic opportunism and adaptability (Hardy et al., 1992). Albert Namatjira, an Aranda man from the western MacDonnell Ranges, took every possible opportunity for artistic expression. Having grown up within the classic Central Australian Aboriginal art traditions, his work as an artist included wood carvings and paintings. Through Namatjira's later work with artist Rex Battarbee, he and his family began a tradition of Aboriginal water-colour landscapes: once again depicting the Central Australian landscape, not only because of its tourist appeal, but because it was familiar country containing particular sites of religious importance. As one writer has put it:

> We now cannot but see Namatjira's paintings as a way of reaffirming his tribal territorial knowledge while simultaneously sharing with outsiders his pride in his land's great beauty. Further, we now perceive the repetition of similar rocks and similar ghost gums as a way of converting them from once-off observations to timeless symbols. [Thomas, 1986: 26]

The fact of showing their country and making statements about it is indisputable, despite the origin of the technique or the materials. The Namatjira movement, like the crayon drawings, can be seen as another Central Australian Aboriginal attempt to reaffirm to outsiders their interests and rights in land, a long-standing "traditional" function of art in this area as in other parts of Aboriginal Australia.

These earlier examples of crayon drawings and water-colours are sometimes obscured by what is probably now the most famous art form of Central Australia, acrylic dot paintings. Acrylic painting has its origins in the community of Papunya, 200 kilometres west of Alice Springs. In the early 1970s, a young school teacher, Geoff Bardon, attempted to get Luritja, Warlpiri and Pintupi schoolchildren to paint in terms of their own culture instead of from the point of view of an introduced one (Bardon, 1991). This perspective offered such serious and significant opportunities that the older men in the community took it over and began painting, on to board, canvas and any other available material, the sacred stories of their origins. Over the years, and with the interest of the art market, a large-scale movement spread to many other communities to the point where, now, hundreds of artists produce thousands of paintings a year. These vary from small canvases sold as souvenirs in Alice Springs to major works sold for large amounts of money to the art museums of the world.

Whether souvenir or fine art, the acrylic paintings of Central Australia depict The Dreaming stories and sites specific to particular artists and groups. The same rules which apply to the other more "traditional" art forms also apply to acrylic works. The aim in both is to state relations with and rights in land. Rock, body and ground paintings co-exist with acrylic painting in the Aboriginal communities of the Centre. In the former case the art is directed inwards. In the latter it is outward. The content, however, is the same (Anderson and Dussart, 1988).

Aboriginal artists have always interacted with the "outside" world in an active, opportunistic, adaptable, flexible way. Aboriginal people, at first contact and since, have always taken the opportunities presented to them via introduced media to express themselves and to achieve explicit aims vis-à-vis their position in the world.

Aboriginal arts today

It is a common view today that the world's interest in Aboriginal art is recent and a function of modern enlightened attitudes. However, the first exhibition of works done by Aboriginal people and exhibited as "art" occurred in Adelaide in the late 1880s. This exhibition, titled the "Dawn of Art", consisted of eighteen drawings of various animals and birds done by Aboriginal men who were inmates or workers at the Palmerston Gaol in Darwin.

Similarly, an exhibition called "Primitive Art" opened at the Museum of Victoria in Melbourne in 1929. This exhibition

> presented a range of Aboriginal art: carved trees from New South Wales, spears and shields, painted ceremonial boards from Groote Eylandt, reproductions of rock paintings from Victoria, ... bark paintings ... and even the design for a wooden grave memorial. [Jones, 1988: 167]

Aboriginal craftsmen were brought to Melbourne from the Lake Eyre region to demonstrate the manufacture of artefacts and ceremonial items.

These exhibitions, unlike the quite common museum displays of exotic "native" domestic paraphernalia, were billed as "art" and attracted considerable public interest. Such exhibitions played an important role in helping to change white attitudes and to bring about policy changes. It seems unlikely that Aboriginal artists were not active participants in this process.

Contemporary Aboriginal art

What is the Aboriginal art scene today? What are artists attempting to do and say about their contemporary position in the broader, European dominated Australian society? Does Aboriginal artists' interaction with the commercial market affect the cultural integrity of the work?

Aboriginal art has been described by international art dealers and critics as the most exciting thing to happen in modern world art circles for many years. The Australian Aboriginal arts and crafts industry is thriving. A recent government report (Altman et al., 1989: 34) estimated that there were over 6,000 artists working in several hundred communities and locations across Australia. The effect on the Australian economy is significant, with a total of $18.5 million generated in 1987–88. In addition, around 50 per cent of this art was sold for export. One in five of the twenty-three million visitors to museums and art galleries yearly in Australia come expressly to see Aboriginal art (Statistical Advisory Group of Cultural Ministers Council and Strategic Development Unit of Australia Council). Exhibitions of Aboriginal works now appear regularly in the United States, Europe and Asia.

Aboriginal writers, poets and playwrights such as Sally Morgan, Jack Davis and the late Oodgeroo Noonuccal (Kath Walker) have met with success worldwide. Aboriginal-run art co-operatives and organisations such as Papunya Tula, Bula Bula, the Japukai and Sydney Dance Theatre groups and so on flourish. Festivals and conferences such as the National Black Playwrights and Aboriginal Writers Conference have been held by and for Aboriginal people. Many initiatives have come out of these forums and they demonstrate the vitality of Aboriginal arts today (see, for example, Davis and Hodge, 1985).

Despite the earlier European belief that there was originally no art in Australia and the not-uncommon belief today that there is no "real" Aboriginal art left, artists have actively adapted and incorporated new elements presented to them, maintaining all the while the basically political thrust of their work in an attempt to alter their social and economic environments.

Aboriginal art today is a success story of the first order. Aboriginal artists demonstrate through their work that they are not victims of the "art machine" or of post-colonial exploitation. Rather, they are actively dealing with their surroundings through means of their cultural heritage. They see their art as playing a critical role both in Aboriginal society today and in the broader Australian and world scene.

Aboriginal visual artists paint to make a living. If people stopped buying their paintings, the artists would stop painting. This does not diminish the "meaning" of the art, for it comes out of a larger, more encompassing system. This demonstrates that the art is directed. Aboriginal artists are not passive victims of cultural commercialisation or of exploitation by a relentless art world. Exploitation obviously occurs. However, to portray the artists only as poor, helpless pawns is to present a distorted, object-oriented and racist view. Aboriginal art today should be viewed from a human-oriented perspective and as a positive force in Aboriginal communities and Aboriginal life. It is a wedge; it is subversive; it is explicitly political; it is active. The interaction is considerable; the blurring between black and white is the hallmark of Aboriginal art. The cultural interaction is both complex and typical.

There is substantial continuity in Aboriginal art from past to present, regardless of the nature and origin of the art. Aboriginal art today is a powerful example of the ability of Aboriginal society to adapt and to incorporate, or absorb, elements of the dominating, non-Aboriginal milieu. Art is a means, used actively by Aboriginal people, from first contact onwards, to challenge the European world view. Art is crucial to the attempt to alter the relationships between Europeans and Aboriginal people and to consciously and explicitly declare Aboriginal rights in land and to assert the validity of Aboriginal culture in the modern world.

Aboriginal art is thus an extremely positive force and a lively, complex and dynamic scene with implications for Australia as a whole, both overseas and in terms of how it sees itself. Aboriginal art, although ever dynamic and changing, continues today based on a fundamental continuity with the past, both in content and in aim. Many events today affirm the vitality of Aboriginal art and culture, its place on the world scene and its positive economic value in the lives of artists and their families: Central Australian artists in Paris at the "Magicians of the Earth" exhibition in 1990 interacting with artists from all over the world; the Aboriginal band, Yothu Yindi, on stage at the World Music Festival in Adelaide in 1993; the Stomping Ground Festival in the Kimberley; international and national tours of the Aboriginal and Islander Dance Company; places such as the Eora Centre in Sydney and Tandanya in Adelaide; the international success of Aboriginal writers and the visual arts; and the prominence of Aboriginal arts in the media. Aboriginal art is here to stay and it is the driving force of significant change in non-Aboriginal people's attitudes about Aboriginal culture.

References

Altman, J., McGuigan, C. and Yu, P. (1989). *The Aboriginal Arts and Crafts Industry: Report of the Review Committee*. Canberra: Australian Government Publishing Service.

Anderson, C. (1993). "The art of the sacred and the art of art: contemporary Aboriginal painting in Central Australia". In *Arts of the Pacific*, edited by Philip Dark. Honolulu. University of Hawaii Press.

——— and Dussart, F. (1988). "Dreamings in acrylic: Western Desert art". In *Dreamings: The Art of Aboriginal Australia*, edited by Peter Sutton. Ringwood: Viking, pp. 89-143.

Bardon, Geoffrey (1991). *Papunya Tula: Art of the Western Desert*. Ringwood: McPhee Gribble.

Berndt, Ronald M. and Catherine H. with John E. Stanton (1982). *Aboriginal Australian Art: A Visual Perspective*. Sydney: Methuen.

Caruana, Wally (1993). *Aboriginal Art*. Melbourne: Thames and Hudson.

Davis, J. and Hodge, N. (1985). *Aboriginal Writing Today: Papers From the First National Conference of Aboriginal Writers, held in Perth WA, in 1983*. Canberra: Australian Institute of Aboriginal Studies.

Dorn, R.J. and Nobbs, M. (1992). "Further support for the antiquity of South Australian rock engravings". *Australian Aboriginal Studies*, no. 1, pp. 56-60.

Edwards, Robert and Guerin, Bruce (1969). *Aboriginal Bark Paintings*. Adelaide: Rigby.

Hardy, J., Megaw, J. V. S. and Megaw, M. R. (eds) (1992). *The Heritage of Namatjira: The Watercolours of Central Australia*. Melbourne: Heinemann.

Isaacs, Jennifer (ed.) (1980). *Australian Dreaming: 40,000 Years of Aboriginal History*. Sydney: Landsdowne Press.

——— (1984). *Arts of The Dreaming. Australia's Living Heritage*. Sydney: Lansdowne Press.

Jones, Philip (1988). "Perceptions of Aboriginal Art: A History". In *Dreamings: The Art of Aboriginal Australia*, edited by Peter Sutton. Ringwood: Viking, pp. 143-79.

—— and Sutton, Peter (1986). *Art and Land: Aboriginal Sculptures of the Lake Eyre Region*. Adelaide: South Australian Museum in association with Wakefield Press.

Kean, J., Alberts, F., Ackerman, K., Giles, K. (1990). *Paper, stone, tin: catalogue of an exhibition at Tandanya, July 1990*. Adelaide: Tandanya.

Smyth, Robert Brough (1972). *Aborigines of Victoria: With Notes Relating to the Habits of the Natives of Other Parts of Australia and Tasmania*. Melbourne: George Robertson.

Sutton, Peter (ed.) (1988). *Dreamings: The Art of Aboriginal Australia*. Ringwood: Viking.

Thomas, D. (1986). "Albert Namatjira and the worlds of art: a re-evaluation". In *Albert Namatjira: The Life and Work of an Australian Painter*, edited by Nadine Amadio et al., South Melbourne: Macmillan, pp. 21-26.

Walsh, Grahame (1988). *Australia's Greatest Rock Art*. Bathurst: E. J. Brill/Robert Brown and Associates.

Chapter 13

Self-determination and the Struggle for Aboriginal Equality

David Roberts

Self-determination

Self-determination has been described as "the cornerstone of government policy" and "the central word" in Aboriginal affairs since the
election of the Whitlam government in 1972 (O'Donoghue, 1992: 7).
It was a significant departure from previous government policies in
that it recognised the demands of Aboriginal and Torres Strait Islanders
for social justice and equality and acknowledged their right to make
decisions about matters affecting their own lives. Since 1972, successive governments have attempted to establish structures and processes
that would facilitate Aboriginal self-determination and self-management within the Australian state.[1]

While there is no commonly agreed definition in Australia of
self-determination and its meaning is contested, there does appear to
be general agreement that central to self-determination is the right of
indigenous Australians to make decisions on issues relating to them
and to manage their own affairs. There is no such agreement as to how
this should be achieved nor has a framework within which this can
occur been established.

The government has defined self-determination as "Aboriginal
communities deciding the pace and nature of their future development
as significant components within a diverse Australia" (O'Donoghue,
1992: 7). This in effect limits the exercise of self-determination to what
is compatible with the interests of the Australian state. Successive
Australian governments have rejected the view that self-determination
includes the right of Aboriginal people to decide their political status
and the exploration of political options such as self-government and
Aboriginal sovereignty. Self-determination has been defined much
more narrowly in Australia than it has been in international forums
where, as part of the decolonisation process, it has been premised on
the right of a people to decide their own political status and future.

The Australian government indicated to the United Nations Working Group on Indigenous Peoples in July 1992 that it had great difficulty with interpretations of self-determination that included the possibility of independence when it stated:

> If self-determination in general means that each people has the option of full independence and forming their own state, it will be very difficult for states to accept the application of that right to many groups (Watson, 1993: 8).

Indeed, the concept underlying the process of reconciliation that the government set in motion in 1991 is for a "bringing together" of Aboriginal and Torres Strait Islander peoples with the rest of the Australian population into the one state, not their separation from it. Prime Minister Keating and his Aboriginal Affairs Minister, Robert Tickner, consistently reinforced this purpose as a central objective of reconciliation. Likewise, the Keating government's "One Nation" policy reinforced the currency of the government's definition of self-determination in terms of Aboriginal and Torres Strait Islander incorporation within the Australian state.

The House of Representatives Standing Committee, in its 1990 report on Aboriginal and Torres Strait Islander community control, management and resources, was of the view that self-determination included the right of indigenous Australians to make decisions over their political status as well as their economic, social and cultural development. It also emphasised the need for an adequate resource and skills base if indigenous Australians' control over the future of their communities was to become a reality. Self-determination, so described, envisaged the possibility of some form of political autonomy, perhaps as self-government and, by extension, even the possibility of independence. Such a view of self-determination reflects the political platform of some Aboriginal groups such as the Provisional Aboriginal Government.

For Aboriginal and Torres Strait Islander peoples, self-determination has taken on different meanings and raises different possibilities to different groups. These meanings reflect the different situations and historical experiences of the diverse range of indigenous communities across Australia.

The indigenous population of Australia is very heterogeneous. Four broad categories of indigenous communities have been identified in

Australia, although care needs to be taken in their use as any more than general descriptors. No two communities are identical. Each reflects its own unique cultural background, historical experiences and local conditions. Communities differ in the degree to which they have been subjected to dispossession, dispersal and the destruction of their economies and law during the colonisation process. Outstations, Aboriginal towns and settlements, small non-Aboriginal towns, and cities and towns of over 20,000 people comprise the four general categories of community settings in which Aboriginal people live. Almost 75 per cent of Aborigines live in or around non-Aboriginal towns and cities, with the remainder living on outstations and Aboriginal settlements.

The situations, needs and options for those living in remote areas are significantly different from the ones for those living in the urban areas. Land rights, for example, have been pursued with much more success in central and northern Australia, and some communities, such as those at Yirrkala, Uluru and Kakadu, have been able to participate in successful commercial developments. Other groups have been able to establish pastoral enterprises which generate some employment and income. Others have used the outstation movement and subsistence activities as a means of lessening their dependence on the government.

The options for those Aboriginal people living in more densely populated parts of Australia are more limited. Unless Aboriginal people break into the employment market and gain jobs, there is little alternative to welfare dependency. Likewise, in remote areas where opportunities for employment (as defined by government agencies) are very limited, welfare dependency is the only option for most members of the community.

The diversity of situations, the varying impact of colonialism on communities and differential access to resources make for different political agendas. Such differences render it difficult for any Aboriginal organisation to speak on behalf of the Aboriginal movement generally and can lead to apparent competing interests and priorities, a situation exacerbated by government-imposed structures. Attempts by activists to promote particular strategies for self-determination often run foul of localised interests trying to maximise their share of government funds or of competing groups pursuing different agendas.

The diversity of positions and the difficulties involved in developing political programs that attract widespread support are illustrated in the comments of lawyer Darryl Cronin:

> Aboriginal people in this country are heading down a long road. This road leads to the proper recognition of our rights … For us to be strong and fight for our rights all Aboriginal people have to go down that road together. My concern is some Aboriginal people are starting to go off the road onto little bush tracks. In the Northern Territory some Aboriginal people are following the Northern Territory Government and are accepting Community Government, while some people are trying to move further away towards being part of the Government system.
>
> Some Aboriginal people are just sitting on the side of the road, watching us fight for our rights. They don't want to get involved.
>
> Some mob call us "radicals" and say they don't want a part of the struggle for our rights. All these Aboriginal people going off the road … are going to find it hard to get back … when we begin negotiating a Treaty and developing our own form of Aboriginal Government. They have sold themselves short and have accepted things too early without looking at all the options. [*Land Rights News*, July 1989: 20]

Cronin's comments provide some insight into the range of different views among Aboriginal people. Some expect the government to provide for them and fix their problems. Some identify equality within Australian society as their main goal. They want the opportunity to obtain employment and have equal access to facilities such as housing, health and education alongside other Australians. For others, the goal is a return of the land and recognition of Aboriginal lifestyles, while others seek new arrangements for political autonomy and even separate nationhood.

For Lois O'Donoghue, Chairperson of the Aboriginal and Torres Strait Islander Commission, self-determination is summarised as "well-being" and social justice. It equals "full citizenship rights" and requires similar employment prospects, education opportunities, housing and municipal facilities and a life expectancy for indigenous Australians which is the same as for other Australians. Her approach has some congruence with the government's definition of self-determination, although she does argue for "appropriate recognition of our status as the First Australians being enshrined in the Australian Constitution" (O'Donoghue, 1992: 15) and advocates the provision of a resource base through the instigation of measures such as a Land

Acquisition Fund in order to reduce Aboriginal dependency on government funding.

Some Aboriginal organisations and leaders have taken a more radical line on self-determination with the National Aboriginal and Islander Legal Service arguing that self-determination must involve a fundamental restructuring of power relations between indigenous and other Australians (NAILS, 1989: 15). The Federal Land Council has taken the position that Aboriginal people have never ceded their sovereign rights as a nation and that negotiations on the future status of Aboriginal people should be not entered into with the Australian government until Aboriginal sovereignty is recognised and Aboriginal people are accorded equal status.

Michael Mansell, representing the Aboriginal Provisional Government (APG), sees in sovereignty the opportunity for separation from the rest of Australia and has called on the federal government to conduct a referendum to enable Aborigines to choose "whether they wish to go down the track of sovereignty or whether they wish to stay in the Australian community" (*Koori Mail*, 21 October 1992: 7). Under his proposal, Aboriginal communities would be granted Crown Land in rural areas of Australia and would become self-governing and no longer dependent on government. The APG's use of sovereignty and self-government keeps the issue of Aboriginal autonomy firmly on the agenda. It also brings into sharp focus recognition that the difficulties being confronted in achieving self-determination remain embedded in colonialism.

The Aboriginal struggle

Throughout most of the history of Aboriginal–European relations, government policies and practices have been imposed. They have been characterised by a lack of consultation with the indigenous population. It has been governments, together with their bureaucracies and advisers, that have controlled the situation for Aborigines and Torres Strait Islanders. They have imposed their will in a manner that serves to emphasise not only the powerlessness of Aborigines and Torres Strait Islanders in Australian society but also the failure to recognise the legitimacy of their ideas, views and aspirations.

Aboriginal people have been involved in an ongoing struggle to improve their situation. Their campaign for social justice and equality was well in train by the time self-determination was adopted as government policy. Their task has largely centred on finding ways to persuade other Australians to support the aims and needs they themselves identify. Their situation as a colonised people, small in population and widely dispersed across Australia, has forced them into working in and around a complex and foreign system of rules, structures, priorities and controls established by the dominant society.

Given the history of disempowerment and marginalisation of Aboriginal and Torres Strait Islander peoples, the small numbers and dispersal across Australia, indigenous Australians have been remarkably successful in bringing their issues to prominence in the national arena. O'Donoghue believes that the political strength of the Aboriginal movement "lies in our weakness; our 1.5 per cent of the national population. We present no threat to mainstream Australia, as on the pastoral frontier we once did." (O'Donoghue, 1992: 13)

The Aboriginal movement has been able to gain influence largely by applying moral and political pressure on the Australian state to right wrongs of the past, for equality and for social justice. In so doing it has made judicious use of international forums to publicise its situation and promote its agenda. Its struggle has resulted in tangible gains which have included the bringing of Aboriginal affairs into the commonwealth government's realm of responsibility (concurrently with state governments), citizenship, voting rights, land rights, significant funding increases in support of Aboriginal health, housing, education, training, municipal services, legal aid and welfare and anti-racial discrimination legislation.

During the 1950s and 1960s, organisations such as the Federal Council for the Advancement of Aborigines and Torres Strait Islanders (FCAATSI) were established and provided a national focus for political activity. Other organisations such as the Victorian Aboriginal Advancement League passed into the control and management of Aboriginal people. The 1964 Freedom Rides through northern New South Wales publicised the second-class status of Aboriginal people and the blatant racism to which they were subjected. At Dagaragu (Wave Hill), the Gurundji Walk-off was to prove the beginning of a new movement for land rights and a secure resource base, while the establishment of the Tent Embassy in 1972 outside Parliament House in Canberra forced the major political parties to address Aboriginal demands.

The land rights campaign that has been waged by Aborigines and Torres Strait Islanders has been a significant element in their attempts to gain a secure base that will provide a social, cultural, economic and political basis for real autonomy. Its successes include the passage of the *Northern Territory Land Rights Act* in 1976, the granting of freehold title to large areas of land in the north-west of South Australia to the Pitjantjatjara and the success of smaller land rights claims in other states such as New South Wales and Victoria. The land rights movement, however, received a major setback when the Hawke Labor government withdrew its proposed national land rights legislation in 1986.

At the community level, Aboriginal people increasingly have taken the initiative in areas such as health, education and legal services. They have set up their own community-based organisations, such as the Aboriginal Medical Service in Redfern, to such an extent that by 1992 there were some 2,000 community organisations servicing the needs of Aboriginal and Torres Strait communities.

More than twenty-five years have passed since Australians voted overwhelmingly in the 1967 referendum to give Aborigines and Torres Strait Islanders "a fair go", include them in the census and give the commonwealth government the responsibility to legislate and provide funding in Aboriginal affairs. The referendum marked the beginning of a new era during which Aboriginal affairs have become predominantly a commonwealth, and hence national, responsibility; funding for Aboriginal affairs has increased dramatically; Aboriginal issues have become a significant part of the national agenda; anti-racial discrimination legislation has been passed; land rights have become a reality for some Aboriginal groups; the principle of Aboriginal consultation has become acknowledged in government processes; the administration of Aboriginal affairs has been placed under the direction of indigenous elected representatives with the establishment of the Aboriginal and Torres Strait Islander Commission; real gains have been made in increasing indigenous access to education and in reducing the high incidence of infant mortality, child health problems and trachoma; the Royal Commission into Aboriginal Deaths in Custody was conducted with additional funding made available to assist the implementation of its recommendations; and self-determination has become the guiding light of government policy.

Commonwealth funding for Aboriginal affairs has increased dramatically since the Labor government came to power in 1972. There was an almost four-fold increase in funding from $31 million in 1971/72 to $117 million in the 1973–74 financial year budget (Howard, 1982: 90). By the mid-1980s, the budget was approaching $400 million and in 1992–93 had grown to $1161 dollars (ATSIC, 1993:158). These sums represent a considerable growth per capita over a twenty-one year period, given an Aboriginal and Torres Strait Islander population of 115,951 in 1971 which had increased to 261,129 by 1991. These funds have been used for housing, education, health, community facilities, legal aid, welfare, employment and training initiatives and for the administration of Aboriginal affairs.

Despite these funding increases, there has been little significant improvement in the overall socioeconomic situation of Aboriginal and Torres Strait Islander people. In terms of health, education, income, housing and employment indicators, they remain significantly worse off than any other sector of the Australian community. In its paper *Social Justice for Indigenous Australians* (1992–93), the commonwealth government acknowledged that the first Australians are the most disadvantaged Australians. In every available measure of social and economic disadvantage, Aboriginal and Torres Strait Islander people record worse outcomes, face greater problems and enjoy fewer opportunities than the rest of the Australian population. This poverty and relative powerlessness of Australia's indigenous people is reflected in inferior education, employment, income and housing. (Commonwealth Government Paper, 1992: 8–15)

The level and extent of disadvantage, particularly in terms of incomes, employment and welfare, had already been documented extensively in the 1985 Report of the Committee of Review of Aboriginal Employment and Training Programs (the *Miller Report*). The *Miller Report* had found that there had been little improvement in real economic status for Aborigines between the Census of 1971 and that of 1981 and that Aboriginal people who had employment continued to be concentrated in lower skilled or unskilled positions. Aboriginal employment opportunities had diminished rapidly as the economy restructured and the report estimated that 50 per cent of the Aboriginal workforce was unemployed — an unemployment rate about six times the rate of all other Australians at the time. Moreover, the 1986 census went on to reveal that Aboriginal median income remained at half the median income for other Australians.

The *Miller Report* also found an overwhelming dependence by Aboriginal and Torres Strait Islander people on government funding. It identified 71 per cent of national Aboriginal income being provided by the government, mainly in the form of social welfare payments. Only 16 per cent of government funding was directed towards economic development. The report pointed out that:

> This clearly demonstrates that current Aboriginal advancement policy is not positively directed towards the long-term economic prospects of Aboriginal people. [*Miller Report*, 1985: 40]

Essentially the *Miller Report* found that the government was achieving little more than providing a minimum level of welfare and living standards for an alarmingly high proportion of the indigenous population. Far too little of the government's funds were being used to enhance long-term employment prospects or to assist Aborigines in establishing and developing viable economic bases for their communities.

The report was highly critical of the failings in the government's administration of its Aboriginal programs and emphasised the need for flexibility. It argued that policies needed to be designed to meet the needs of different Aboriginal situations and that responsibility for planning and use of programs should rest with Aboriginal people at the local level. It went on to:

> urge the government to adopt a policy of support to Aboriginal people which goes beyond welfare, housing and municipal services industries and which should be directed towards Aboriginal people becoming more independent by enabling them to provide for their livelihood. Programs to achieve this end will be longer term, involve real training and result in Aboriginal control of resources, as well as access to jobs in the regular labour market. [*Miller Report*, 1985: 10]

In 1991, the Academy of Social Sciences in Australia and the Centre for Aboriginal Economic Policy Research at the Australian National University conducted a workshop entitled "Aboriginal Employment Equity by the Year 2000". The papers presented at the workshop portrayed a rather depressing picture which, six years on from the *Miller Report*, served to confirm its findings and to show that further progress had been very limited. Examination of the impact of greater opportunities in schooling, for example, had proved far less encouraging than had been expected. While education opportunities had increased and more educated Aborigines overall were gaining employment and higher incomes, for those who lived in rural or remote areas, the opportunities for employment and higher income status were largely non-existent. Education alone was found insufficient to improve the socioeconomic status of Aborigines (Sanders, 1991: 15–16). Aborigines and Torres Strait Islanders remained overwhelmingly dependent on the welfare system for their incomes.

Charles Perkins has identified welfare as an instrument which has forced Aboriginal people into dependency and which maintains them in it. When giving the Frank Archibald Memorial Lecture in October 1990, he called for a total reorganisation and redirection of Aboriginal affairs in order to "project Aboriginal people out of this degrading, and self perpetuating dependency welfare system" (Perkins, 1990: 1). He warned against the dangers of becoming resigned to and accepting of welfare dependency and exhorted Aborigines to "throw off the old social welfare system".

> The time has come for our people to break out of this unworthy, enforced western dreamtime and charter a new course, not only for our people, and particularly for our children, but for our nation. We must throw off the yoke of welfare and the soul destroying concept of welfare and the subsequent dependency syndrome. It is destroying us and will continually do so … We are running out of time … [Perkins, 1990: 6]

Internal colonialism

Over the past 200 years Australia has moved from colonial status to independence while Aboriginal and Torres Strait Islander peoples have remained in a situation described by Beckett (1987) as one of *internal colonialism*. Internal colonialism is characterised by relations of dominance and subordination, the expropriation of the land and natural resources of the colonised peoples, the exploitation of their labour and their marginalisation to the fringes of the majority society. It involves systematic discrimination of the subject peoples by the conquering group in a manner that serves to separate them and entrench inequality. Their subordination is justified and rationalised by the emergence of ideologies based on beliefs of racial and cultural superiority and becomes institutionalised throughout the structures of society. Some insight into its continued manifestation in contemporary Australia can be gleaned from the report of the Royal Commission into Aboriginal Deaths in Custody when the Royal Commissioner, Mr Elliott Johnston QC, wrote:

> until I examined the files of the people who had died and the other materials which have come before the Commission and listened to Aboriginal people speaking, I had no conception of the degree of pin-pricking domination, abuse of personal power, utter paternalism, open contempt and total indifference with which so many Aboriginal people were visited on a day to day basis. [cited in O'Donoghue, 1992: 10]

Beckett's analysis is supported by Howard (1982) and Jennett (1987), who demonstrate that welfare has been a long-standing government policy which has been used to order and control Aborigines, first under the reserve system and then, as that collapsed, through the social welfare system. They argue that the colonial structures that have been imposed and the forms of incorporation that have been forced upon Aboriginal and Torres Strait Islander peoples have served to obstruct their movement for greater autonomy and have continued to perpetuate their unemployment, inequality and powerlessness.

Given this context of internal colonialism, it is hardly surprising that there has been so little progress in breaking out of welfare dependency over the past two decades for the Aboriginal and Torres Strait Islanders. As Howard (1982) points out, the government is not a neutral force which can improve the situation just by expanding funding and setting up new programs. For Aborigines, the government and its instrumentalities are part of the problem. It is through its actions and those of its predecessors that Aboriginal people have been denied the capacity and opportunity to be economically independent. Government agencies, by their very nature, seek to gain and maintain hegemonic control. They are not well placed to be agents of Aboriginal self-determination and their responses to Aboriginal demands have been essentially based on the provision of social welfare, thereby fostering continued dependency.

Government policies in general have reflected an inability to accommodate the interests of Aborigines and Torres Strait Islanders. The structures within which the latter have been obliged to operate have been imposed upon them by coercion, persuasion and welfare.

Throughout their experience of colonisation, their interests have not been protected by the state and where conflicts of interests exist, particularly over resource issues, they invariably lose out.

Governments, together with other vested interests, have continued in recent years to go to great lengths to protect "the public interest" in order to set aside Aboriginal interests. Over the critical issue of land rights, a key economic resource and one of central spiritual significance, the mining lobby, together with the Western Australian and Queensland governments, in the mid-1980s waged a relentless campaign against proposed national land rights legislation. They were instrumental in the commonwealth government's decision to first remove any reference to an Aboriginal right of veto on mining and then in its decision to withdraw and abandon the legislation altogether. Aboriginal bodies such as the National Aboriginal Conference and the Federation of Land Councils protested about the lack of consultation and against the changes that were "steamrolled" through, but to no effect.

While the abandonment of the national land rights legislation did not mean that the federal government had abandoned land rights altogether, and it did pass title over to the Mutitjulu people at Uluru in 1985, it does serve to emphasise the dependent status and lack of power of Aboriginal people in relation to the Australian state. This powerlessness is further illustrated by the Hawke government's amendments to the *Northern Territory Land Rights Act* 1976, which in effect enabled the government to allow mining on Aboriginal-owned land, and the 1993 decision of the Keating Government to permit the Northern Territory to extinguish native title at McArthur River for the purpose of mining.

The state and territory governments also have operated to frustrate Aboriginal efforts to gain an economic base and control over their resources. In 1980 the Court Liberal government in Western Australia conducted a military-style operation to overcome Aboriginal resistance to oil drilling at Noonkanbah, even though the company concerned was prepared to drill elsewhere. The government was determined to show that Aborigines had no control or rights over mining in Western Australia, even on land they possessed. In the early 1980s, despite being reputedly more progressive, the South Australian Bannon Labor government ignored Kokotha protests against the Roxby Downs uranium and gold mine which was situated on land they claimed. In the Northern Territory the government used an array of legal and administrative devices to frustrate Aboriginal land claims. In Darwin the town's area was increased to 4,350 square kilometres to defeat the Kuntai land claim on Cox Peninsula. Darwin is now the world's largest city in terms of area. A similar tactic was used to frustrate a Jawoyn land claim at Katherine and a Waramungu land claim at Tennant Creek. In Western Australia the government even circumvented its own *Aboriginal Heritage Act* in its efforts in the late 1980s to permit the development of the Nyungar sacred Waugal (Swan Brewery) site.

Such actions have demonstrated very clearly to Aboriginal people how their rights are not guaranteed and protected by the Australian political and legal systems. In the case of the Nyungar struggle, one commentator observed that:

> the hoops that the protesters have had to leap through in taking legal actions and making Heritage Act applications under both Federal and State legislation have convincingly demonstrated to them the ethnocentric nature of the whitefella Courts and the whitefella Acts. [Ansara, 1989: 12]

Government frameworks for self-determination

In pursuing their objectives, Aboriginal and Torres Strait Islander people have had to operate within the constraints of the structures and processes imposed by the Australian states. Their capacity to effect self-determination and self-management goals defined and determined for them by successive Australian governments is limited by the internal colonial framework within which they are forced to operate.

Beckett points out, though, that one of the paradoxes of welfare colonialism is the fostering of political autonomy while simultaneously incorporating the colonised through welfare dependency. The extension of citizenship to Aborigines and Torres Strait Islanders in 1967 brought with it an obligation to facilitate their participation and gain their consent (Beckett, 1987: 175). The Whitlam government's response was to adopt a policy of self-determination and to establish mechanisms for consultation and community management. These attempts to involve Aborigines in the political process have served to foster Aboriginal political activity and autonomy. In particular, they have provided Aboriginal and Torres Strait Islander people with organisational structures, albeit imposed ones, at both grass roots and national levels with which to pursue their various agendas.

Following its extensive investigation into indigenous management and community control, the House of Representatives Standing Committee on Aboriginal Affairs described it as "ironic" that Aboriginal and Torres Strait Islander communities were being required to establish and use non-Aboriginal structures in order to have more control over their own affairs. The Committee found that:

> The imposition of council management structures on Aboriginal communities by and large has ignored the existence of traditional decision making processes. [House of Representatives Standing Committee on Aboriginal Affairs, 1990: 20]

Not only was the grafting of non-Aboriginal institutions on to Aboriginal communities and the continued failure to recognise the authority of Aboriginal organisations in the non-Aboriginal power structure seen as inappropriate, the government was also criticised for not assisting Aboriginal people to develop the instrumental capacity to manage their communities according to its requirements.

The Committee was also very critical of the means by which policies of self-determination and self-management had been implemented, characterising them as "hurried" and lacking adequate consultation. The Committee found this to be a major contradiction, arguing that:

> the imposition of programs, policies and structures without adequate consultation is inconsistent with the notion of Aboriginal communities being self determining and having the ability to influence and control their own affairs. [Standing Committee, 1990: 8]

The Committee concluded that the policies of self-determination and self-management had been a failure "in many circumstances", with the Department of Aboriginal Affairs in its evidence to the Committee noting that:

> many Aboriginal communities have yet to make the transition to self-determination and that in some cases communities are just as dependent upon outside agencies as they have been in the past, despite the implementation of the policy of self-determination. [Standing Committee, 1990: 5)

The Committee found that there were two broad categories of reasons for this failure. The first group of reasons was located with the government and its agencies and the second was located with the communities themselves. Government agencies needed to improve their performance, provide more appropriate and better coordinated services and develop more appropriate and sensitive executive management infrastructures. The Committee also found that there was often a lack of commitment and involvement in the government's community management structures among community members which the Department of Aboriginal Affairs claimed placed "almost insuperable obstacles in the way of the transition of self-determination" (Standing Committee, 1990: 7). The Department's position completely failed to recognise the contradictions involved in the imposition of alien structures on communities in the name of self-determination.

In order to provide for a mechanism for consultation at the national level, the government established the National Aboriginal Consultative Committee (NACC) in 1973. Significantly, its existence, structure and functions were all determined by the federal government and the NACC had no decision-making or policy-making powers. Its function was solely advisory.

In addition to setting up the NACC, the government also encouraged and financially supported the development of indigenous organisations at the community level.

Despite such initiatives, and its policy of self-determination, the Whitlam government proved extremely reluctant to relinquish its control over Aboriginal affairs. When the National Aboriginal Consultative Committee delegates, dissatisfied with their purely advisory role, voted to change their body into a National Aboriginal Congress with policy-making powers and control over the budget of the Department of Aboriginal Affairs, the government moved rapidly to quash the move, isolating those it identified as radicals and threatening to sack the delegates.

While the government supported the establishment of Aboriginal organisations with funding, in so doing it ensured its own capacity to oversee and control activities. This it strengthened in 1975 with the introduction of a new set of administrative guidelines designed to increase administrative control over expenditure and to reduce the autonomy of Aboriginal communities and organisations. It also ruled that assets bought with government funds were to be vested in and owned by the Department of Aboriginal Affairs, the department it had set up in 1973 to administer Aboriginal affairs. Such actions served to undermine Aboriginal efforts to build an assets base and a measure of economic independence. They worked towards the maintenance of a colonial situation of dependency, rather than the declared purpose of self-determination.

With the election in 1975 of the coalition government under the leadership of Malcolm Fraser, the policy of self-determination was replaced with the less politically contentious policy of self-management and self-sufficiency. The Fraser government was no more willing to hand over real control to Aborigines than its predecessor. It replaced the NACC with a new consultative body, whose role was advisory only, and which it named the National Aboriginal Conference (NAC).

Like the NACC, the NAC had a government-determined structure with delegates elected on the Westminster principle of representative democracy, a principle which bore no relation to Aboriginal community authority and decision-making processes.

The NAC was a much-criticised body, and was tagged as being a "token". In 1984, following a formal review of its structure and function, it was found to have had little influence on the government and its agencies, no capacity to deliver services or provide funding and tenuous links with the communities (Jennett, 1990: 259). While such criticisms serve to expose some of the problems NAC delegates had in operating within such a structure, especially when the Minister for Aboriginal Affairs did not make significant use of his capacity to refer matters to the Conference for advice, they mask its efforts to provide a national voice for Aborigines on the issue of a treaty and on land rights.

When the NAC came to the end of its term in June 1985, it was not replaced. It was not until 1990, when the Aboriginal and Torres Strait Islander Commission (ATSIC) was established, that a structure to enable broad representation of Aboriginal and Torres Strait Islanders was to re-emerge.

In ATSIC the government attempted to amalgamate the representative functions of former bodies such as the NAC with the administrative functions of the Department of Aboriginal Affairs and the funding role of the Aboriginal Development Commission. In so doing, the government hoped to overcome the inter-bureaucratic rivalry that had characterised relations between the former bodies and to provide a more effective mechanism with which to pursue self-determination. Community representation in the management of ATSIC was incorporated initially through the establishment of sixty regional councils, organised into seventeen zones, across Australia. Each zone elected a commissioner to ATSIC with the remaining three commissioners, including the chairperson, being appointed by the government.

The government promoted ATSIC as a conduit that would facilitate Aboriginal self-determination and self-management with Prime Minister Hawke stating: "via ATSIC we are going to have a better way of getting the views of the Aboriginal community" (Brennan, ALB: 5). Lois O'Donoghue, on her appointment as the chairperson of ATSIC, claimed that ATSIC was the "voice of Australia's Aboriginal and Torres Strait Islander peoples" and described its establishment as the commencement of a "unique and productive partnership with the government" (Brennan, ALB: 4). In an address to the National Press Club in May 1992, O'Donoghue argued that ATSIC's establishment was an acknowledgment that previous administrative and political arrangements had failed and that real progress in Aboriginal affairs was proving elusive. She described ATSIC as "the culmination of a long line of attempts to achieve Aboriginal self-determination at the governmental level and as a radical shift away from previous Aboriginal Affairs institutions" (O'Donoghue, 1992).

Organisations such as the Aboriginal Provisional Government and the Federation of Land Councils (FLC) have been strongly critical of suggestions that ATSIC has the authority to speak on behalf of Aborigines and Torres Strait Islanders and that it is a vehicle for Aboriginal self-determination. The FLC sees ATSIC as a body whose central function is to administer government services and argues that it does not have the capacity or authority to negotiate on behalf of Aborigines and Torres Strait Islanders on matters of significance such as a treaty, or even to provide a structure for consultation on such issues.

How well placed ATSIC is to actively foster self-determination is problematic, however. While its processes for representation and advice from communities and its declared intention to decentralise and delegate decision-making to regional and local levels have been welcomed, it remains a bureaucratic organisation, operating within the confines of the *Public Service Act* and staffed accordingly. It is still a semi-government body subject to government policy, funded by the government and accountable to the Minister for Aboriginal Affairs who retains the power to direct the Commission. ATSIC has to operate under so tight a regime of financial accountability that the Minister for Aboriginal Affairs informed Parliament:

> There is no other department or statutory authority in existence in the Commonwealth which will be as accountable as ATSIC. I defy Honourable Members opposite to find me any organisation under this Government or any other Government that will be as accountable as this structure. [Brennan, ALB: 5]

So restrictive are these requirements that Rowse (1992) and the Foundation for Aboriginal and Islander Research Action (1991) argue that ATSIC lacks the capacity to devolve decision making and funding to the regional and local levels and, therefore, will be unable to give real substance to self-determination. ATSIC also lacks the financial capacity to provide Aboriginal communities with the infrastructure and funds for capital development required for sustained economic development. As O'Donoghue admits:

> We remain very much dependent on the patronage and goodwill of governments — for recurrent funding of Aboriginal organisations, for special pieces of legislation such as the *Northern Territory Land Rights Act* and the *ATSIC Act* ... Though the ultimate aim of self-determination is an end to this situation, Aboriginal people clearly have a long way to go. [O'Donoghue, 1992: 14]

Native title: A chance for real progress?

The High Court's decision on *native title* in June 1992 provided a new basis upon which Aborigines and Torres Strait Islanders could pursue the return of land and compensation. The decision overthrew the doctrine of *terra nullius*, recognised indigenous prior ownership and provided an opportunity for Aborigines and Torres Strait Islanders to pursue their rights to the title of land with which they had maintained traditional ties and where native title had not already been extinguished.

Opening the International Year for the World's Indigenous Peoples at Redfern Park in December 1992, Prime Minister Keating described the High Court's decision as a practical building block for change, adding that:

By doing away with the bizarre concept that this continent had no owners prior to the settlement of Europeans, Mabo establishes a fundamental truth and lays the basis for justice ... Mabo is an historic decision — we can make it an historic turning point, the basis of a new relationship between indigenous and non-Aboriginal Australians. [Keating, 1993: 4]

The Council for Aboriginal Reconciliation also viewed the High Court's decision with optimism, describing it as an

opportunity to set right the relationship [between Aborigines and other Australians] in a way that was not possible in the beginning. [Dodson, 1993: 7]

According to Dodson, the decision not only provided a new basis for Aboriginal land tenure but also elevated into the forefront of the national political agenda issues of self-determination, self-government, recognition of customary law, protection of cultural and sacred sites and the rights of indigenous Australians to choose the way of life that they want to follow. (Seminar, University of South Australia, 19 August 1993).

The recognition of native title by the High Court has led to many indigenous groups across Australia pursuing claims for land title. The economic and cultural significance of gaining ownership of land was emphasised by John Dalungdalu Jones of the Fraser Island Land Council when he explained the reasons for the Council's proclamation of ownership of Kgari (Fraser Island) and its claim to about $6 million a year in tourist levies to help fund education, social welfare, tourism and environmental management projects:

Instead of our people having to have their hand out forever to get social welfare, we can use that money to establish economic and culturally viable jobs for our own young people for the future, just as Uluru does. [*Australian*, 21 July 1993: 2)

The High Court's decision proved a highly contentious issue throughout most of 1993, as different groups of powerful vested interests sought to protect their interests and resolve what they described as "uncertainty" over land title. The pastoral and mining industries in particular pursued a vigorous campaign aimed at securing the validation of their titles and the extinguishment of native title. The Australian Chamber of Commerce and Industry, the Australian Coal Association, the Australian Mining Industry Council, the Australian

Petroleum Exploration Association, the Australian Tourism Industry Association, the National Association of Forest Industries and the National Fishing Industry Council joined forces to release a paper to give the community a better understanding of the issues raised by Mabo. While the paper conceded that Aborigines may be entitled to some compensation, it argued that they should not have any right to veto development, asserting that experience in Western Australia and the Northern Territory had demonstrated that such powers have had quite dire consequences on industry. In some quarters the campaign against native title reached extreme heights with Hugh Morgan, managing director of Western Mining and a long-standing opponent of land rights, arguing that the future of Australia had been put at risk, that its territorial integrity was under threat and that "all titles to property in Australia have been devalued as a result of Mabo" (*Australian*, 1 July 1993: 1). He demanded that Prime Minister Keating retract from his "uncompromising" support for Mabo, arguing that his position "could only lead to a very rapid economic decline and to a partitioning of the continent. Mabo directly threatens the unity of Australia." (*Australian*, 1 July 1993: 2)

As Social Justice Commissioner Mick Dodson was to observe, the campaign against a just settlement of native title poignantly captured the conflict and challenge that faced all Australians:

> Powerful vested interests have worked relentlessly to maintain the social and economic systems which structurally exclude other groups of peoples.
>
> They use their powerful voices to argue that human rights concerns must not be allowed to stand in the way of economic development. They use their powerful voices to induce paranoia in the attempt to convince the people of this country that their interest lay in supporting the status quo, regardless of its legal or moral basis. And there have been political figures who have been willing to support those interests and to ignore the voices of those seeking justice. [cited in Roberts, 1993: 20]

The government sought to reassure non-Aboriginal Australians that they had nothing to fear from the native title decision and continued to link it with "reconciliation", stating that the High Court's judgment must be used to support the broader goal of reconciling Aboriginal and non-Aboriginal Australia and rectifying the dispossession of those Aborigines whose links with their traditional land have been broken.

The commonwealth government decided to resolve the "uncertainty" over native title through the means of legislation and in September 1993 it released its draft legislation for public comment. Aboriginal groups responded angrily to the draft legislation, denouncing it as an empty promise and for failing to safeguard their interests. Of particular concern was the government's proposal to suspend the *Racial Discrimination Act* to extinguish native title in order to validate existing title, and the prime role given to the states in determining native title claims.

Confronted by trenchant criticism from Aboriginal leaders, the churches, human rights groups and members of its own backbench, the government entered into further rounds of negotiations with Aboriginal and Islander representatives, state governments and mining and pastoral interests. It abandoned its proposal to suspend the *Racial Discrimination Act* and undertook to legislate to protect native title interests so that they could coexist with leasehold title. It also agreed to provide Aboriginal groups with the right to take their case for native title to a Commonwealth Tribunal. Alongside the legislation, the government also committed itself to providing a "social justice package" that would include a Land Acquisition Fund to enable Aboriginal communities to purchase land. The Prime Minister described the changes as a "win–win for everybody", a position not endorsed by the Coalition, which decided to oppose the legislation, nor the Western Australian government, which moved to introduce its own legislation on native title.

Certainly the government's changes to its proposed legislation went some way towards addressing Aboriginal concerns but, even assuming the passage of the legislation through parliament, just how many Aborigines will benefit and in what ways remains uncertain. Estimates vary as to how many Aboriginal people will directly benefit from native title, but it is likely that the number will be relatively small, no more than 5 per cent of the Aboriginal population. Even for the beneficiaries, it will be quite some time — a matter of years rather than months — before native title claims are heard and settled and, in cases where compensation is due, compensation determined and paid. The situation for the large majority of Aboriginal people remains problematic in that they will not directly benefit from native title. The federal government's Thirty-Three Point Plan for the resolution of Mabo, which was presented to the Council of Australian Governments' meeting in June, had recognised this in its emphasis that the native title decision must be used for the far broader goal of reconciliation and to rectify the dispossession of Aborigines whose links with their traditional land had been broken. The plan, however, had left the details of how this might be achieved open for negotiation within the constraints of "budget realities". It is at this point that the proposed social justice legislation and land acquisition program become critical. As Charles Perkins states:

> One of our problems is that we don't have this independent economic base, away from Government ... we have got to really create it in the sense that we have to empower people at the local level with assets they control and they in fact own. And that is not the situation at the current time. [ABC Education TV, 1993]

If the government's legislation and social justice package are able to provide a basis upon which real gains can be made in the acquisition and control of resources by the indigenous Australians, they will constitute a significant step forward in the struggle to break free from welfare dependency and to pursue self-determination. Beyond this, Aboriginal communities also need an injection of capital and the acquisition of managerial and labour skills appropriate to the direction they choose to take. Furthermore, self-determination also requires the eradication of structural disadvantage and institutional racism within the broader Australian society. Until real progress is made in overcoming these obstacles, and governments themselves are prepared to relinquish an overseeing and veto role for themselves in Aboriginal affairs, self-determination will remain both illusory and elusive.

Ultimately, Aboriginal self-determination will only be achieved through Aboriginal endeavour and struggle, as Charles Perkins observes:

> The essential element in Aboriginal affairs that is most important and that a lot of Aboriginal people should never lose sight of, all the time, is that the only people who are going to make a change to Aboriginal affairs are Aboriginal people.
>
> White people will never change anything for you. Governments, good or bad, of whatever political colour, will never change anything for you.
>
> There's only one person that is going to do it, and that is that black face you see in the mirror when you wake up in the morning.

That is the person that is going to change Aboriginal affairs for the better, and for your children. [ABC Education TV, 1993]

Note

1. The state is here defined as the totality of institutions, structures and processes which together control and manage power in contemporary Australian society.

References

ABC Education TV (1993). "Towards the future: policies and practice". *Windows on Aboriginal Australia*, OLAA Series, Melbourne, episode 13.

Altman, J.C. (ed.) (1991). *Aboriginal Employment Equity by the Year 2000*. Canberra: Centre for Aboriginal Economic Policy Research, Australian National University.

Ansara, M. (1989). "Self determination". *Bulletin of the Olive Pink Society*, vol. 1, no. 2, pp. 11-13.

Aboriginal & Torres Strait Islander Commission (1991–92). *Annual report*.

Beckett, J. (1987). *Torres Strait Islanders: Custom and Colonialism*. Sydney: Cambridge University Press.

Beckett, J. (1988). "Aboriginality, citizenship and nation state". *Social Analysis*, vol. 24, pp. 3-18.

Brennan, F. (1990). "ATSIC: seeking a national mouthpiece for local voices". *Aboriginal Law Bulletin*, vol. 2, no. 43, pp. 4-6.

——— (1991). *Sharing the Country: The Case for an Agreement Between Black and White Australians*. Ringwood: Penguin.

Cunneen, C. (1992). "Aboriginal imprisonment during and since the Royal Commission into Aboriginal Deaths in Custody". *Aboriginal Law Bulletin*, vol. 2, no. 55, pp. 13-14.

Cowlishaw, G. (1988). *Black, White or Brindle: Race in Rural Australia*. Cambridge: Cambridge University Press.

Department of Prime Minister and Cabinet (1992a). *Council for Aboriginal Reconciliation: An Introduction*. Canberra: AGPS.

——— (1992b). *Aboriginal Reconciliation: An Historical Perspective*. Canberra: Australian Government Publishing Service.

——— (1993). *Making Things Right: Reconciliation After the High Court's Decision on Native Title*. Canberra: Council for Aboriginal Reconciliation.

Dodson, P. (1989). "Statehood for Northern Territory". *Aboriginal Law Bulletin*, vol. 2, no. 39, pp. 14-16.

——— (1993). "Reconciliation and the high court's decision on native title". *Aboriginal Law Bulletin*, vol. 3, no. 61, pp. 6-9.

Foundation for Aboriginal and Islander Research Action (1991). "ATSIC: a limited step forward?" *Aboriginal Law Bulletin*, vol. 2, no. 43, pp. 7-9.

Hiatt, L. R. (1987). "Treaty, compact or makarrata?" *Oceania*, vol. 58, no. 2.

House of Representatives Standing Committee on Aboriginal Affairs (1990). *Our Future Ourselves: Aboriginal and Torres Strait Islander Community Control, Management and Resources*. Canberra: AGPS.

Howard, M. (1982). "Australian Aboriginal politics and perpetuation of inequality". *Oceania*, vol. 53, no. 1, pp. 82-101.

Jennett, C. (1987). "Incorporation or independence? the struggle for Aboriginal equality". In *Three Worlds of Inequality: Race, Class and Gender*, edited by C. Jennett and R. Stewart. Melbourne: Macmillan, pp. 57-93.

_____ "Aboriginal affairs policy". In *Hawke and Australian Public Policy*, edited by C. Jennett and R. Stewart. Melbourne: Macmillan.

Johnston, E. (1991). *National Report: Overview and Recommendations, Royal Commission into Aboriginal Deaths in Custody*. Canberra: AGPS.

Jull, P. (1993). "Political strategies for indigenous peoples: levels of practical action". Mimeo. Darwin: North Australian Research Unit, Australian National University.

Keating, P. (1993). "Australian Launch of the International Year for the World's Indigenous People, 10 December 1992". *Aboriginal Law Bulletin*, vol. 3, no. 61, pp. 4-5.

Koori Mail. Various issues.

Land Rights News, various issues.

Lavery, D. (1992). "When the CAR Stops on reconciliation day will indigenous Australians have gone anywhere?" *Aboriginal Law Bulletin*, vol. 2, no. 58, pp. 7-8.

Mansell, M. (1992). "Beyond 2001: the white man's dream may be an Aboriginal nightmare". Mimeo. Hobart: Aboriginal Provisional Government.

Committee of Review of Aboriginal Employment and Training Programs (1985). *Aboriginal Employment and Training Programs: Report of the Committee of Review.* Canberra: AGPS.

Moizo, B. (1990). "Implementation of the community development employment scheme in Fitzroy Crossing: a preliminary report". *Australian Aboriginal Studies*, no. 1, pp. 37-40.

Morris, B. (1989). *Domesticating Resistance: The Dhan-gadi Aborigines and the Australian State*. London: Berg.

Mowbray, M. (1990). "Mainstreaming as assimilation in the Northern Territory". *Australian Aboriginal Studies*, no. 2, pp. 20-26.

National Aboriginal and Islander Legal Services (1989). "An interesting and informative chat was not what I had in mind …". *Aboriginal Law Bulletin*, vol. 2, no. 36, pp. 12-15.

O'Donoghue, L. (1992). *One Nation: Promise or Paradox?* Speech at the National Press Club. Canberra: ATSIC.

Perkins, C. (1989). "Governments and Aboriginal communities". *Australian Journal of Public Administration*, vol. 48, no. 1, pp. 21-28.

_____ (1990). "Welfare and Aboriginal people in Australia: time for a new direction". The Frank Archibald Memorial Lecture. Armidale: University of New England.

Reynolds, H. (1991). "Who is reconciling whom, and to what?" *Australian Society*, pp. 3-4.

Roberts, D. (1993). "Reconciliation and the Mabo Factor". *Kaurna Journal of Higher Education,* vol. 4, pp. 16-24.

Rowse, T. (1992a). "Can ATSIC really contribute to Aboriginal self-determination?" *Modern Times,* pp. 22-23.

—— (1992b). *Remote Possibilities: The Aboriginal Domain and the Administrative Imagination.* Darwin: Northern Australia Research Unit, Australian National University.

Ryan, L. (1989). "Aboriginals and Islanders". In *From Fraser to Hawke,* edited by Brian Head and A. Patience. Melbourne: Longman Cheshire, pp. 394-408.

Sanders, W. (1991). "Destined to fail: the Hawke government's pursuit of statistical equality in employment and income status between Aborigines and other Australians by the year 2000". *Australian Aboriginal Studies,* no. 2, 13-17.

Social Justice for Indigenous Australians (1992–93). Budget Related Paper No. 7. Canberra: Australian Government Publishing Service.

Stephenson, M.A. and Ratnapala, S. (eds) (1993). *Mabo, a Judicial Revolution: The Aboriginal Land Rights Decision and the Impact on Australian Law.* St Lucia: University of Queensland Press.

Tatz, C. (1983). "Aborigines and the age of atonement". *The Australian Quarterly,* vol. 55, no. 3, pp. 291-306.

Taylor, J. (1993). "Industry segregation among employed Aborigines and Torres Strait Islanders". *ANZJS,* vol. 29, no. 3, pp. 3-20.

Watson, I. (1992). "International Year for Indigenous Peoples 1993: How far is there to travel in achieving indigenous rights?" Kaurna public lecture. Adelaide: University of South Australia.

—— "Has Mabo turned the tide for justice?" *Social Alternatives,* vol. 12, no. 1, pp. 5-9.

Wright, J. (1988). "What became of that treaty?" *Australian Aboriginal Studies,* no. 1, pp. 40-44.